MEMOIRS

OF

THE JACOBITES

OF 1715 AND 1745.

BY MRS. THOMSON,

AUTHOR OF

"MEMOIRS OF THE COURT OF HENRY THE EIGHTH, "
"MEMOIRS OF SARAH, DUCHESS OF MARLBOROUGH, " ETC.

VOLUME II.

1845.

Memoirs of the Jacobites of 1715 and 1745 - Volume II

Mrs. Thomson

DODO PRESS

CONTENTS TO THE SECOND VOLUME.

WILLIAM MAXWELL, EARL OF NITHISDALE.

COUNTESS OF NITHISDALE.

FROM A DRAWING BY CHARLES KIRKPATRICK SHARPE, ESQ[RE].
TAKEN FROM THE ORIGINAL PICTURE BY SIR GODFREY KNELLER AT TERREGLES.

It is happily remarked by the editor of the Culloden Papers, with regard to the devotion of many of the Highland clans to the exiled family of Stuart, that "it cannot be a subject requiring vindication; nor, " adds the writer, "if it raise a glow on the face of their descendants, is it likely to be the blush of shame. " The descendants of William Maxwell, Earl of Nithisdale, have reason to remember, with a proud interest, the determined and heroic affection which rescued their ancestor from prison, no less than the courage and fidelity which involved their chief in a perilous undertaking, and in a miserable captivity.

The first of that ancient race, who derived their surname from the Lordship of Maxwell, in the county of Dumfries, was Robert de Maxwell of Carlaverock, who, in 1314, was killed at the battle of Bannockburn, fighting under the banners of King James the Third. From that period until the seventeenth century, the house of Maxwell continued to enjoy signal proofs of royal favour; it was employed in important services and on high missions, extending its power and increasing its possessions by intermarriages with the richest and noblest families in Scotland. An enumeration of the honours and privileges enjoyed by this valiant race will show in how remarkable a degree it was favoured by the Stuarts, and how various and how forcible were the reasons which bound it to serve that generous and beloved race of Scottish monarchs.

Herbert, who succeeded John de Maxwell, was one of the Commissioners sent by Alexander the Second to England, to treat for a marriage with one of the daughters of that crown; and, having concluded the negotiation favourably, was endowed with the office of Lord Great Chamberlain of Scotland, which he held during his life-time, and which was afterwards bestowed on his son.

Eustace de Maxwell, in the time of Robert de Bruce, was among those patriots who adhered to the Scottish King. The Castle of Carlaverock, one of the most ancient possessions of the brave Maxwells, stands a memento, in its noble ruins, of the disinterested loyalty of its owners.

The remains of Carlaverock afford but a slight notion of its former strength. The importance of its situation is, however, undoubted. Situated on the south borders of the Nith, near to Glencapel Quay, it constituted a stronghold for the Scottish noble, who scarcely feared a siege within its walls, and when the army of Edward advanced to invest it, refused to surrender; "for the fortress was well furnished, " says Grose, "with soldiers, engines, and provisions. "

But this defiance was vain; after sustaining an assault, Carlaverock was obliged to capitulate; when the generosity of Edward's measures excited the admiration of all humane minds. The troops, only sixty in number, were taken into the King's service, as a token of his approval of their brave defence; they were then released, ransom free, and received each a new garment, as a gift from the King.

Carlaverock was, some time after, retaken by the Scotch, and Sir Eustace de Maxwell resumed his command over the garrison. It was again invested by King Edward; but, on this occasion, Eustace drove the English from the attack, and retained possession of the fortress.

Afterwards, of his own free will, he demolished the fortress, that no possession of his might favour the progress of the enemy. He was rewarded by several grants of lands, and twenty-two pounds in money.

In the fifteenth century, Herbert de Maxwell marrying a daughter of the Maxwells of Terregles (Terre Eglise), the son of that marriage was ennobled, and was dignified by the title of Lord de Maxwell. His successor perished at Flodden, but the grandson of the first Lord had a happier fortune, and was entrusted by James the Fifth to bring over Mary of Guise to Scotland, first marrying her as the King's proxy.

The house of Maxwell prospered until the reign of James the Sixth; by whom John, Lord Maxwell, was created Earl of Morton, and made Warden of the Marches: but a reverse of fortune ensued. From some court intrigue, the Warden was removed from office, and his place supplied by the Laird of Johnstones; all the blood of the Maxwells was aroused; a quarrel and a combat were the result; and, in the scuffle, the new-made Earl of Morton was killed. The injury was not forgotten, and John, who succeeded the murdered man, deemed it incumbent upon him to avenge his father. In consequence, the Laird of Johnstone soon fell a sacrifice to this notion of honour, or outbreak of offended pride. The crime was not, however, passed over by law; the offender was tried, and executed, in 1613, at the Cross in Edinburgh; and his honours were forfeited. But again the favour of the Stuarts shone forth; the title of Morton was not restored, but Robert, the brother of the last Earl of Morton, was created Earl of Nithisdale, and restored to the Lordship of Maxwell; with precedency, as Earl, according to his father's creation as Earl of Morton.

This kindness was requited by a devoted loyalty; and, in the reign of Charles the First, the Earl of Nithisdale suffered much, both by sequestration and imprisonment, for the royal cause.

In 1647, in consequence of failure of the direct line, the title and estates of the Nithisdale family devolved on a kinsman, John Lord Herries, whose grandson, William, the subject of this memoir, proved to be the last of the Maxwell family that has ever enjoyed the Earldom.

He was served heir male, and of line male and entail of his father, on the twenty-sixth of May, 1696; and heir male of his grandfather, the Earl of Nithisdale, on the sixteenth of the same month. [1] At his accession to his title, the Earl of Nithisdale possessed no common advantages of fortune and station. "He was allied, " says the Scottish Peerage, "to most of the noble families in the two kingdoms. " His mother, the Lady Lucy, was daughter to the Marquis of Douglas; his only sister, Lady Mary Maxwell, was married to Charles Stewart, Earl of Traquair; and he had himself wedded a descendant of that noble and brave Marquis of Worcester who had defended Ragland Castle against Fairfax.

In addition to these family honours, Lord Nithisdale possessed rich patrimonial estates in one of the most fertile and luxuriant counties in Scotland. The Valley of the Nith, from which he derived his title, owned his lordship over some of its fairest scenes. Young, rich, and happily married, he was in the full sunshine of prosperity when, in the year 1715, he was called upon to prove the sincerity of that fidelity to the house of Stuart for which his family had so greatly suffered, and for which it had been so liberally repaid.

It is remarkable that the adventurers in the unfortunate cause of the Chevalier St. George were, with rare exceptions, men of established credit, men who had vast stakes in their country, and who had lost no portion of their due consideration in the eyes of others by extravagance or profligacy. This fact marks the insurrection of 1715, as presenting a very different aspect to that of other insurrections raised by faction, and supported by men of desperate fortunes. So early as the year 1707, it appears by Colonel Hooke's secret negotiations in favour of the Stuarts, that the bulk of the Scottish nobility had their hearts engaged in the cause, and that their honour was pledged to come forward on the first occasion. In the enumeration given by one of the agents employed in traversing the country, Lord Nithisdale and his relatives are mentioned as certain and potent allies. "In Tweedale, " writes Mr. Fleming to the Minister of Louis the Fourteenth, "the Earl of Traquair, of the house of Stuart, and the Laird of Stanhope are powerful. In the shires of Annandale, Niddesdale, and Galloway, are the Earl of Niddesdale, with the Viscount of Kenmure, the Laird of Spinkell, with the numerous clan of the Maxwells; and there is some hope also of the Earl of Galloway; Thus the King's party is connected through the whole kingdom, and we are certain of being masters of all the shires, except Argyleshire, Clydesdale, Renfrew, Dumbarton, and Kyle. "[2] "An affair of this nature, " adds Mr. Fleming, "cannot be communicated to all the well affected; and it is a great proof of the zeal of those to whom it is trusted, that so many people have been able to keep this secret so inviolably. " Such was the commencement of that compact which, held together by the word of Scotchmen, was in few instances broken; but was maintained with as scrupulous a regard to honour and fidelity by the poorest Highlander that ever trod down the heather, as by the great nobleman within his castle hall.

Among the list of the most considerable chiefs in Scotland, with an account of their disposition for or against the Government, the Earl of Nithisdale is specified by contemporary writers as one who is able to raise three hundred men, and willing to employ that force in the service of the Pretender. [3]

In the resolution to carry the aid of his clansmen to the service of either side, the chieftain of that day was powerfully assisted by the blind devotion of the brave and faithful people whom he led to battle. Unhappily, the influence of the chief was often arbitrarily, and even cruelly exerted, in cases of doubtful willingness in their followers.

It will be interesting to scrutinize the motives and characters of those who occupied the chief posts in command, upon the formation of this Southern party in favour of the Chevalier. Although some of these chiefs have obtained celebrity in history, yet their efforts were sincere; their notions of patriotism, be they just, or be they erroneous, deserve a rescue from oblivion; their sufferings, and the heroism with which they were encountered, show to what an extent the fixed principle to which the Scotch are said ever to recur, will carry the exertions, and support the fortitude, of that enduring and determined people.

To William Gordon, Viscount Kenmure and Baron of Lochinvar, was entrusted, in a commission from the Earl of Mar, the command of the insurgents in the south of Scotland. This choice of a General displayed the usual want of discernment which characterized the leaders of the Rebellion of 1715. Grave, and as a contemporary describes him, "full aged; " of extraordinary knowledge in public affairs, but a total stranger to all military matters; calm, but slow in judgment; of unsullied integrity, —endowed, in short, with qualities truly respectable, but devoid of energy, boldness, and address, yet wanting not personal courage, there could scarcely have been found a more excellent man, nor a more feeble commander. At the head of a troop of gentlemen, full of ardour in the cause, the plain dress and homely manners of Lord Kenmure seemed inappropriate to the conspicuous station which he held; for the exercise of his functions as commander was attended by some circumstances which required a great combination of worldly knowledge with singleness of purpose.

George Seaton, the fifth Earl of Wintoun, was another of those noblemen who raised a troop of horse, and engaged, from the very first commencement of the rebellion, in its turmoils. The family of Seaton, of which the Earl of Wintoun was the last in the direct line, "affords in its general characteristics, " says a celebrated Scottish genealogist, "the best specimen of our ancient nobility. They seem to have been the first to have introduced the refined arts, and an improved state of architecture in Scotland. They were consistent in their principles, and, upon the whole, as remarkable for their deportment and baronial respectability, as for their descent and noble alliances. "[4]

In consequence of so many great families having sprung from the Seatons, they were styled "*Magnæ Nobilitatis Domini*; " and their antiquity was as remarkable as their alliances, the male representation of the family, and the right to the honours which they bore, having been transmitted to the present Earl of Eglintoun, through an unbroken descent of seven centuries and a half.

The loyalty of the Seatons was untainted. The first Earl of Wintoun had adopted as one of his mottoes, "*Intaminatis fulget honoribus,* " and the sense of those words was fully borne out by the testimony of time. The Seatoun Charter Chest contained, as one of their race remarked, no remission of any offence against Government, a fact which could not be affirmed of any other Scottish family of note. But this brave and ancient house had signal reason for remaining hitherto devoted to the monarchs of the Scottish throne.

Four times had the Seatons been allied with royalty: two instances were remarkable. George Seatoun, second Earl of Huntly, married the Princess Annabella, daughter of James the First, and from that union numerous descendants of Scottish nobility exist to this day: and George, the third Lord Seaton, again allied his house with that of Stuart, by marrying the Lady Margaret Stuart, daughter of the Earl of Buchan, and granddaughter of Robert the Second. In consequence of these several intermarriages, it was proverbially said of the house of Seaton, "the family is come of princes, and reciprocally princes are come of the family. " And these bonds of relationship were cemented by services performed and honours conferred. The devotion of the Seatons to Mary, Queen of Scots, has been immortalised by the pen of Sir Walter Scott. George, the seventh Lord Seaton, attended on that unhappy Princess in some of the most brilliant scenes of her eventful life, and clung to her in every vicissitude of her fate. He, as Ambassador to France, negotiated her marriage with the Dauphin, and was present at the celebration of the nuptials. He afterwards aided his royal mistress to escape from Lochleven Castle, in 1568, and conducted her to Niddry Castle, his own seat. When, in gratitude for his fidelity, Mary would have created him an Earl, Lord Seaton declined the honour, and preferred his existing rank as Premier Baron of Scotland. Mary celebrated his determination in a couplet, written both in French and in Latin:

> "Il y a des comtes, des rois, des ducs aussi,
> Ce't assez pour moy d'estre Signeur de Seton."

The successor of Lord Seaton, Robert, judged differently from his father, and accepted from James the Sixth the patent for the Earldom of Wintoun; distinguishing the new honour by a courage which procured for him the appellation of "Greysteel. "[5]

George, the fifth Earl of Wintoun, and the unfortunate adherent to the Jacobite cause, succeeded to the honours of his ancestors under circumstances peculiarly embarrassing. His legitimacy was doubted: at the time when his father died, this ill-fated young man was abroad, his residence was obscure; and as he held no correspondence with any of his relations, little was known with regard to his personal character. In consequence partly of his absence from Scotland, partly, it is said, of an actual hereditary tendency, a belief soon prevailed that he was insane, or rather, as a contemporary expresses it, "mighty subject to a particular kind of caprice natural to his family. "[6]

The Viscount Kingston, next heir to the title of Wintoun, having expressed his objections to Lord Wintoun's legitimacy, the young man, in 1710, took steps to establish himself as his father's heir. Two witnesses were produced who were present at the marriage of his parents, and bonds were found in the family chests, designating Lord Wintoun as "our eldest lawful son, " by Dame Christian Hepburn Countess of Wintoun, "our spouse. " This important point being established, Lord Wintoun served himself heir to his father and became the possessor of the family estates, chiefly situated in East Lothian, their principal residence being the palace of Seaton, so recognized in the royal charters, from its having been the favourite resort of royalty, the scene of entertainment to Mary of Scots, and her court, and the residence of Charles the First, when in Scotland in 1633. It was afterwards the place of meeting for the Jacobite nobles, and their adherents. [7]

Differing from many of his companions in arms, Lord Wintoun was a zealous Protestant; but without any regard to the supremacy of either mode of faith, it appears to have been a natural consequence of his birth and early associations that he should cling to the house of the Stuarts. One would almost have applied to the young nobleman the term "recreant, " had he wavered when the descendant of Mary Stuart claimed his services. But such a course was far from his inclination. It was afterwards deemed expedient by his friends to plead for him on the ground of natural weakness of intellect; "but, " says a contemporary, "Lord Wintoun wants no courage, nor so much capacity as his friends find it for his interest to suggest. "[8] He was forward in action, and stimulated the military ardour of his followers, as they rushed with their ancient cry of "Set-on" to the combat. The earliest motto borne on these arms by the Seatons, "Hazard, yet forward, " might indeed be mournfully applied to all who engaged in the hopeless Rebellion of 1715.

Lord Wintoun, like Lord Derwentwater, was in the bloom of his youth when he summoned his tenantry to follow him to the rendezvous appointed by Lord Kenmure. He took with him three hundred men to the standard of James Stuart; but he appears to have carried with him a fiery and determined temper, —the accompaniment, perhaps, of noble qualities, but a dangerous attribute in times of difficulty.

Robert Dalzell, sixth Earl of Carnwath, was another of those Scottish noblemen whose adherence to the Stuarts can only be regarded as a natural consequence of their birth and education. The origin of his family, which was of great antiquity in the county of Lanark, but had been transplanted into Nithisdale, is referred to in the following anecdote. In the reign of Kenneth the Second, a kinsman of the King having been taken and hung by the Picts, a great reward was offered by Kenneth, if any one would rescue and restore the corpse of his relation. The enterprise was so hazardous, that no one would venture on so great a risk. "At last, " so runs the tale, "a certain gentleman came to the King, and said, 'Dalziel, ' which is the old Scottish word for 'I dare. ' He performed his engagement, and won for himself and his posterity the name which he had verified, and an armorial bearing corresponding to the action. "

To James the First and to Charles the First the Dalziels owed their honours, and had the usual fortune of paying dearly for them, during the Great Rebellion, by sequestration, and by the imprisonment of Robert, first Earl of Carnwath, after the battle of Worcester, whither he attended Charles the Second. Undaunted by the adversities which his house had formerly endured, Robert Dalzell, of Glenæ, sixth Earl of Carnwath, again came forward in 1715 to maintain the principles in which he had been nurtured, and to assist the family for whom his ancestors had suffered. During his childhood, the tutor of this nobleman had made it his chief care to instil into his mind the doctrine of hereditary right, and its consequent, passive obedience and non-resistance. At the University of Cambridge, young Dalzell had imbibed an affection for the liturgy and discipline of the Church of England; whilst his attainments had kept pace with the qualities of his heart, and the graces of his deportment. He was, in truth, a young man of fair promise, and one whose fate excited great interest, when a sombre tranquillity had succeeded to the turbulence of rebellion. Gentle in his address, affable, kind-hearted, Lord Carnwath had a natural and ready wit, and a great command of language, to which his English education had doubtless contributed. He was related by a former marriage between the families to the Earl of Wintoun, whose troop was commanded by Captain James Dalzell, the brother of Lord Carnwath. This young officer had served in the army of George the First, but he threw up his commission at the beginning of the Rebellion, —a circumstance which saved him from being shot at Preston as a deserter. [9]

Robert Balfour, fifth Earl of Burleigh, was among the chiefs who, shortly after the outbreak, avowed their adherence to the Pretender's party. He was one of the few Jacobites whose personal character has reflected discredit upon his motives, and disgraced his compeers: his story has the air of romance, but is perfectly reconcilable with the spirit of the times in which Lord Burleigh figured.

When a very young man he became attached to a girl of low rank, and was sent abroad by his friends in hopes of removing his attachment. Before he quitted Scotland, he swore, however, that if the young woman married in his absence, he would kill her husband. Upon returning home, he found that the unfortunate object of his affections had been united to Henry Stenhouse, the schoolmaster at Inverkeithing. The threat had not been uttered without a deep meaning: young Balfour kept his word, and hastening to the school where Stenhouse was pursuing his usual duties, he stabbed him in the midst of his scholars. The victim of this murderous attack died twelve days afterwards.

Nearly eight years had elapsed since the crime had been perpetrated, and the wretched murderer had encountered, since that time, his trial, in the Court of Justiciary, and had received sentence of death by beheading; but he escaped from prison a few days previously, by exchanging clothes with his sister. He was then a commoner; but in 1714, the title of Lord Burleigh, and an estate of six hundred and ninety-seven pounds yearly, devolved upon him. When the Rebellion broke out, his restless spirit, as well, perhaps, as the loss of reputation, and the miseries of reflection, impelled him to enter into the contest.

Such were the principal promoters of the insurrection in the south of Scotland; they were held together by firm bonds of sympathy, and their plans were concerted in renewed conferences at stated periods.

The twenty-ninth of May was, of course, religiously observed by this increasing and formidable party. During the previous year (1714) the Jacobite gentry had met at Lochmaben, under pretence of a horse-racing; and, although it does not appear that the Earl of Nithisdale was among those who assembled on that occasion, yet several of his kinsmen attended. The plates which were the prizes had significant devices: on one of them were wrought figures of men in a falling posture; above them stood one "eminent person, " the Pretender, underneath whom were inscribed the words from Ezekiel, xxi. 27, "I will overturn, overturn, overturn it: and it shall be no more, until he come whose right it is, and I will give it him. " When the races were ended, Lord Burleigh, then Master of Burleigh, led the way to the Cross of Lochmaben, where, with great solemnity, drums beating, and colours displayed, those there colected drank to *"their King's health; "* the Master of Burleigh giving the toast, and uttering an imprecation on all such as should refuse to pledge it. These meetings had been continued for several years, and, during the reign of Queen Anne, without any molestation from Government. [10] Lord Nithisdale took a decided part in all these measures, and was one of those who were considered as entirely to be trusted by the Earl of Mar, with regard to the projected arrival of the Pretender in Scotland. On the sixth of August, 1715, that project was communicated by Mar to the Earl of Nithisdale, through the medium of Captain Dalzell, who was despatched likewise to Lord Kenmure, and to the Earl of Carnwath. Lord Nithisdale obeyed the summons, and met the great council of the Jacobite nobles at Braemar, where the decisive and irrevocable step was taken.

Lord Nithisdale, in common with the other members of what was now termed the Jacobite Association, had been diligently preparing the contest. Meetings of the Association had been frequent, and even public. The finest horses had been bought up at any cost, with saddles and accoutrements, and numbers of horse-shoes. Many country gentlemen, who were in the habit of keeping only two or three saddle-horses at a time, now collected double the number; and a suspicion prevailed that it was the intention of some, who were Jacobites, to mount a troop. But no seizure had been made of their property in the last reign, there being few justices of the peace in Dumfriesshire, nominated by Queen Anne, who were not in the service of the Chevalier. [11] Trained bands were, however, soon raised by the well-affected gentry of the county for the protection of the neighbourhood; and Nithisdale was traversed by armed bands, —Closeburn House, then the residence of Sir Thomas Kirkpatrick,

[12] being a frequent point of union for the friends of the Hanoverian interests to assemble. [13] At Trepons, in the upper part of Nithisdale, was the first blood drawn that was shed in this disastrous quarrel, Mr. Bell of Nimsea, a Jacobite gentleman, being there shot through the leg by one of the guards, on his refusing to obey orders. [14] The occurrence was typical of the remorseless cruelty which was afterwards exhibited towards the brave but unfortunate insurgents.

By a clause in the act "for encouraging loyalty in Scotland, " passed on the thirtieth of August, power was given to the authorities to summon to Edinburgh all the heads of the Jacobite clans, and other suspected persons, by a certain day, to find bail for their good conduct. Among the long list of persons who were thus cited to appear, was the Earl of Nithisdale. Upon his non-appearance, he was, with the rest, denounced, and declared a rebel. [15] This citation was followed by an outbreak on the part of Lord Kenmure and his followers, simultaneous to that on which the Northumberland Jacobites had decided. And the borders now became the chief haunts of the insurgents, who continued moving from place to place, and from house to house, in order to ripen the scheme which involved, as they considered, their dearest interests.

The loyal inhabitants of Dumfries were engaged, one Saturday, in the solemnities of preparation for the holy sacrament, when they received intimation of a plot to surprise and take possession of the town on the following sabbath, during the time of communion. This project was defeated by the prompt assembling of forces, notwithstanding that Lord Kenmure, with one hundred and fifty-three horsemen, advanced within a mile and a half of the town, on his march from Moffat. Upon being advised of the preparations made for defence, this too prudent commander addressed his troops, and said, "that he doubted not there were, in the town, as brave gentlemen there as himself, and that he would not go on to Dumfries that day. " He returned to Lochmaben, where, on the following Thursday, the Pretender's standard was proclaimed: Lochmaben is a small market-town about fifteen miles from Dumfries; it served for some time as the head-quarters of the Jacobite party. "At their approach, " relates the historian of that local insurrection, "the people of that place had put their cattle into a fold to make room for their horses; but the beasts having broken the fold, some of them drew home to the town a little before day; and a townsman, going to hunt one of 'em out of his yeard, called on his dog nam'd 'Help. '

Hereupon the sentries cried 'Where? ' and apprehending it had been a party from Dumfries to attack them, gave the alarm to the rebels, who got up in great confusion. "

Lord Kenmure, attended by the Jacobite chiefs, and Lord Nithisdale, soon quitted the town of Lochmaben; and proceeding to Ecclefechan, and thence marching to Langholme, reached Hawick on the fifteenth of September, and determined on proceeding from that place into Teviotdale. Meantime measures were taken by the Duke of Roxburgh, who was Lieutenant Governor of Dumfriesshire, to prevent the Castle of Carlaverock being made available for the Jacobite forces. The Duke gave orders that the back bridge of the isle should be taken off, and a communication thus cut off between the Papists in the lower part of Galloway and the rebels in the borders. The inhabitants of the parish of Carlaverock were also strictly watched, being tenants, mostly, of the Earl of Nithisdale; and the same precaution was taken with regard to his Lordship's tenantry in Traquair, Terregles, and Kirkcunyean; yet, according to the statement of Mr. Reay, a most violent partisan against the Jacobites, the humble dwellers on these estates were but little disposed to follow their chieftain, who took, so the same account declares, "only two or three domestic servants with him. "[16] This, however, is contradicted by the assertion of Mr. Patten, who specifies that Lord Nithisdale was followed by three hundred of his tenantry; and also by the expectations which were founded, upon a close survey and scrutiny, by the agents of the Chevalier before the outbreak. [17]

Lord Nithisdale had now taken a last farewell of the beautiful and smiling country of his forefathers; with what bright hopes, with what anticipations of a successful march and a triumphant return he may have quitted Terregles, it is easy to conjecture. Unhappily his enterprise was linked to one over which a man, singularly ill-fitted for the office of command, presided: for it was decreed that the Jacobite forces, under the command of Lord Kenmure, should proceed to the assistance of Mr. Forster's ill-fated insurrection in the north of England.

The history of that luckless and ill-concerted enterprise has been already given. [18] The Earl of Nithisdale was taken prisoner after the battle of Preston, but little mention is made of his peculiar services at that place.

Lord Nithisdale was, with other prisoners of the same rank, removed to London. The prisoners of inferior rank were disposed of, under strong guards, in the different castles of Lancaster, Chester, and Liverpool. The indignities which were wreaked upon the unfortunate Jacobites as they entered London have been detailed in the life of Lord Derwentwater. Amid the cries of a savage populace, and the screams of "No warming pan, " "King George for ever! " an exclamation which proves how deeply the notion of spurious birth had sunk into the minds of the people, the Earl of Nithisdale was conducted, his arms tied with cords, and the reins of his horse taken from him, with his unfortunate companions, into the Tower. He arrived in London on the 9th of December, 1715. [19]

Of the manner in which the State prisoners of that period were treated, there are sufficient records left to prove that no feeling of compassion for what might be deemed a wrong, but yet a generous principle of devotion to the Stuarts, no high-toned sentiment of respect to bravery, nor consideration for the habits and feelings of their prisoners, influenced the British Government during that time of triumph. The mode in which those unfortunate captives were left in the utmost penury and necessity to petition for some provision, after their estates were escheated, plainly manifests how little there was of that sympathy with calamity which marks the present day. [20]

But if the State prisoners in London were treated with little humanity, those who were huddled together in close prisons at Preston, Chester, Liverpool, and the other towns were in a still more wretched condition.

In the stores of the State Paper Office are to be found heartrending appeals for mercy, from prisoners sinking under dire diseases from too close contiguity, or from long confinement in one apartment. Consumption seems to have been very prevalent; and in Newgate the gaol fever raged. For this rigorous confinement the excuse was, that it had been found impossible to give the prisoners air, without risk of escape. In Chester, the townspeople conspired to assist the poor wretches in this endeavour; and perhaps, in regard to those of meaner rank, the authorities were not very averse to the success of such efforts, for the prisons were crowded, and the expense of even keeping the unfortunate captives alive began to be a source of complaint on the part of Government.

The great majority of the prisoners of the north were country gentlemen, Roman Catholics, from Cumberland and Northumberland, —men who were hearty and sincere in their convictions of the righteousness of their cause—men, whose ancestors had mustered their tenantry in the field for Charles the First. To those whose lives were spared, a petition was recommended, and taken round for signature, praying that their sentence of death or of imprisonment might be exchanged for transportation. But, whether these high-spirited gentlemen expected that another insurrection might act in their favour, or whether they preferred death to a final farewell, under circumstances so dreadful, to their country, does not appear. They mostly refused to sign the petition, which was offered to them singly: and the commandant at Preston, Colonel Rapin, in his correspondence with Lord Townshend, expresses his annoyance at their obstinacy, and expatiates on the inconvenience of the numbers under his charge at Preston. At length, after Captain John Dalzell, brother to the Earl of Carnwath, had signed the petition, a large body of the prisoners were ordered to be transported without their petitioning, and to be put in irons. They were hurried away to Liverpool, to embark thence for the Colonies, gentlemen and private soldiers mingled in one mass; but orders were afterwards sent by Lord Townshend to detain the gentlemen. Three hundred and twenty-seven prisoners had, however, been already shipped off. Those who remained were not permitted to converse, even with each other, without risk, —one Thomas Wells being appointed as a spy to write to the Jacobites, and to discourse with them, under the garb of friendliness, in order to draw out their real sentiments. [21]

From this digression, which may not be deemed irrelevant, since it marks the spirit of the times, we return to the unhappy prisoners in the Tower, which was now thickly tenanted by the fallen Jacobites.

Lord Nithisdale had the sorrow of knowing that many of his friends and kinsmen were in the same gloomy and impenetrable fortress to which he had been conducted. It is possible that the Jacobite noblemen were not hopeless; and that remembering the clemency of William the Third to those who had held a treasonable correspondence with the Court of St. Germains, they might look for a similar line of policy from the reigning monarch.

It must be acknowledged, however, that Government had been greatly exasperated by acts of violence and of wanton destruction on the part of the Jacobites throughout the country; and that the general disaffection throughout the North, and, in particular, the strong Tory predilections at Oxford, must have greatly aggravated the dangers, and consequently, in a political view, have enhanced the crimes of the Chevalier's adherents. "The country, " writes Colonel Rapin to Lord Townshend, "is full of them [the Jacobites], and the same spirit reigns in London. "

"Oxford, " writes an informant, under the name of *Philopoliticus,* "is debauched by Jacobitism. They call the Parliament the Rump; and riots in the street, with cries of 'Down with the Rump! ' occur daily. " Even the fellows and heads of the colleges were disposed to Jacobite opinions; and the Jacobites had expected that the city would become the Chevalier's head-quarters as it had been that of Charles the First. [22]

But that which hastened the fate of the Earl of Nithisdale and of his friends, was the landing of James Stuart, at Peterhead, in Scotland, on the twenty-second of December, —an event which took place too late for his friends and partisans, and fatally increased the calamities of those who had suffered in his cause. On Monday, the ninth of January, he made his public entry into Perth, and, on the same day, the reigning monarch addressed his Parliament. [23]

"Among the many unavoidable ill consequences of this Rebellion, " said the King, "none affects me more sensibly than that extraordinary burden which it has, and must, create to my faithful subjects. To ease them as far as lies in my power, I take this first opportunity of declaring that I freely give up all the estates that shall become forfeited to the Crown by this Rebellion, to be applied towards defraying the extraordinary expense incurred on this occasion. " As soon as a suitable address had been returned by both Houses, a debate concerning the prisoners taken in rebellion ensued, and a conference was determined on with the House of Lords. Mr. Lechmere, who was named to carry up the message to the Lords, returned, and made a long and memorable speech, concerning the rise, depth, and extent of the Rebellion; after which it was resolved, *nemine contradicente,* to impeach the Earl of Derwentwater, William Lord Widdrington, William Earl of Nithisdale, Robert Earl of Carnwath, George Earl of Wintoun, William Viscount Kenmure, and William Lord Nairn, of high treason.

The same evening, a committee was appointed to draw up articles of impeachment; and so great was the dispatch used, and so zealous were the committee, that in two hours the articles were prepared, agreed to, and ordered to be engrossed with the usual saving clause. During this time, the Lords remained sitting, and before ten o'clock the articles were presented before that assembly.

On the following day, the prisoners were conducted before the Bar of the House, where the articles of impeachment were read to them, and they were desired to prepare their replies on the sixteenth day of the month. Thus only six days were allowed for their answers; upon application, however, two days more were granted. The prisoners were allowed to choose counsel, and also to have a free communication with any persons, either peers or commoners, whom they might name.

On the twenty-first of January, the King again addressed his Parliament, and referred to the recent landing of the "Pretender" in Scotland. The reply of the two Houses to this speech emphatically declares, "that the landing of the Pretender hath increased their indignation against him and his adherents, and that they were determined to do everything in their power to assist his Majesty, not only in subduing the present Rebellion, but in destroying the seeds and causes of it, that the like disturbance may never rise again to impair the blessings of his Majesty's reign. "[24]

On the ninth of February the six impeached lords were brought, at eleven in the morning, to the Court erected in Westminster Hall, wherein both Lords and Commons were assembled. The ceremonial of opening this celebrated Court was conducted in the following manner: —

The Lords being placed on their proper seats, and the Lord High Steward on the woolsack, the Clerk of the Crown in the Court of Chancery, after making three reverences to the Lord Steward, presented, on his knees, the King's commission; which, after the usual reverences, was placed on the table. A proclamation for silence was then heard. The High Steward stood up and addressed the Peers, "His Majesty's commission is going to be read; your Lordships are desired to attend. "

The Peers hereupon arose, uncovered themselves, and stood while the commission was being read. The voice of the Sergeant-at-arms exclaimed, "God save the King! " The Herald and Gentleman Usher of the Black Rod, after three reverences, kneeling, then presented the White Staff to his Grace, the High Steward; upon which his Grace, attended by the Herald, the Black Rod, and Seal Bearer, removed from the woolsack to an armed chair which was placed on the uppermost step but one next to the throne.

The Clerk of the Crown ordered the Serjeant-at-arms to make another proclamation for silence; and amidst the stillness, the Lieutenant of the Tower brought in, amid an assembly of their compeers, his prisoners. Lord Wintoun was alone absent; for he had obtained a few days of delay. [25]

The Earl of Nithisdale pleaded guilty, with his companions in misfortune. On Thursday, the nineteenth of January, when called upon for his answer, his defence was couched in the following terms: "It is with the greatest confusion, " he began, "the said Earl appears at your Lordships' Bar, under the weight of an impeachment by the Commons of Great Britain for high treason. " He went on to declare that he had ever been a zealous assertor of the liberties of his country, and never engaged in any design to subvert the established Government and good laws of the kingdom.

When summoned by those who were entrusted with the administration of the government in Scotland to Edinburgh, he did, he alleged, not obey the summons, being assured that if he went thither he would be made a close prisoner. He was therefore forced to abscond; for being at that time in ill-health, a confinement in Edinburgh Castle would have endangered his life. The Earl also stated that he had remained in privacy, until several of the persons mentioned in the impeachment had appeared in arms very near the place where they had lain concealed. He then "inconsiderately and unfortunately" joined them, with four domestics only, and proceeded in their company to the places named in the indictment; but knew nothing of the intended insurrection until the party "were actually in arms. " After some expressions, stating that he was deeply sensible of his offence, he confessed, with "a sorrow equal to his crime, " that he was guilty; "but referred to his hopes of mercy, grounded on his having capitulated at Preston, where he performed the duty of a Christian in preventing effusion of blood; and on his reliance on his Majesty's mercy. "

On being further asked by the Lord High Steward whether he had anything to say "why judgment should not pass upon him according to law, " Lord Nithisdale recapitulated the points in his answer in so weak a voice, that the Lord Steward reiterated the former question: "Have you pleaded anything in arrest of judgment? " "No, my Lord, I have not, " was the reply.

The Earl of Nithisdale received the sentence of condemnation with the other Lords; and, like them, had the misery of hearing his doom prefaced by a long and admired harangue. The sentence was then pronounced in all its barbarous particularities; the law being in this, as the Lord High Steward declared, deaf to all distinctions of rank, "required that he should pronounce them. " But his Grace intimated the most ignominious and painful parts of the sentence were usually remitted.

Lord Nithisdale, unlike Lord Widdrington and Lord Kenmure, who had referred in terms of anguish to their wives and children, had made no appeal on the plea of those family ties, to which few of his judges could have been insensible. He returned to the Tower, under sentence of death, to be saved by the heroism of a woman; according to some accounts, of his mother; [26] but actually, by the fearless, devoted affection of his wife.

Winifred, Countess of Nithisdale, appears, from her portrait by Kneller, to have conjoined to an heroic contempt of danger a feminine and delicate appearance, with great loveliness of countenance. [27] She was descended from a family who knew no prouder recollection than that their castle-towers had been the last to welcome the unhappy Charles the First in the manner suited to royalty. Her mother was the Lady Elizabeth Herbert, daughter of Edward, the second Marquis of Worcester, and author of "The Century of Inventions. " Lady Nithisdale was therefore the great-granddaughter of that justly honoured Marquis of Worcester whose loyalty and disinterestedness were features of a character as excellent in private life, as benevolent, as sincere, as it was conspicuous in his public career. Yet, so universal, so continual has been the popular prejudice against Popery in this country, that even the virtues of this good man could scarcely rescue him from the imputation, as Lord Clarendon expresses it, of being "that sort of Catholics, the people rendered odious, by accusing to be most Jesuited. "

The maternal family of Lady Nithisdale were, therefore, of the same faith with her husband, and, like his family, they had suffered deeply for the cause of the Stuarts; and it is remarkable that, with what some might deem infatuation, many descendants of those who had seen their fairest possessions ravaged, their friends and kindred slain, should be ready to suffer again. It is impossible for any reasoning to dispel the idea that this must be a true and fixed principle, independent, in many noble instances, of the hope of reward, —a far less enduring motive, and one which would be apt to change with every change of fortune.

Lady Nithisdale, on her father's side, was descended from the Herberts of Powis Castle, who were ennobled in the reign of James the First. She was the fourth daughter of William, Marquis of Powis, who followed James the Second, after his abdication, to France, and was created by that monarch Duke of Powis, a title not recognised in England. [28] The titular Duke of Powis, as he is frequently called in history, chose to remain at St. Germains, and was at length outlawed for not returning within a certain period. He died at St. Germains in 1696. Upon the death of her father, Lady Winifred Herbert was placed with her elder sister, the Lady Lucy, in the English convent at Bruges, of which Lady Lucy eventually became Abbess. A less severe fate was, however, in store for the younger sister.

Under these adverse circumstances, so far as related to the proper maintenance of her father's rank in England, was Winifred Herbert reared. How and where she met with Lord Nithisdale, and whether the strong attachment which afterwards united them so indissolubly, was nurtured in the saloons of St. Germains, or in the romantic haunts of Nithisdale, we have no information to decide, neither have the descendants of the family been able even to ascertain the date of her marriage.

It is not improbable, however, that, before his marriage, Lord Nithisdale visited Paris and Rome, since the practice of making what was called "the grand tour" not only prevailed among the higher classes, but especially among the Jacobite nobility, many of whom, as in the case of Lord Derwentwater, were educated abroad; and this is more especially likely to have been the case in the instance of Lord Nithisdale, since, as Lady Nithisdale remarks in her narrative, her husband was a Roman Catholic in a part of Scotland peculiarly adverse to that faith, "the only support, " as she calls him, "of the

Catholics against the inveteracy of the Whigs, who were very numerous in that part of Scotland. "

In her participation of those decided political opinions, which were inbred in Lady Nithisdale, she appears not to have departed from that feminine character which rises to sublimity when coupled with a fearless sacrifice of selfish considerations. It was the custom of the day for ladies to share in the intrigues of faction, more or less. Lady Fauconbridge, the Countess of Derwentwater, Lady Seaforth, all appear to have taken a lively part in the interests of the Jacobites. The Duchess of Marlborough was, politically speaking, extinct; but the restless love of ascendancy is never extinct. The fashionable world were still divided between her, and the rival whom she so despised, Catherine Sedley, Duchess of Buckingham.

But Lady Nithisdale, living in the North, and possibly occupied with her two children, remained, as she affirms, in the country, until the intelligence of her lord's committal to the Tower brought her from her seclusion years afterwards; she writes thus to her sister, the Lady Lucy Herbert, Abbess of the English Augustine Nuns at Bruges, who had, it seems, requested from her an account of the circumstances under which Lord Nithisdale escaped from the Tower.

"I first came to London, " Lady Nithisdale writes, "upon hearing that my lord was committed to the Tower. I was at the same time informed that he had expressed the greatest anxiety to see me, having, as he afterwards told me, no one to console him till I came. I rode to Newcastle, and from thence took the stage to York. When I arrived there, the snow was so deep that the stage could not set out for London. The season was so severe, and the roads so bad, that the post itself was stopped: however, I took horses and rode to London, though the snow was generally above the horses' girths and arrived safe without any accident. "

After this perilous journey, the determined woman sought interviews with the reigning Ministers, but she met with no encouragement; on the contrary, she was assured that, although some of the prisoners were to be saved, Lord Nithisdale would not be of the number.

"When I inquired, " she continues, "into the reason of this distinction, I could obtain no other answer than that they would not flatter me. But I soon perceived the reasons, which they declined alleging me. A Roman Catholic upon the frontiers of Scotland, who headed a very considerable party, a man whose family had always signalized itself by its loyalty to the royal house of Stuart, would, " she argued, "become a very agreeable sacrifice to the opposite party. They still, " so thought Lady Nithisdale, "remembered the defence of the castle of Carlaverock against the republicans by Lord Nithisdale's grandfather, and were resolved not to let his grandson escape from their power. "

Upon weighing all these considerations, Lady Nithisdale perceived that all hope of mercy was vain; she determined to dismiss all such dependance from her mind, and to confide in her own efforts. It was not impossible to bribe the guards who were set over the state prisoners: indeed, from the number of escapes, there must either have been a very venal spirit among the people who had the charge of the prisoners generally, or a compassionate leaning in their favour.

Having formed her resolution, Lady Nithisdale decided to communicate it to no one, except to her "dear Evans, " a maid, or companion, who was of paramount assistance to her in the whole affair.

Meantime, public indications of compassion for the condemned lords, seemed to offer better hopes than the dangerous enterprise of effecting an escape.

On the eighteenth of February, orders were sent both to the Lieutenant of the Tower and to the Sheriffs of London and Middlesex for the executions of the rebel lords. [29] Great solicitations had, meantime, been made for them, and the petitions for mercy not only reached the Court, but came down to the two Houses of Parliament, and being seconded by some members, debates ensued. That in the Commons ended in a motion for an adjournment, carried by a majority of seven only, and intended to avoid any further interposition in that House. Many who used to vote with the Government, influenced, says a contemporary writer, by "the word *mercy*, voted with the contrary party. " In the House of Peers, however, the question being put, whether the petitions should be received and read, it was carried by a majority of nine or ten voices.

But the sanguine hopes of those who were hanging upon the decisions of the Lords for life or death, were again cruelly disappointed. After reading the petitions, the next question was, whether in case of an impeachment, the King had power to reprieve? This was carried by an affirmative, and followed by a motion to address his Majesty, humbly to desire him to reprieve the lords who lay under sentence of death. These relentings, and the successive tides of feeling displayed in this high assembly, prove how divided the higher classes were on the points of hereditary monarchy, and others also at issue; but the Whig ascendancy prevailed. There was a clause introduced into the address, which nullified all former show of mercy; and the King was merely petitioned "to reprieve such of the condemned lords as deserve his mercy; and that the time of the respite should be left to his Majesty's discretion. " This clause was carried by five votes only.

To the address the following inauspicious answer was returned from King George: "That on this, and other occasions, he would do what he thought most consistent with the dignity of his Crown, and the safety of his people. "

This struggle between the parties ended, says the author of the Register, "in the execution of two of these condemned lords, and the removal of some others from their employments, that had been most solicitous for their preservation. "

The objects of this petty tyranny could well afford to succumb under the workings of that mean and revengeful spirit, whilst they might cherish the conviction of having used their efforts in the true spirit of that Christianity which remembers no considerations of worldly interest, when opposed to duty. Lady Nithisdale's relation of this anxious and eventful day, the twenty-third of February, is far too animated to be changed in a single expression. She had refused to remain confined with Lord Nithisdale in the Tower, on the plea of infirm health; but actually, because she well knew that she could better aid his cause whilst herself at liberty. She was then forbidden to see her husband; but by bribing the guards, she often contrived to have secret interviews with him, until the day before that on which the prisoners were condemned.

"On the twenty-second of February, which fell on a Thursday, our general petition was presented to the House of Lords, the purport of which was to interest the Lords to intercede with his Majesty to pardon the prisoners. We were, however, disappointed. The day before the petition was to be presented, the Duke of St. Albans, who had promised my Lady Derwentwater to present it, when it came to the point, failed in his word. However, as she was the only English Countess concerned, it was incumbent on her to have it presented. We had but one day left before the execution, and the Duke still promised to present the petition; but for fear he should fail, I engaged the Duke of Montrose to secure its being done by one or the other. I then went in company with most of the ladies of quality then in town, to solicit the interest of the Lords as they were going to the House. They all behaved to me with great civility, but particularly the Earl of Pembroke, who, though he desired me not to speak to him, yet he promised to employ his interest in my favour, and honourably kept his word, for he spoke very strongly in our behalf."[30]

"The subject of the debate was, whether the King had the power to pardon those who had been condemned by Parliament: and it was chiefly owing to Lord Pembroke's speech that it was carried in the affirmative. However, one of the Lords stood up and said that the House could only intercede for those who should prove themselves worthy of their intercession, but not for all of them indiscriminately. This salvo quite blasted all my hopes, for I was assured that it was aimed at the exclusion of those who should refuse to subscribe to the petition, which was a thing I knew my lord would never submit to; nor, in fact, could I wish to preserve his life on those terms. As the motion had passed generally, I thought I could draw from it some advantage in favour of my design. Accordingly I immediately left the House of Lords, and hastened to the Tower, where, affecting an air of joy and satisfaction, I told the guards I passed by, that I came to bring joyful tidings to the prisoners. I desired them to lay aside their fears, for the petition had passed the House in their favour. I then gave them some money to drink to the Lords and his Majesty, though it was trifling; for I thought if I were too liberal on the occasion, they might suspect my designs, and that giving them something would gain their good will and services for the next day, which was the eve of the execution. "

On the following day Lady Nithisdale was too much occupied in preparations for her scheme to visit the Tower; the evening of the eventful twenty-third of February arrived; and when all things were put in readiness, this resolute and well-judging woman threw herself upon the confidence of one in whose power she was, to a certain degree, and whose co-operation she could only secure by such a proceeding. She sent for the landlady of the house in which she lodged, and told her that she had made up her mind to effect Lord Nithisdale's escape, since there was no chance of his being pardoned. She added those few but thrilling words: "This is the last night before his execution! " While she spoke, perhaps, the condemned nobleman was supplicating on his knees to God for that mercy which was withheld by man. Imagination paints the despondency of Lord Derwentwater; the calm and dignified sorrow of the justly pitied Kenmure.

Lady Nithisdale then made a request calculated to alarm a woman of an ordinary character; but she seems to have understood the disposition of the person whom she thus addressed.

"I told her that I had every thing in readiness, and that I trusted she would not refuse to accompany me, that my lord might pass for her. I pressed her to come immediately, as we had no time to lose. " This sudden announcement, which a less sagacious mind might have deemed injudicious, had the effect which Lady Nithisdale expected; the undertaking was one of such risk, that it could only be an enterprise of impulse, except to her whose affections were deeply interested in the result. The consent of Mrs. Mills was carried by storm, as well as that of another coadjutor, a Mrs. Morgan, who usually bore the name of Hilton, to whom Lady Nithisdale dispatched a messenger, begging her to come immediately. "Their surprise and astonishment, " remarks Lady Nithisdale, speaking of these, her two confidantes, "made them consent, without ever thinking of the consequences. " The scheme was, that Mrs. Mills, who was tall and portly, should pass for Lord Nithisdale; Mrs. Morgan was to carry concealed the bundle of "clothes that were to serve Mrs. Mills when she left her own behind her. " After certain other preparations, all managed with infinite dexterity and shrewdness, these three heroines set out in a coach for the Tower, into which they were to be admitted, under the plea of taking a last leave of Lord Nithisdale. Lady Nithisdale, even whilst her heart throbbed with agitation, continued to support her spirits. "When we were in the coach; " she relates, "I never ceased talking, that they her companions might have no leisure to repent.

"On our arrival at the Tower, the first I introduced was Mrs. Morgan (for I was only allowed to take in one at a time). She brought in the clothes which were to serve Mrs. Mills when she left her own behind her. When Mrs. Morgan had taken off what she had brought for my purpose, I conducted her back to the staircase; and in going I begged her to send my maid to dress me, that I was afraid of being too late to present my last petition that night if she did not come immediately. I dispatched her safe, and went partly down stairs to meet Mrs. Mills, who had the precaution to hold her handkerchief to her face, as is natural for a woman to do when she is going to take her last farewell of a friend on the eve of his execution. I had indeed desired her to do so, that my lord might go out in the same manner. Her eyebrows were rather inclined to be sandy, and my lord's were very dark and very thick. However, I had prepared some paint of the colour of hers, to disguise his with; I also brought an artificial head-dress of the same coloured hair as hers, and I painted his face and his cheeks with rouge to hide his long beard, which he had not had time to shave.

"All this provision I had before left in the Tower. The poor guards, whom my slight liberality the day before had endeared me to, let me go quietly out with my company, and were not so strictly on the watch as they usually had been; and the more so, as they were persuaded, from what I had told them the day before, that the prisoners would obtain their pardon. I made Mrs. Mills take off her own hood, and put on that which I had brought for her. I then took her by the hand and led her out of my lord's chamber; and in passing through the next room, in which were several people, with all the concern imaginable I said, 'My dear Mrs. Catherine, go in all haste, and send me my waiting-maid; she certainly cannot reflect how late it is. I am to present my petition to-night, and if I let slip this opportunity I am undone, for to-morrow is too late. Hasten her as much as possible, for I shall be on thorns till she comes.' Everybody in the room, who were chiefly the guards' wives and daughters, seemed to compassionate me exceedingly, and the sentinel officiously opened me the door. When I had seen her safe out, I returned to my lord and finished dressing him. I had taken care that Mrs. Mills did not go out crying, as she came in, that my lord might better pass for the lady who came in crying and afflicted; and the more so, as he had the same dress that she wore. When I had almost finished dressing my lord in all my petticoats except one, I perceived it was growing dark, and was afraid that the light of the candles might betray us, so I resolved to set off. I went out leading him by the hand, whilst he held his handkerchief to his eyes. I spoke to him in the most piteous and afflicted tone, bewailing bitterly the negligence of Evans, who had ruined me by her delay. Then I said,

'My dear Mrs. Betty, for the love of God, run quickly and bring her with you; you know my lodging, and if you ever made dispatch in your life, do it at present: I am almost distracted with this disappointment. ' The guards opened the door, and I went down stairs with him, still conjuring him to make all possible dispatch. As soon as he had cleared the door I made him walk before me, for fear the sentinel should take notice of his walk, but I continued to press him to make all the dispatch he possibly could. At the bottom of the stairs I met my dear Evans, into whose hands I confided him. I had before engaged Mr. Mills to be in readiness before the Tower to conduct him to some place of safety, in case we succeeded. He looked upon the affair as so very improbable to succeed, that his astonishment, when he saw us, threw him into such a consternation that he was almost out of himself; which Evans perceiving, with the greatest presence of mind, without telling him anything, lest he should mistrust them, conducted him to some of her own friends on whom she could rely, and so secured him, without which we certainly should have been undone. When she had conducted him and left him with them, she returned to Mr. Mills, who had by this time recovered himself from his astonishment. They went home together; and having found a place of security, they conducted him to it. In the mean time, as I had pretended to have sent the young lady on a message, I was obliged to return up stairs and go back to my lord's room in the same feigned anxiety of being too late, so that everybody seemed sincerely to sympathise in my distress. When I was in the room, I talked as if he had been really present. I answered my own questions in my lord's voice, as nearly as I could imitate it. I walked up and down as if we were conversing together, till I thought they had time enough thoroughly to clear themselves of the guards. I then thought proper to make off also. I opened the door and stood half in it, that those in the outward chamber might hear what I said, but held it so close that they could not look in. I bade my lord formal farewell for the night, and added, that something more than usual must have happened to make Evans negligent on this important occasion, who had always been so punctual in the smallest trifles, that I saw no other remedy than to go in person. That if the Tower was then open, when I had finished my business, I would return that night; but that he might be assured I would be with him as early in the morning as I could gain admittance into the Tower, and I flattered myself I should bring more favourable news. Then, before I shut the door, I pulled through the string of the latch, so that it could only be opened in the inside.

"I then shut it with some degree of force, that I might be sure of its being well shut. I said to the servant as I passed by (who was ignorant of the whole transaction), that he need not carry in candles to his master till my lord sent for them, as he desired to finish some prayers first. "[31]

Thus ended this singular, successful, and heroic scheme. It was now necessary that the devoted Lady Nithisdale should secure her own safety.

She had, it seems, been bent upon proffering a last petition to King George, in case her attempt had failed. She drove home to her lodgings, where a friend, named Mackenzie, waited to take her petition. "There is no need of a petition, " were the words that broke from the agitated woman; "my lord is safe, and out of the Tower, and out of the hands of his enemies, though I know not where he is. " Lady Nithisdale then discharged the coach which had brought her to her lodgings, a precaution which she always observed for fear of being traced, —never going in the same vehicle to more than one place. She sent for a chair, and went to the Duchess of Buccleugh, who had promised to present her petition, having taken her precaution against all events. The Duchess expected her, but had company with her; and Lady Nithisdale barely escaped being shown into the room where her friend was with her company. She, however, excused herself, and, sending a message to her Grace, proceeded to the residence of the Duchess of Montrose. "This lady had ever, " said Lady Nithisdale, "borne a part in my distresses; " she now left her company to see and console the wife of the rebel lord, of whom, she conjectured, Lady Nithisdale must have taken, that night, a last farewell. As the two friends met, the Duchess, to her astonishment, found her visitor in a transport of joy; "she was extremely shocked and frightened, " writes Lady Nithisdale; "and has since confessed to me that she thought my troubles had driven me out of myself. " She cautioned Lady Nithisdale to secrecy, and even to flight; for the King had been extremely irritated by the petition already sent in by Lady Nithisdale. The generous Duchess was, among those who frequented the Court, the only person that knew Lady Nithisdale's secret. After a brief interview, Lady Nithisdale, sending for a fresh chair, hurried away to a house which her faithful attendant Evans had found for her, and where she was to learn tidings of Lord Nithisdale. Here she learned that Lord Nithisdale had been removed from the lodging to which he had at first been conducted, to the mean abode of a poor woman just opposite the guard-house. Here the former Lord of Carlaverock and of Nithisdale met his wife. Lady Nithisdale hurries over the meeting, but her simple account has its own powers of description.

The good woman of the house had, it seems, but one small room up a pair of stairs, and a very small bed in it. "We threw ourselves on the bed that we might not be heard walking up and down. She left us a bottle of wine and some bread, and Mrs. Mills brought us some more in her pockets the next day. We subsisted on this provision from Thursday till Saturday night, when Mr. Mills came and conducted my lord to the Venetian Ambassador's. We did not communicate the affair to his Excellency, but one of the servants concealed him in his own room till Wednesday, on which day the Ambassador's coach-and-six was to go down to Dover to meet his brother. My lord put on a livery, and went down in the retinue, without the least suspicion, to Dover; where Mr. Michel (which was the name of the Ambassador's servant) hired a small vessel, and immediately set sail for Calais. The passage was so remarkably short, that the captain threw out this reflection, —that the wind could not have served better if the passengers had been flying for their lives, little thinking it to be really the case.

"Mr. Michel might have easily returned without suspicion of being concerned in my lord's escape; but my lord seemed inclined to have him with him, which he did, and he has at present a good place under our young master. This is an exact and as full an account of this affair, and of the persons concerned in it, as I could possibly give you, to the best of my memory, and you may rely upon the truth of it. For my part, I absconded to the house of a very honest man in Drury Lane, where I remained till I was assured of my lord's safe arrival on the Continent. I then wrote to the Duchess of Buccleugh (everybody thought till then that I was gone off with my lord) to tell her that I understood I was suspected of having contrived my lord's escape, as was very natural to suppose; that if I could have been happy enough to have done it, I should be flattered to have the merit of it attributed to me; but that a bare suspicion without proof, would never be a sufficient ground for my being punished for a supposed offence, though it might be motive sufficient for me to provide a place of security; so I entreated her to procure leave for me to go about my business. So far from granting my request, they were resolved to secure me if possible. After several debates, Mr. Solicitor-General, who was an utter stranger to me, had the humanity to say, that since I showed such respect to Government as not to appear in public, it would be cruel to make any search after me. Upon which it was resolved that no further search should be made if I remained concealed; but that if I appeared either in England or Scotland, I should be secured. But this was not sufficient for me, unless I could submit to see my son exposed to beggary. My lord sent for me up to town in such haste, that I had not time to settle anything before I left Scotland. I had in my hand all the family papers, and I dared trust them to nobody: my house might have been searched without warning, consequently they were far from being secure there. In this distress, I had the precaution to bury them in the ground, and nobody but myself and the gardener knew where they were. I did the same with other things of value. The event proved that I had acted prudently; for after my departure they searched the house, and God only knows what might have transpired from those papers! All these circumstances rendered my presence absolutely necessary, otherwise they might have been lost; for though they retained the highest preservation after one very severe winter, (for when I took them up they were as dry as if they came from the fire-side,) yet they could not possibly have remained so much longer without prejudice. "

Lord Nithisdale went to Rome, and never revisited his native country; indeed, the project of the Rebellion of 1745, and the unceasing efforts and hopes by which it was preceded on the part of the Jacobites, must have rendered such a step impracticable to one who seems to have been especially obnoxious to the house of Hanover.

His escape, according to Lady Nithisdale, both infuriated and alarmed George the First, "who flew into an excessive passion, " as she expresses it, on the news transpiring; and exclaimed that he was betrayed, and that it could not have been done without a confederacy. He instantly dispatched messengers to the Tower, to give orders that the prisoners who were still there, might be the more effectually secured. He never forgave Lady Nithisdale; and the effects of his powerful resentment were such, as eventually to drive her for ever from England.

Inexperienced, young, a stranger in the vast metropolis, Lady Nithisdale was now left alone, to skulk from place to place that she might avoid the effects of the royal displeasure. She absconded to the house of an "honest man" in Drury Lane, where she remained in concealment until she heard of her husband's safe arrival on the

Continent. A report, meantime, prevailed of her having been the means of Lord Nithisdale's escape; and it was generally believed that she had gone with him. To the surprise of the Duchess of Buccleugh, Lady Nithisdale one day appeared before her, the object of that sudden and perhaps undesired visit being to obtain, by the influence of the Duchess, leave to quit London; and to disseminate, through her Grace, a belief that the safety of Lord Nithisdale was not procured by his wife's means. It must have been one of the most aggravating circumstances to that noble and affectionate being, to have employed so much artifice in the conduct of this affair; but, if ever artifice be allowable, it is when opposed as a weapon to tyranny. Besides, Lady Nithisdale had now not only her own safety to consider; she had to protect the interests of her son.

Those whom she had mortally offended were eager to punish her courage by imprisonment.

The Solicitor-General, however, showed a more compassionate spirit than his employers, and in the course of several debates in the House of Commons, submitted that if Lady Nithisdale paid so much respect to Government as not to appear in public, it would be cruel to make any farther search after her. It was therefore decided that unless the lady were seen in England or Scotland, she should be unmolested; but if she were observed in either of those countries, she should be secured. This might be a decision of mercy, but Lady Nithisdale could not submit to it, unless she left her son's estate to be ruined by waste and plunder. Hurried as she had been to London, she had found time only to make one arrangement, which proved to be of the utmost importance.

"I had in my hands, " she relates, "all the family papers, and dared trust them to nobody. My house might have been searched without warning, consequently they were far from being secure there. In this distress I had the precaution to bury them in the ground, and nobody but myself and the gardener knew where they were: I did the same with other things of value. The event proved that I had acted prudently to save these papers. "

Lady Nithisdale determined to return, at all risks, to Scotland; and it was, perhaps, from her care in concealing the important documents to which she refers, that the estates were not escheated. She soon put into execution the heroic determination, of which she made no boast. Her journey was full of perils; not only those incident to the time and season of the year, but the great risk of being betrayed and discovered. Little respect was paid, in that reign, when truly the spirit of chivalry was extinguished, to the weaker sex. Ladies, active and instrumental as they were in political intrigues, if found out, were made to pay the penalty of their dissaffection with hard imprisonment; or, if at large, wandered from place to place, conscious that the eye of the law pursued their footsteps. Lady Seaforth, the wife of one of the rebel lords, was reduced to necessity, even of the common necessaries of life; and Lady Widdrington and her children shared the same cruel privations. [32]

Believing herself, also, to be an object of peculiar dislike to George the First, Lady Nithisdale's courage in braving the royal displeasure a second time, certainly appears to border upon folly and a rash temerity. But she knew well that if she could once reach the land of the Maxwells, the strict respect paid to the head of the clan, and the remarkable fidelity of all ranks of the Scotch to those who trust to their honour, would there prove her safeguard. The great danger was in making the journey. But the young heroic Countess dismissed all fear from her mind, and prepared for her enterprise.

"In short, " she thus prefaces her narrative, "as I had once exposed my life for the safety of the father, I could not do less than hazard it once more for the fortune of the son. I had never travelled on horseback but from York to London, as I told you; but the difficulties did not arise now from the severity of the season, but the fear of being discovered and arrested. To avoid this, I bought three saddle-horses, and set off with my dear Evans and a very trusty servant, whom I brought with me out of Scotland. We put up at all the smallest inns on the road, that could take in a few horses, and where I thought I was not known; for I was thoroughly known at all the considerable inns on the northern road. Thus I arrived safe at Traquhair, where I thought myself secure, for the lieutenant of the county being a friend of my lord's, would not permit any search to be made after me without sending me previous notice to abscond. Here I had the assurance to rest myself two whole days, pretending that I was going to my own house with leave from Government. I sent no notice to my house, that the magistrates of Dumfries might not make too narrow enquiries about me. So they were ignorant of my arrival in the country till I was at home, where I still feigned to have permission to remain. To carry on the deceit the better, I sent to all my neighbours and invited them to come to my house. I took up my papers at night and sent them off to Traquhair. It was a particular stroke of providence that I made the dispatch I did, for they soon suspected me, and by a very favourable accident, one of them was overheard to say to the magistrates of Dumfries, that the next day they would insist on seeing my leave from Government. This was bruited about, and when I was told of it, I expressed my surprise that they should be so backward in coming to pay their respects; 'but, ' said I, 'better late than never: be sure to tell them that they shall be welcome whenever they choose to come. '

"This was after dinner, but I lost no time to put everything in readiness with all possible secrecy; and the next morning before day-break, I set off again for London with the same attendants, and, as before, put up at the smallest inns and arrived safe once more. "[33]

The report of her journey into Scotland had preceded Lady Nithisdale's return to London; and, if we may credit her assertions, which are stated with so much candour as to impart a certain conviction of their truthfulness, their King was irritated beyond measure at the intelligence. Orders were immediately issued for her arrest; and the Monarch protested that Lady Nithisdale did whatever she pleased in spite of him; that she had given him more trouble than any other woman in Europe. Again driven into obscurity, Lady Nithisdale took the opinion of a very celebrated lawyer, whose name she does not specify, and, upon his opinion, determined to retire to the Continent. The reasons which her legal adviser assigned for this counsel was, that although, in other circumstances, a wife cannot be prosecuted for saving her husband, yet in cases of high treason, according to the rigour of the law, the head of a wife is responsible for that of a husband. Since the King was so incensed against Lady Nithisdale there could be no answering for the consequences, and he therefore earnestly besought her to leave the kingdom.

Lady Nithisdale, conscious of the wisdom of this recommendation, and wearied, perhaps, of a life of apprehension, determined to adopt the plan recommended.

It is evident that she joined Lord Nithisdale at Rome, whither he had retired; for the statement which she has left concludes in a manner which shows that the devoted and heroic wife had been enabled to rejoin the husband for whom she had encountered so much anxiety, contumely, and peril. Her son, it appears, also accompanied her, from her reference to "our young Master, " meaning the Master of Nithisdale; since, when she wrote, the Prince Charles Edward could not be endowed with that appellation, his father being then alive. Her narrative is thus concluded: [34]—

"This is the full narrative of what you desired, and of all the transactions which passed relative to this affair. Nobody besides yourself could have obtained it from me; but the obligations I owe you, throw me under the necessity of refusing you nothing that is in my power to do. As this is for yourself alone, your indulgence will excuse all the faults which must occur in this long recital. The truth you may, however, depend upon; attend to that and overlook all deficiencies. My lord desires you to be assured of his sincere friendship. I am, with the strongest attachment, my dear sister, yours most affectionately,

"WINIFRED NITHISDALE. "

Little is known of the Earl of Nithisdale after his escape to Rome, where he died in 1744. He thus lived through a period of comparative quiet, till his native country was again on the eve of being embroiled in a civil war, more replete with danger, sullied by greater crimes, and more disastrous to his native country, than the short-lived struggle of 1715. An exile from his Scottish possessions, Lord Nithisdale possibly implanted in the mind of his own son that yearning to establish the rights of the Stuarts which appears not to have been eradicated from the hearts of the Scottish Jacobites until their beloved and royal race had become lineally extinct.

The descendants of William, Earl of Nithisdale, have never been able to ascertain where his Lordship is buried. His noble and admirable wife died at Rome, as well as her husband; but her remains were brought to this country, and they are deposited at Arundel Castle.

John Maxwell, who assumed the title of Earl of Nithisdale, appears to have remained absent from Scotland until the troubles of 1745 began. It was probably on the death of his father in 1744, that he returned to take possession of the family estates, —that this, the representative of the family of Maxwell, ventured to appear in Dumfriesshire.

The following correspondence which passed between the Earl of Nithisdale, popularly so called, and his friend, Mr. Craik, of Arbigland[35] in Dumfriesshire, is a curious commentary upon the motives and reasons which actuated the minds of the Jacobites in the second attempt to re-establish the Stuart family. The first letter from Mr. Craik is dated October the thirteenth, 1745, when Edinburgh Castle was blockaded by Charles Edward, who was publishing his manifestoes from the saloons of Holyrood House. The answer from Lord Nithisdale is written in reply to one of remonstrance addressed to him by his friend. There is no date, but it is obviously written at Edinburgh.

The remonstrances from Mr. Craik were instantly dispatched, to avert, if possible, any decided step on the part of Lord Nithisdale. The arguments which it contains shew the friendly intention of the earnest writer. Lord Nithisdale had, in his former letter, challenged his friend to assign his reasons for dissuading him from the enterprise.

LETTER FROM MR. CRAIK TO LORD NITHISDALE.

"My waiting for a safe hand to convey this to you has prevented my answering yours of the thirteenth sooner. It must give me great pleasure that you have not determined to engage in the present enterprize, which from several apparent symptoms I had reason to apprehend; and if you stick by your promise of doeing nothing rashly (fitt only for desperados indeed!) in a matter of such moment, I shall be sett at ease from the anxiety I felt on your account.

"In mine which gave occasion to yours, I really had no intention to enter into the merits of the cause: all I meant was, to make experiment how far my interest with you could prevail to keep you undetermined till meeting, when I might promise myself more success in reasoning upon the subject, than while you remained in town, where the spirit of the place, the people you converse with, the things you hear and see, all unite to inflame your passions and confound your understanding. But since it has, beyond my intention, engaged you to explain your sentiments at large, and to call upon you to give my opinion, and since I suppose your arguments contain all that can be said by those of the party who would be thought to judge coolly and act reasonably at this juncture, I shall, with the freedom and openness of a friend, consider them as they lye before me in yours; and if I am forced to exceed the limits of a letter, you may blame yourself, who drew me in. You tell me you are ready to believe; I agree in opinion with you, that as matters are come to this length, it's now greatly to the interest of Scotland to wish success to the undertaking, and that nothing but the improbability of success should hinder every Scotsman to join in it. This tho' a verrie material point, you take for granted without assigning a single reason; but as I know it is one of their delusive arguments, now much in use where you are, and the chief engine of the party to seduce well-meaning men to concur in the ruin of the constitution and their country, I shall give you what I apprehend you must mean by it in the most favourable light it will bear; and then from an impartial stating of the fact as it truely stands, leave yourself to judge how far an honest man, a wise one, and a lover of his country, can justify either to himself or the worlde, his being of this opinion. The meaning of your argument I take to be this: that by the unaccountable success of the enterprize and the tame submission of the people in general, if the scheme misgive all Scotland becomes involved in the guilt, and may expect the outmost severitys this Government and the people of England can afflict them with; but on the other hand, should the undertaking be crowned with success, as Scotesmen have the merit of it, they must become the peculiar favourites of the family they have raised to the throne, and reap all the advantages they can promise themselves from a grateful and generous prince. I hope I have done justice to your argument, allow me allso to do justice to facts and truth.

"The people of Great Britain having found, from repeated experiments, how precarious their libertys were in the hands of the princes who founded their title to govern them in hereditary right, —that however absurd the pretence was in itself, no example could make them forego a claim which so much flattered their ambition, and upon which only, with any shew of reason, arbitrary power and tyranny can be built at last, —determined to secure (as far as human prudence can) the possession of that inestimable blessing to themselves and posterity by fixing the royal power in a family whose only title should be the free choice of the people, and who, should they attempt, would be restrained from inslaving those they governed, and would not only act most absurdly, but might reckon upon having the same voice of the people against them.

"The maxims by which our hereditary princes conducted themselves, were sufficiently felt to the sad experience of our forefathers; thank God we were reserved for happier times! History will inform you of their repeated and unwearied attempts to subvert the constitution and inslave a free people. Their sacrifizing the interest of the nation to France, their violating their oaths and promises, their persecutions and their schemes to establish a religion which in its nature is inconsistent with the toleration of any other, though reasons of state may make it wink at this on particular occasions, —but should I descend to particulars, it would lead me beyond the limites I have prescribed myself.

"The present family have now reigned over us these thirty years, and though during so long a time they may have fallen into errors, or may have committed faults, (as what Government is without?) yett I will defy the most sanguin zealot to find in history a period equal to this in which Scotland possessed so uninterrupted a felicity, in which liberty, civil and religious, was so universally enjoyed by all people of whatever denomination—nay, by the open and avowed ennemys of the family and constitution, or a period in which all ranks of men have been so effectually secured in their property. Have not trade, manufactures, agriculture, and the spirit of industry in our country, extended themselves further during this period and under this family than for ages before? Has any man suffered in his liberty, life, or fortune, contrary to law? Stand forth and name him if you can. Tho' the King's person, his family, his government, and his ministers, have been openly abused a thousand times in the most scurrilous and reproachful terms, could it ever provoke him to one arbitrary act or to violate those laws which he had made the rule of his government? Look into the reigns of the James's and the Charles's, and tell me wither these divine and hereditary princes were guided by the same spirit of mildness and forgivness?

"I am sensible how often and how many destructive designs have been imputed to the prince upon the throne and his ministers, of the cry raised against standing armies, of the complaints of corruption, long parliaments, and Hanoverian interest pursued in opposition to that of Britain; but I am allso sensible there is not a true friend to liberty, a dispassionate and sober man, but who (now the mask is laid aside) perceives they were, at bottom, the artifices and popular pretences of men struggling to force themselves into power, or of those who in the dark were aiming the destruction of our happy constitution.

"Men endued with popular talents, of figure and fortune in the world, and without the advantages of apparent disinterestedness on their side, will allways have address enough, with a seeming plausibility, to pervert every act of Government at home, and to defame and run down every publick transaction abroad; and disciples will never be wanting of capacity and passions fitted to become the dupes of such false apostles. The corruption complained of is but too universal, and it's to be feared too deep-rooted to be cured; it is the constant attendant of peace and wealth; and such is the depravity of our natures, that these blessings cannot be enjoyed without having this plague, the most sordid and detestable of all vices, accompanying them. But if it is in our governours, it is also in the people, and change your kings and ministers as often as you please, whoever is in possession, or whoever is in quest of power, will allways lay hold of the vices, the follys, or the prejudices of mankind to exclude others from it or to acquire it to themselves.

"It's to be hoped most people now perceive with what views they were taught to exclaim against and oppose a standing body of native and freeborn troops; but it is to be lamented their eyes were reserved to be opened only by the greatest of all publick calamitys. "

It appears, however, from the following letter of Mr. Craik, that Lord Nithisdale was really implicated in the insurrection: —

"My Lord,

"I am sincerely and deeply touched with your Lordship's situation, and can honestly assure you it would give me a real satisfaction could I any how contribute to save you on this unhappy occasion. As you have done me the honour to ask my opinion how you are to conduct yourself, and as the Doctor has informed me of the circumstances of your journey, I should but ill deserve the character of humanity and good nature you are pleased to give me, if I did not, with freedom and candour, lay before you what, after this day having fully considered it, appears to me most for your honour, and the safty and preservation of your life and family.

"It is certain the Habeas Corpus Act is suspended, and I doubt not but as soon as the lenth you have gone and your being returned is known above, warrants will be issued to carrie you up to London; if you retire out of the kingdom, it will not prevent your being attainted; and I am afraid the unfortunate step you have made will putt your estate but too much within the reach of the law, and your family is undone. If you stay till you are apprehended, not only your estate, but your person is in the mercy of the Government, and how far severitys on this occasion may be carried, is not for me to prescribe; only I am apprehensive your religion, quality, and estate, will make you but too obnoxious to the Government, and when the affair is over, informers will not be wanting to furnish them with materials.

"We are not ignorant what arts and industry have been employed to draw you out of the retirement and quiet you were well disposed to remain in. We are sensible you were imposed upon by those already embarked; and it will acquit you before God and every sober man, if you no longer keep measures with those who have deceived you in a matter of such moment, when your life and fortune were at stake. My lord, I have impartially laid before you the present circumstance you are in, as far as my abilities enable me to judge, that you may have it under your Lordship's consideration; I shall next take the freedom to suggest what to me appears the safest and most prudent part now left to you to act, and which I likeways submit to your Lordship's own judgment, without taking upon me to decide. What I mean is this, that your Lordship should, without loss of time, surrender your person to the Governor of Carlisle, and acquaint him you came to throw yourself upon the clemency of the Government; at the same time, your Lordship would, by express, have some proper friend at London advised of your intention, and one of some weight and interest, and who was fitt to put your conduct in the most favourable light. You will easily perceive that this confidence in the Government, and voluntary surrender of your person, and your preventing all others in an early repentance must distinguish you, in the eyes of the Government, from every other person who has embarked, and entitle you to its favour and protection: whereas, if you wait till you are apprehended, or leave the kingdom, your case, tho' quite different, will be ranked with those who have gone the greatest lengths. If your Lordship approve of this, if you think proper to lett me know by a line to-morrow, I shall not faill to be in town on Tuesday; and as I have a friend at London who I know is very capable and well disposed to serve you, if it be agreeable to you, shall, with the Doctor, concert the letter proper to be sent. "

The answer of Lord Nithisdale contains a curious summary of some of the motives which actuated the Jacobites of 1745.

LETTER FROM LORD NITHISDALE TO MR. CRAIK.

"Dear Sir,

"I have both yours, giving your opinion on the present affairs, without assigning your reasons, and as I take it, urging an answer from me, whether I am determined to take a share in the present enterprise, which you seem to think I should not. I shall answer the last first, by telling you that I have not yet fully digested my thoughts on that matter; only be assured I'll do nothing rashly—that's only for desperados. As to the other, I'm ready to believe you agree in opinion with me, that as matters are come this length, it's now greatly the interest of Scotland to wish success to the undertaking; and that nothing but the improbability of success should hinder every Scotsman to join in it; and indeed I don't think there's great reason to fear that either, unless vast numbers of foreign forces are poured into the country for support of the party in possession.

"The Militia of England are little to be feared, nor do I believe they'll be trusted with arms, as there's a chance what way they may be used, particularly by that part of the country who only know how to handle them. As to the Dutch who are come over, there's now greater reason to believe they'll be recalled, and it may be some time before others are sent in their place, if at all. I do believe the United States, if they dare, will give all the support they can; but if France shall really prove in earnest, I imagine they'll consider it necessary to be quiet. Other foreign forces may be sent in, but on the other hand there's a very great improbability; thir people will likewise get aid, and here there's assembling a very numerous resolute army. The prospect of the situation of the country for some time to come, must affect every well-wisher to it, and the consequences to this part, if the undertaking shall misgive, appear to me terrible; if it succeed, what have we to fear? You'll answer, the introduction of Popery and arbitrary government; but I don't imagine, considering the success and fate of his grandfather and uncle, that will be attempted; and as to any fear that we may be made dependant and tributary to the foreign powers giving aid to the present adventure, that I'm not apprehensive of, nor do I imagine it would be in his power to accomplish, tho' inclinable to it. I shall say no more on the subject; only it's easier preventing an evil than remedying, and that may be applyed to both sides; only this one further I observe, that I think it's the interest of the nation to have a sovereign settled whose title is unquestionable: we see the inconveniencys attending the other. You'll perhaps answer, there will still be a Pretender; but I reply, not so dangerous an one, if at all. You write, in your letter, that people may, without meaning, be treated and led away with popular arguments. I assure you I'm none of these—what I have said now, is on a Sunday forenoon. However, I should wish you communicate my mind to nobody. If any material news occur before the bearer leave Edinburgh, you shall have them; and to-morrow I'll mind your commission, and any other you shall give with respect to your nursery, &c., which I hope you're still carrying on, and that your garden-wall is now completed. If you had some pieces of cannon to place in it, would it not keep out against an army not provided with battering-pieces, seeing it's at a sufficient distance from the thundering of any castle? Were it not for fear of your horses, I should wish you came in here and saw the fortifications made on our city-wall, and the army against which they were intended; the last is worth your while. No Court in Europe is filled with such a set of well-look'd brave fellows.

"I hope my dykers are going on, and beg you'll acquaint the tenants to have the rents ready, in regard I'm to be soon in the country, and won't make any stay above a day or two; this to you, but to yourself I can yet fix no time for coming out as I can't think of leaving Edinburgh till I see how matters turn, and it's also necessary to stay and take care of my house, furniture, papers, &c. I believe I shall eat my Christmas goose with you, if I don't go into England, which I would incline for sake of a jaunt, if I thought it safe and had a right set with me. I ever am, dear Sir,

"Your's &c. "

Another letter from a kinsman of Lord Nithisdale's shews that he was not alone in his inclination to join in the Insurrection of 1745.

LETTER FROM MR. MAXWELL OF CARRUCHAN.

"October 13th.

"Dr. Willie,

"By accounts this day from Edinburgh, allmost everybody is going along with the stream, so that a short delay wou'd lose all the merit. This has determined me to do the thing so suddenly, that I have not time to send for you, unless it were to see me go off, which is impossible. I depend upon your protection for those I leave behind. What gives me the greatest concern is least some such creditors as have still my father's security, should molest him in my absence. I recommend particularly to you, that if you can hear of any, you'll endeavour to make them sensible that they are as safe as before, and tell the comissary that I expect the same piece of friendship from him, who lyes more in the way of hearing what passes of that kind. I believe there are three or four thousand French or Irish landed in Wales, with Lord John Drummond. The Highland army marches south the beginning of the week. Farewell dear Willie. God bless you! Ever your's

(Signed) Ja. Maxwell. "

"Saturday. —I set out before daylight to-morrow. "

From Mr. Maxwell of Carruchan, to Mr. Craik of Arbigland.

Since Lord Nithisdale's name did not appear in the list of the young Chevalier's officers, we must conclude that he did not persevere in his resolutions. There is no date to Mr. Craik's second letter, but it must have been written after Carlisle had surrendered to the Duke of Cumberland, —an event which took place on the thirtieth of December, 1745.

The Earl of Nithisdale, as he was styled, lived until the year 1776, and possibly in peace and prosperity, since the family estates were spared to him. He married his first cousin, Lady Catherine Stewart, daughter of the Earl of Traquhair by Lady Mary Maxwell, and left an only daughter.

This lady, named after her celebrated grandmother Winifred, was also, by courtesy, endowed with the honours of the forfeited rank, and styled Lady Winifred Maxwell. Her Ladyship would have inherited the Barony of Herries, of Terregles, but for the attainder of her grandfather. The estates of Lord Nithisdale were inherited by her son, Marmaduke William Constable, Esq., of Everingham Park, in the county of York; who, on the death of his mother, assumed, by royal licence, the surname of Maxwell. The title of Nithisdale, except for the attainder, would have descended upon the next heir, Mr. Maxwell of Carruchan. [36]

FOOTNOTES:

[1] There is no statement of the date of Lord Nithisdale's birth in any of the usual authorities, neither can his descendant, William Constable Maxwell, Esq., of Terregles, supply the deficient information.

[2] Secret History of Colonel Hooke's Negotiations, by himself, p. 175. London, 1740.

[3] Patten's History of the Rebellion, of 1715, p. 234.

[4] Service of the Earl of Eglintoun, as heir male of the Earl of Wintoun. Printed for the family. Extract from "Peerage Law by Riddell, " p. 201. Published in 1825.

[5] Service of the Earl of Eglintoun, p. 8.

[6] Buchan's Account of the Earls Marischal, p. 125.

[7] Eglinton Case.

[8] Patten, p. 52.

[9] Patten, p. 54. Life of the Earls Marischal, p. 130.

[10] Reay's History of the Late Rebellion. Dumfries, 1718.

[11] Reay, p. 139.

[12] Now of Sir Charles Stuart Menteath, Bart.

[13] Reay, p. 184.

[14] Id.

[15] Id. p. 211.

[16] Reay, p. 257.

[17] Patten, pp. 224-235. Colonel Hooke's Negotiations.

[18] In the Life of Lord Derwentwater.

[19] Reay, p. 326.

[20] See Letters in the State Paper Office from Lord Widdrington, and many others of inferior rank, No. 3. 1715.

[21] State Papers, 1716, No. 3.

[22] State Papers, No. 3, July 26, 1715.

[23] Reay, p. 355.

[24] Reay, p. 359.

[25] A Faithful Register of the Late Rebellion, London, p. 65, 1718.

[26] Faithful Register, p. 86.

[27] Her picture, painted in the bloom of her youth, is still at Terregles, in Dumfriesshire, the seat of William Constable Maxwell, Esq., the descendant of Lord Nithisdale. To Mrs. Constable Maxwell, of Terregles, I am indebted for the following interesting description of the portrait of Lady Nithisdale, to which I have referred. "Her hair is light brown, slightly powdered, and she is represented with large soft eyes, regular features, and fair, rather pale complexion. Her soft expression and delicate appearance give little indication of the strength of mind and courage which she displayed. Her dress is blue silk, with a border of cambric, and the drapery a cloak of brown silk."

[28] His son was restored to his father's honours. The title of Marquis of Powis became extinct; but the estates devolved on Lord Herbert of Cherbury, husband to the last Marquis's niece; and ultimately to Lady Henrietta Herbert, who married Lord Clive, created Earl of Powis. —*Burke's Extinct Peerage.*

[29] Faithful Register, p. 84.

[30] Faithful Register, p. 86.

[31] Burke's History of the Commoners of Great Britain and Ireland, vol. i. p. 329.

[32] See Letters and Petitions in the State Papers, No. iii. p. 1716.

[33] See Burke's Commoners, vol. i. p. 333.

[34] See Burke's Commoners, vol. i. p. 334.

[35] I am indebted to the present Mr. Craik, of Arbigland, for this correspondence.

[36] I am indebted for some of these particulars to the courtesy of William Constable Maxwell, Esq., present owner of Terregles, Carlaverock, and also of the beautiful hereditary property of Lincluden.

WILLIAM GORDON, VISCOUNT KENMURE.

The origin of the distinguished surname of Gordon is not clearly ascertained: "some, " says Douglass, "derive the Gordons from a city of Macedonia, named Gordonia; others from a manor in Normandy called Gordon, possessed by a family of that name. The territory of Gordon in Berwickshire was, according to another account, conferred by David the First upon an Anglo-Norman settler, who assumed from it the name of Gordon. "

William Gordon, sixth Earl of Kenmure, was descended from a younger son of the ducal house of Gordon; in 1633 Sir John Gordon of Lochinvar was created Viscount Kenmure and Lord of Lochinvar; and the estates continued in an unbroken line until they descended to William, the sixth Viscount, who was the only Scottish peer in 1715 who suffered capital punishment.

This unfortunate nobleman succeeded his father in 1698; and possessed, up to the period of his taking the command of the army in the south, the estates belonging to his family in the Stuartry of Kirkcudbright. Kenmure Castle, still happily enjoyed by the family of Gordon, stands upon an eminence overlooking the meadows, at that point where the river Ken expands into a lake. The Castle was originally a single tower, to which various additions have been made according to the taste of different owners. The Castle Keep is now ruinous and unroofed, but the body of the house is in good repair. A fine prospect over the scenery of the Glenhens is commanded by the eminence on which the castle stands. An ancient avenue of lime-trees constitutes the approach to the fortress from the road.

In this abode dwelt the Viscount Kenmure until the summons of Lord Mar called him from the serene tenour of a course honoured by others, and peaceful from the tranquillity of the unhappy nobleman's own disposition; for his was not the restless ambition of Mar, nor the blind devotion of the Duke of Perth; nor the passion for fame and ascendancy which stimulated Lord George Murray in his exertions. Lord Kenmure was, it is true, well acquainted with public business, and an adept in the affairs of the political world, in which he had obtained that insight which long experience gives. His acquaintance with books and men was said to be considerable; he is allowed, even by one who had deserted the party which Lord Kenmure espoused, to be of a "very extraordinary knowledge. "[37]

But his calm, reflective mind, his experience, his resources of learning, rather indisposed than inclined this nobleman from rising when called upon to lend his aid to the perilous enterprise of James Stuart. Beloved in private life, of a singularly good temper, calm, mild, of simple habits, and plain in his attire, he was as it was generally observed, the last man whom one might have expected to rush into the schemes of the Jacobite party.

That one so skilled in human affairs should venture, even in a subordinate degree, to espouse so desperate a cause as that of James was generally reputed to be, might seem to prove that even the wise were sanguine, or that they were carried away by the enthusiasm of the hour. Neither of these circumstances appear to bear any considerable weight in revolving the conduct of Lord Kenmure.

A stronger influence, perhaps, than that of loyalty operated on the conduct of Viscount Kenmure. He was married: his wife, the spirited and energetic Mary Dalzell, was the only sister of Robert, sixth Earl of Carnwath. Her family were deeply imbued with the principles of hereditary right and of passive obedience; and Lady Kenmure cherished these sentiments, and bestowed the energies of her active mind on the promotion of that cause which she held sacred. The house of Dalzell had been sufferers in the service of the Stuarts. By her mother's side, Lady Kenmure was connected with Sir William Murray of Stanhope, and with his singular, and yet accomplished son, Sir Alexander Murray of Stanhope, who was taken prisoner at Preston, fighting for the Jacobites. The Earl of Carnwath, Lady Kenmure's brother, was one of those men whose virtues and acquirements successfully recommend a cause to all who are under the influence of such a character. Having been educated at Cambridge, he had imbibed an early affection for the liturgy of the Church of England; his gentle manners, his talents, and his natural eloquence, established him in the affections of his friends and acquaintance. This nobleman was, like his sister, ready to sacrifice everything for conscience sake: like her, he was a sufferer for that which he esteemed to be justice. He was afterwards taken prisoner at Preston, impeached before the House of Peers in 1716, and sentenced to be executed as a traitor, and his estate forfeited; but eventually he was respited and pardoned. He survived to be four times married.

Another of Lady Kenmure's brothers, John Dalzell, was, it is true, a captain in the army upon the breaking out of the Rebellion in 1715;

but, at the summons of him whom he esteemed his lawful Sovereign, he threw up his commission, and engaged in the service of James.

When Lord Kenmure received a commission from the Earl of Mar to head the friends of the Chevalier in the South, he had ties which perhaps were among some of the considerations which led him to hesitate and to accept the proffered honour unwillingly. On his trial he referred to his wife and "four small children, " as a plea for mercy. But Lady Kenmure, sanguine and resolute, did not view these little dependent beings as obstacles to a participation in the insurrection. If she might be considered to transgress her duty as a mother, in thus risking the fortunes of her children, she afterwards compensated by her energy and self-denial for her early error of judgment.

It had been arranged that the insurrection in Dumfriesshire was to break out in conjunction with that headed in Northumberland by Mr. Forster. To effect this end, numbers of disaffected, or, as the Jacobite writers call them, well-affected noblemen and gentlemen assembled in parties at the houses of their friends, moving about from place to place, in order to prepare for the event.

It was on the twelfth of October, 1715, that Viscount Kenmure set out in the intention of joining the Earl of Wintoun, who was on his road to Moffat, and who was accompanied by a party of Lothian gentlemen and their servants. It is said by the descendants of Viscount Kenmure, on hearsay, that his Lordship's horse three times refused to go forward on that eventful morning; nor could he be impelled to do so, until Lady Kenmure taking off her apron, and throwing it over the horse's eyes, the animal was led forward. The Earl of Carnwath had joined with Lord Kenmure, and rode forwards with him to the rencontre with Lord Wintoun. Lord Kenmure took with him three hundred men to the field. [38]

At the siege of Preston, in which those who fell dead upon the field were less to be compassionated than the survivors, Lord Kenmure was taken prisoner. His brother-in-law, the Earl of Carnwath, shared the same fate. They were sent with the principal state prisoners to London. The same circumstances, the same indignities, attended the removal of Lord Kenmure to his last earthly abode, as those which have been already related as disgracing the humanity of Englishmen, when the Earl of Derwentwater was carried to the Tower.

The subsequent sufferings of these brave men were aggravated by the abuses which then existed in the state prisons of England. The condition of these receptacles of woe, at that period, beggars all description. Corruption and extortion gave every advantage to those who could command money enough to purchase luxuries at an enormous cost. Oppression and an utter carelessness of the well-being of the captive, pressed hardly upon those who were poor. No annals can convey a more heartrending description of the sufferings of the prisoners confined in county gaols, than their own touching and heartfelt appeals, some of which are to be found in the State Paper Office.

In the Tower, especially, it appears from a diary kept by a gentleman who was confined there, that the greatest extortion was openly practised. Mr. Forster and a Mr. Anderton, who were allowed to live in the Governor's house, were charged the sum of five pounds a-week for their lodging and diet, —a demand which, more than a century ago, was deemed enormous. Several of the Highland chiefs, and among them the celebrated Brigadier Mackintosh, were "clapped up in places of less accommodation, for which, nevertheless, they were charged as much as would have almost paid the rent of the best houses in St. James's Square and Piccadilly. " Mr. Forster, it must be added, was obliged to pay sixty guineas for his privilege of living in the governor's house; and Mr. Anderton to give a bribe of twenty-five guineas for having his irons off. A similar tax was made upon every one who entered, and who could pay, and they were thankful to proffer the sum of twenty guineas, the usual demand, to be free from irons. It was, indeed, not the mere freedom from chains for which they paid, but for the power of effecting their escape. Upon every one who did not choose to be turned over to the common side, a demand was made of ten guineas fee, besides two guineas weekly for lodging, although in some rooms men lay four in a bed. Presents were also given privately, so that in three or four months' time, three or four thousand pounds were paid by the prisoners to their jailers.

Many of the prisoners being men of fortune, their tables were of the most luxurious description; forty shillings was often paid for a dish of peas and beans, and thirty shillings for a dish of fish; and this fare, so unlike that of imprisonment, was accompanied by the richest French wines. The vicious excesses and indecorums which went on in the Tower, among the state prisoners, are said to have scandalized the graver lookers on. [39] The subsequent distress and misery which ensued may, of course, be traced, in part to this cause.

Lord Derwentwater, ever decorous and elevated in his deportment, was shocked at the wayward and reckless conduct of some of the Jacobites on their road to London, told one of the King's officers at Barnet that these prisoners "were only fit for Bedlam." To this it was remarked, that they were only fit for Bridewell. Whilst hopes of life continued, this rebuke still applied. The prisoners were aided in their excesses by the enthusiasm of the fair sex. The following extract from another obscure work, "The History of the Press-yard," is too curious to be omitted. "That while they [the prisoners] flattered themselves with hopes of life, which they were made to believe were the necessary consequences of a surrender at discretion, they did, without any retrospect to the crimes they were committed for, live in so profuse a manner, and fared so voluptuously, through the means of daily visitants and helps from abroad, that money circulated very plentifully; and while it was difficult to change a guinea almost at any house in the street, nothing was more easy than to have silver for gold to any quantity, and gold for silver, in the prison, —those of the fair sex, from persons of the first rank to tradesmen's wives and daughters, making a sacrifice of their husbands' and parents' rings, and other precious moveables, for the use of those prisoners; so that, till the trial of the condemned lords was over, and that the Earl of Derwentwater and Viscount Kenmure were beheaded, there was scarce anything to be seen amongst them but flaunting apparel, venison pasties, hams, chickens, and other costly meats, with plenty of wine."

Meantime the trial of the attainted lords took place, and checked, like the sudden appearance of a ghostly apparition, this horrible merriment, —with which, however, few names which one desires to cherish and to respect are connected. The same forms that attended the impeachment and trial of his companions, were carried on at the trial of Lord Kenmure. The unhappy nobleman replied in few and touching words, and, in a voice which could not be heard, pleaded guilty; an inconsistency, to express it in the mildest terms, of which he afterwards sincerely repented.

At the end of the trial, to the question "What have you to say for yourself why judgment should not be passed upon you according to law?" "My lords," replied Lord Kenmure, "I am truly sensible of my crime, and want words to express my repentance. God knows I never had any personal prejudice against his Majesty, nor was I ever accessory to any previous design against him. I humbly beg my noble Peers and the honourable House of Commons to intercede with the King for mercy to me, that I may live to show myself the dutifullest of his subjects, and to be the means to keep my wife and four small children from starving; the thoughts of which, with my crime, makes me the most unfortunate of all gentlemen. "

After the trial, great intercessions were made for mercy, but without any avail, as far as Lord Derwentwater and Lord Kenmure were concerned. They were ordered for execution on the 24th of February, 1716.

The intelligence of the condemnation of these two lords, produced the greatest dismay among their fellow sufferers in the Tower; and the notion of escape, a project which was singularly successful in some instances, was resorted to, in the despair and anguish of the moment, by those who dreaded a cruel and ignominious death.

Lord Kenmure, meantime, prepared for death. A very short interval was, indeed, allowed for those momentous considerations which his situation induced. He was sentenced on the ninth of February, and in a fortnight afterwards was to suffer. Yet the execution of that sentence was, it seems, scarcely expected by the sufferer, even when the fatal day arrived.

The night before his execution, Lord Kenmure wrote a long and affecting letter to a nobleman who had visited him in prison a few days previously. There is something deeply mournful in the fate of one who had slowly and unwillingly taken up the command which had ensured to him the severest penalties of the law. There is an inexpressibly painful sentiment of compassion and regret, excited by the yearning to live—the allusion to a reprieve—the allusion to the case of Lord Carnwath as affording more of hope than his own—lastly, to what he cautiously calls "an act of indiscretion, " the plea of guilty, which was wrung from this conscientious, but sorrowing man, by a fond value for life and for the living. So little did Lord Kenmure anticipate his doom, that, when he was summoned to the scaffold the following day, he had not even prepared a black suit, — a circumstance which he much regretted, since he "might be said to have died with more decency. "

The following is the letter which he wrote, and which he addressed to a certain nobleman.

"My very good Lord,

"Your Lordship has interested yourself so far in mine, and the lords, my fellow prisoners' behalf, that I should be the greatest criminal now breathing, should I, whether the result of your generous intercession be life or death, be neglectful of paying my acknowledgments for that act of compassion.

"We have already discoursed of the motives that induced me to take arms against the Prince now in possession of the throne, when you did me the honour of a visit three days since in my prison here; I shall therefore wave that point, and lament my unhappiness for joining in the rest of the lords in pleading guilty, in the hopes of that mercy, which the Generals Wills and Carpenter will do us the justice to say was promised us by both of them. Mr. Piggot and Mr. Eyres, the two lawyers employed by us, advised us to this plea, the avoiding of which might have given us further time for looking after the concerns of another life, though it had ended in the same sentence of losing this which we now lie under. Thanks be to the Divine Majesty, to whose infinite mercy as King of Kings, I recommend myself in hopes of forgiveness, tho' it shall be my fate to fail of it here on earth. Had the House of Commons thought fit to have received our petition with the same candour as yours has done, and recommended us to the Prince, we might have entertained some hopes of life; but the answer from St. James's is such as to make us have little or no thoughts of it.

"Under these dismal apprehensions, then, of approaching dissolution, which, I thank my God for his holy guidance, I have made due preparation for, give me leave to tell you, that howsoever I have been censured on account of the family of the Gordons, which I am an unhappy branch of, that I have ever lived and will die in the profession of the Protestant religion, and that I abhor all king-killing doctrines that are taught by the church of Rome as dangerous and absurd. And though I have joined with some that have taken arms, of that persuasion, no other motive but that of exercising to the person called the Pretender, whom I firmly believe to be the son of the late King James the Second, and in defence of whose title I am now going to be a sacrifice, has induced me to it. Your Lordship will remember the papers I have left with you, and deliver them to my son. They may be of use to his future conduct in life, when these eyes of mine are closed in death, which I could have wished might have stolen upon me in the ordinary course of nature, and not by the hand of the executioner. But as my blessed Saviour and Redeemer suffered an ignominious and cruel death, and the Son of God, made flesh, did not disdain to have his feet nailed to the Cross for the sins of the world; so may I, poor miserable sinner, as far as human nature will allow, patiently bear with the hands of violence, that I expect suddenly to be stretched out against me.

"Your Lordship will also, provided there is no hopes of a reprieve this night, make me acquainted with it as soon as possible, that I may meet that fate with readiness which, in a state of uncertainty, I expect with uneasiness. I must also be pressing with your Lordship that if, in case of death, any paper under my name should come out as pretended to have been written by me, in the manner or form of a speech, you will not believe it to be genuine; for I, that am heartily sorry for disowning my principles in one spoken before your Lordship and the rest of my peers, will never add to that act of indiscretion by saying anything on the scaffold but my prayers for the forgiveness of my poor self and those that have brought me to be a spectacle to men and angels, especially since I must speak in my last moments according to the dictates of my conscience, and not prevaricate as I did before the Lords, for which I take shame to myself. And such a method of proceeding might do injury to my brother Carnwath, who, I am told, is in a much fairer way than I am of not being excluded from grace. I have nothing farther than to implore your Lordships to charge your memory with the recommendations I gave you to my wife and children, beseeching God that he will so sanctify their afflictions, that after the pains and terrors of this mortal life they may with me be translated to the regions of everlasting joy and happiness, to which blessed state of immortality your Lordship shall also, while I am living, be recommended in the prayers of, my very good Lord, your most affectionate kinsman,

Kenmure. "

"From my prison, in the Tower of London, Feb. 23, 1715. "

The following paper, the original of which is still in the hands of his descendants, was written by Lord Kenmure the night before his execution: —

"It having pleased the Almighty God to call me now to suffer a violent death, I adore the Divine Majesty, and cheerfully resign my soul and body to His hands, whose mercy is over all His works. It is my very great comfort that He has enabled me to hope, through the merits and by the blood of Jesus Christ, He will so purifie me how that I perish not eternally. I die a Protestant of the Church of England, and do from my heart forgive all my enemies. I thank God I cannot accuse my selfe of the sin of rebellion, however some people may by a mistaken notion think me guilty of it for all I did upon a laite occasione; and my only desire ever was to contribute my small endeavour towards the re-establishing my rightfull Sovereigne and the constitutione of my countrie to ther divine rights and loyall setlment; and by pleading guilty I meant no more then ane acknowledgment of my having been in armes, and (not being bred to the law) had no notion of my therby giving my assent to any other thing contained in that charge. I take God to wittnes, before whom I am very soon to apear, that I never had any desire to favour or to introduce Popery, and I have been all along fully satisfied that the King has given all the morall security for the Church of England that is possible for him in his circumstances. I owne I submitted myselfe to the Duck of Brunswick, justly expecting that humantity would have induced him to give me my life, which if he had done I was resolved for the future to have lived peaceably, and to have still reteaned a greatfull remembrance of so greatt a favour, and I am satisfied the King would never have desired me to have been in action for him after; but the caice is otherways. I pray God forgive those who thirst after blood. Had we been all putt to the sword immediatly upon our surrender, that might have born the construction of being don in the heatt and fury of passion; but now I am to die in cold blood, I pray God it be not imputed to them. May Almighty God restore injured right, and peace, and truth, and may He in mercy receave my soull.

Kenmure. "[40]

It was decreed that the Earl of Derwentwater and the Viscount Kenmure should suffer on the same day. On the morning of the twenty-fourth of February, at ten o'clock, these noblemen were conducted to the Transport Office on Tower Hill, where they had separate rooms for their private devotions, and where such friends as desired to be admitted to them could take a last farewell. It had been settled that the Earl of Nithisdale should also suffer at the same time, but during the previous night he had escaped. Whether the condemned lords, who were so soon to exchange life for immortality, were made aware of that event or not, has not transpired. What must have been their emotions, supposing that they were conscious that one who had shared their prison, was likely to be restored to his liberty and to his family!

Lord Kenmure conducted himself with a manly composure and courage during this last trial of his submission and fortitude. His reserve, however, on the scaffold was remarkable. It proceeded from a fear, incidental to a conscientious mind, of saying anything inconsistent with his loyalty and principles; and from an apprehension, natural in the dying husband and father, of injuring the welfare of those whom he was to leave at the mercy of Government.

Lord Derwentwater suffered first: his last ejaculation, "Sweet Jesus be merciful unto me! " was cut short by the executioner severing his head from his body. Then, after the body and the head had been carried away, the scaffold was decently cleared, and fresh baize laid upon the block, and saw-dust strewed, that none of the blood might appear to shock the unhappy man who was to succeed the young and gallant Derwentwater in that tragic scene.

Lord Kenmure then advanced. He was formally delivered from the hands of one sheriff to those of the other, who had continued on the stage on which the scaffold was erected all the time, and who then addressed the condemned man. The first question related to the presence of clergy, and of other friends; and Lord Kenmure stated, in reply, that he had the assistance of two clergymen, and desired the presence of some friends who were below. These persons were then called up, and Lord Kenmure retired with his friends and the two clergymen to the south side of the stage, where they joined in penitential prayers, some of them written for the occasion, and others out of a printed book, not improbably the Book of Common Prayer, since Lord Kenmure was a Protestant and an Episcopalian. Lord Kenmure employed himself for some time in private supplications; and afterwards a clergyman, in a prayer, recommended the dying man to the mercy of God. A requiem completed the devotions of the unfortunate Kenmure.

Sir John Fryer, one of the sheriffs, then inquired if his Lordship had had sufficient time; and expressed his willingness to wait as long as Lord Kenmure wished. He also requested to know if Lord Kenmure had anything to say in private; to these questions a negative was returned.

The executioner now came forward. Lord Kenmure was accompanied by an undertaker, to whom the care of his body was to be entrusted; he was also attended by a surgeon, who directed the executioner how to perform his office, by drawing his finger over that part of the neck where the blow was to be given. Lord Kenmure then kissed the officers and gentlemen on the scaffold, some of them twice and thrice; and being again asked if he had anything to say, answered, "No. " He had specified the Chevalier St. George in his prayers, and he now repeated his repentance for having pleaded guilty at his trial. He turned to the executioner, who, according to the usual form, asked forgiveness. "My Lord, " said the man, "what I do, is to serve the nation; do you forgive me? " "I do, " replied Lord Kenmure; and he placed the sum of eight guineas in the hands of the headsman. The final preparations were instantly made. Lord Kenmure pulled off, unassisted, his coat and waistcoat: one of his friends put a white linen cap on his head; and the executioner turned down the collar of his shirt, in order to avoid all obstacles to the fatal stroke. Then the executioner said, "My Lord, will you be pleased to try the block? " Lord Kenmure, in reply, laid down his head on the block, and spread forth his hands. The headsman instantly performed his office. The usual words, "This is the head of a traitor! " were heard as the executioner displayed the streaming and ghastly sight to the multitude.

The body of Lord Kenmure, after being first deposited at an undertaker's in Fleet Street, was carried to Scotland, and there buried among his ancestors. A letter was found in his pocket addressed to the Chevalier, recommending to him the care of his children; but it was suppressed. [41]

Thus died one of those men, whose honour, had his life been spared, might have been trusted never again to enter into any scheme injurious to the reigning Government; and whose death inspires, perhaps, more unmitigated regret than that of any of the Jacobite lords. Lord Kenmure's short-lived authority was sullied by no act of cruelty; and his last hours were those of a pious, resigned, courageous Christian. He was thrust into a situation as commander in the South, peculiarly unfitted for his mild, reserved, and modest disposition: and he was thus carried away from that private sphere which he was calculated to adorn. [42]

After her husband's death, the energies of Lady Kenmure were directed to secure the estates of Kenmure to her eldest son. She instantly posted down to Scotland, and reached Kenmure Castle in time to secure the most valuable papers. When the estates were put up for sale, she contrived, with the assistance of her friends, to raise money enough to purchase them; and lived so carefully as to be able to deliver them over to her son, clear of all debt, when he came of age. Four children were left dependent upon her exertions and maternal protection. Of these Robert, the eldest, died in 1741 unmarried, in his twenty-eighth year. James also died unmarried. Harriet, the only daughter, was married to her mother's cousin-german, Captain James Dalzell, uncle of Robert Earl of Carnwath. John Gordon, the second and only surviving son of Lord Kenmure, married, in 1744, the Lady Frances Mackenzie, daughter of the Earl of Seaforth; and from this marriage is descended the present Viscount Kenmure, to whom the estate was restored in 1824.

Lady Kenmure survived her husband sixty-one years. In 1747, she appears to have resided in Paris, where, after the commotions of 1745, she probably took refuge. Here, aged as she must have been, the spirit of justice, and the love of consistency were shewn in an anecdote related of her by Drummond of Bochaldy, who was mingled up in the cabals of the melancholy Court of St. Germains. It had become the fashion among Prince Charles's sycophants and favourites, to declare that it was not for the interest of the party that there should be any restoration while King James lived; this idea was diligently circulated by Kelly, a man described by Drummond as full of trick, falsehood, deceit, and imposition; and joined to these, having qualities that make up a thorough sycophant.

It was Kelly's fashion to toast the Prince in all companies first, and declare that the King could not last long. At one of the entertainments, which he daily frequented, at the house of Lady Redmond, the dinner, which usually took place at noon, being later than usual, Lady Kenmure, in making an afternoon's visit, came in before dinner was over. She was soon surprised and shocked to hear the company drinking the Prince's health without mentioning the King's. "Lady Kenmure, " adds Drummond, "could not bear it, and said it was new to her to see people forget the duty due to the King. " Kelly immediately answered, "Madam, you are old fashioned; these fashions are out of date. " She said that she really was old fashioned, and hoped God would preserve her always sense and duty enough to continue so; on which she took a glass and said "God preserve our King, and grant him long life, and a happy reign over us! "[43]

Lady Kenmure died on the 16th of August, 1776, at Terregles, in Dumfriesshire, the seat of the Nithisdale family.

FOOTNOTES:

[37] Patten, p. 52

[38] Patten. Reay.

[39] "Secret History of the Rebels in Newgate; " a scarce Sixpenny Tract, in the British Museum. Third Edition.

[40] For this interesting paper I am indebted to the Hon. Mrs. Bellamy, sister of the present and niece of the late Viscount Kenmure.

[41] Faithful Register of the late Rebellion, p. 93; also State Trials.

[42] The impression on the minds of Lord Kenmure's descendants is, that he was by no means a man of feeble character, but one of great fortitude and resolution.

[43] Memoirs of Sir Ewen Cameron of Lochiel, p. 284. Presented to the Abbotsford Club.

WILLIAM MURRAY, MARQUIS OF TULLIBARDINE.

Among the nobility who hastened to the hunting-field of Braemar, was William Marquis of Tullibardine and eldest son of the first Duke of Athole.

The origin of the powerful family of Murray commences with Sir William De Moraira, who was Sheriff in Perth in 1222, in the beginning of the reign of King Alexander the Second. The lands of Tullibardine were obtained by the Knight in 1282, by his marriage with Adda, the daughter of Malise, Seneschal of Stratherio. After the death of William De Moraira, the name of this famous house merged into that of Murray, and its chieftains were for several centuries known by the appellation of Murray of Tullibardine. It was not until the seventeenth century that the family of Murray was ennobled, when James the Sixth created Sir John Murray Earl of Tullibardine.

The unfortunate subject of this memoir was the son of one of the most zealous promoters of the Revolution of 1688. His father, nearly connected in blood with William the Third, was appointed to the command of a regiment by that Monarch, and entrusted with several posts of great importance, which he retained in the time of Queen Anne, until a plot was formed to ruin him by Lord Lovat, who endeavoured to implicate the Duke in the affair commonly known by the name of the Queensbury plot. The Duke of Athole courted inquiry upon that occasion; but the business having been dropped without investigation, he resigned the office of Privy Seal, which he then held, and became a warm opponent of the Act of Union which was introduced into Parliament in 1705.

After this event the Duke of Athole retired to Perthshire, and there lived in great magnificence until, upon the Tories coming into power, he was chosen one of the representatives of the Scottish peerage in 1710, and afterwards a second time constituted Lord Privy Seal.

It is singular that, beholding his father thus cherished by Government, the Marquis of Tullibardine should have adopted the cause of the Chevalier: and not, as it appears, from a momentary caprice, but, if we take into consideration the conduct of his whole life, from a fixed and unalienable conviction. At the time of the first Rebellion, the Marquis was twenty-seven years of age; he may therefore be presumed to have been mature in judgment, and to have passed over the age of wild enthusiasm. The impulses of fanaticism had no influence in promoting the adoption of a party to which an Episcopalian as well as a Roman Catholic might probably be peculiarly disposed. Lord Tullibardine had been brought up a Presbyterian; his father was so firm and zealous in that faith, as to excite the doubts of the Tory party, to whom he latterly attached himself, of his sincerity in their cause. According to Lord Lovat, the arch-enemy of the Athole family, the Duke had not any considerable portion of that quality in his character, which Lord Lovat represents as one compound of meanness, treachery, and revenge, and attributes the hatred with which Athole persecuted the brave and unfortunate Duke of Argyle, to the circumstance of his having received a blow from that nobleman before the whole Court at Edinburgh, without having the spirit to return the insult. [44]

It appears, from the same authority, that the loyalty which the Duke of Athole professed towards King William was of a very questionable description. It becomes, indeed, very difficult to ascertain what were really the Duke of Athole's political tenets. Under these conflicting and unsettled opinions the young Marquis of Tullibardine was reared.

There seems little reason to doubt that his father, the Duke of Athole, continued to act a double part in the troublous days which followed the accession of George the First. It was, of course, of infinite importance to Government to secure the allegiance of so powerful a family as that of Murray, the head of whom was able to bring a body of six thousand men into the field. It nevertheless soon appeared that the young heir of the house of Athole had imbibed very different sentiments to those with which it was naturally supposed a nobleman, actually in office at that time, would suffer in his eldest son. The first act of the Marquis was to join the Earl of Mar with two thousand men, clansmen from the Highlands, and with fourteen hundred of the Duke of Athole's tenants; [45] his next, to proclaim the Chevalier King. Almost simultaneously, and whilst his tenantry were following their young leader to the field, the Duke of Athole was proclaiming King George at Perth. [46] The Duke was ordered, meantime, by the authorities, to remain at his Castle of Blair to secure the peace of the county, of which he was Lord-Lieutenant.

The Marquis of Tullibardine's name appears henceforth in most of the events of the Rebellion. There exists little to shew how he acquitted himself in the engagement of Sherriff Muir, where he led several battalions to the field; but he shewed his firmness and valour by remaining for some time at the head of his vassals, after the unhappy contest of 1715 was closed by the ignominious flight of the Chevalier. All hope of reviving the Jacobite party being then extinct for a time, the Marquis escaped to France, where he remained in tranquillity for a few years; but his persevering endeavours to aid the Stuart cause were only laid aside, and not abandoned.

During his absence, the fortunes of the house of Athole sustained no important change. The office of Privy Seal was, it is true, taken from the Duke and given to the Marquis of Annandale; but by the favour of Government the estates escaped forfeiture, and during the very year in which the Rebellion occurred, the honours and lands which belonged to the unfortunate Tullibardine were vested, by the intercession of his father, in a younger son, Lord James Murray. The effect of this may have been to render the Marquis still more determined in his adherence to the Stuart line. He was not, however, the only member of the house of Murray who participated in the Jacobite cause.

No less consistent in his opinions than the Marquis of Tullibardine, William, the second Lord Nairn, came forward to espouse the cause of the Stuarts. This nobleman was the uncle of Lord Tullibardine, and bore, before his marriage with Margaret, only daughter of the first Lord Nairn, the appellation of Lord William Murray. The title was, however, settled by patent upon him and his heirs; and this obligation, conferred by Charles the Second, was bestowed upon one whose gratitude and devotion to the line of Stuart ceased only with his life. Lord Nairn had been educated to the naval service, and had distinguished himself for bravery. He refused the oaths at the Revolution, and consequently did not take his seat in Parliament. His wife, Margaret, appears to have shared in her husband's enthusiasm, and to have resembled him in courage. In the Earl of Mar's correspondence frequent allusion is made to her under the name of Mrs. Mellor. "I wish, " says the Earl on one occasion, "our men had her spirit. " And the remembrances which he sends her, and his recurrence to her, show how important a personage Lady Nairn must have been. Aided by these two influential relations, the Marquis of Tullibardine had engaged in the dangerous game which cost Scotland so dear. Upon the close of the Rebellion, Lord Nairn was not so fortunate as to escape to France with his relation. He was taken prisoner, tried, and condemned to be executed. At his trial he pleaded guilty; but he was respited, and afterwards pardoned. His wife and children were eventually provided for out of the forfeited estate; but neither punishment nor favour prevented his sons from sharing in the Rebellion of 1745.

Another individual who participated in the Rebellion of 1715 was Lord Charles Murray, the fourth surviving son of the Duke of Athole, and one of those gallant, fine-tempered soldiers, whose graceful bearing and good qualities win upon the esteem even of their enemies. At the beginning of the Rebellion, Lord Charles was an officer on half-pay in the British service; he quickly joined the insurgent army, and obtained the command of a regiment. Such was his determination to share all dangers and difficulties with his troops, that he never could be prevailed upon to ride at the head of his regiment, but went in his Highland dress, on foot, throughout the marches. This young officer crossed the Forth with General Mackintosh, and joined the Northumbrian insurgents in the march to Preston. At the siege of that town Lord Charles defended one of the barriers, and repelled Colonel Dormer's brigade from the attack. He was afterwards made prisoner at the surrender, tried by a court-martial, and sentenced to be shot as a deserter from the British army. He was, however, subsequently reprieved, but died only five years afterwards. [47]

The Marquis of Tullibardine was not, however, the only Jacobite member of the family who had been spared after the Rebellion of 1715, to renew his efforts in the cause. His brother, the celebrated Lord George Murray, was also deeply engaged in the same interests. In 1719, the hopes of the party were revived by the war with Spain, and their invasion of Great Britain was quietly planned by the Duke of Ormond, who hastened to Madrid to hold conferences with Alberoni. Shortly afterwards the Chevalier was received in that capital, and treated as King of England. In March, 1719, the ill-fated expedition under the Duke of Ormond was formed, and a fleet, destined never to reach its appointed place of rendezvous, sailed from Cadiz.

The enterprise met with the usual fate of all the attempts formed in favour of the Stuarts. With the exception of two frigates, none of the ships proceeded farther than Cape Finisterre, where they were disabled by a storm. These two vessels reached the coast of Scotland, having on board of them the Earl of Seaforth, the Earl Marischal, the Marquis of Tullibardine, [48] three hundred Spaniards, and arms for two thousand men. They landed at the island of Lewes, but found the body of the Jacobite party resolved not to move until all the forces under Ormond should be assembled. During this interval of suspense, disputes between the Marquis of Tullibardine and the Lord Marischal, which should have the command, produced the usual effects among a divided and factious party, of checking exertion by diminishing confidence.

It appears, however, that the Marquis had a commission from the Chevalier to invade Scotland; in virtue of which he left the island of Lewes, whence he had for some time been carrying on a correspondence with the Highland chieftains, and landed with the three hundred Spaniards on the main land. The Ministers of George the First lost no time in repelling this attempt by a foreign power, and it is singular that they employed Dutch troops for the purpose; and that Scotland, for the first time, beheld her rights contested by soldiers speaking different languages, and natives of different continental regions. The Government had brought over two thousand Dutch soldiers, and six battalions of Imperial troops from the Austrian Netherlands, and these were now sent down to Inverness, where General Wightman was stationed. As soon as he was informed of the landing of the Spanish forces, that commander marched his troops to Glenshiel, a place between Fort Augustus and Benera. He attacked the invaders: the Highlanders were quickly repulsed and fled to their hills; the Spaniards were taken prisoners; but the Marquis of Tullibardine and the Earl of Seaforth escaped, and, retreating to the island of Lewes, again escaped to France.

During twenty-six years the Marquis of Tullibardine, against whom an act of attainder was passed, remained in exile. He appears to have avoided taking any active part in political affairs. "These seven or eight years, " he says in a letter addressed to the Chevalier, "have sufficiently shewn me how unfit I am for meddling with the deep concerns of state. "[49] He resided at Puteaux, a small town near Paris, until called imperatively from his retreat.

During the period of inaction, no measures were taken to reconcile those whom he had left, the more gallant portion of the Highlanders, to the English Government. "The state of arms, " says Mr. Home, "was allowed to remain the same; the Highlanders lived under their chiefs, in arms; the people of England and the Lowlanders of Scotland lived, without arms, under their sheriffs and magistrates; so that every rebellion was a war carried on by the Highlanders against the standing army; and a declaration of war with France or Spain, which required the service of the troops abroad, was a signal for a rebellion at home. Strange as it may seem, it was actually so. "[50]

During the interval between the two Rebellions of 1715 and 1745, the arts of peace were cultivated in England, and the national wealth augmented; but no portion of that wealth altered the habits of the Highland chieftains, who, looking continually for another rebellion, estimated their property by the number of men whom they could bring into the field. An anecdote, illustrative of this peculiarity, is told of Macdonald of Keppoch, who was killed at the battle of Culloden. Some low-country gentlemen were visiting him in 1740, and were entertained with the lavish hospitality of a Highland home. One of these guests ventured to ask of the landlord, what was the rent of his estate. "I can bring five hundred men into the field, " was the reply. It was estimated, about this time, that the whole force which could be raised by the Highlanders amounted to no more than twelve thousand men; yet, with this inconsiderable number, the Jacobites could shake the British throne.

The danger which might arise to the Government, in case of a foreign war, from the Highlanders, was foreseen by Duncan Forbes of Culloden, and a scheme was formed by that good and great man, and communicated to Lord Hay, adapted to reconcile the chieftains to the sovereignty of the house of Hanover, and at the same time to preserve the peace of the country. This was, to raise four or five Highland regiments, appointing an English or Scotch officer of undoubted loyalty to King George, to be colonel of each regiment, and naming all the inferior officers from a list drawn up by President Forbes, and comprising all the chiefs and chieftains of the disaffected clans. Most unhappily this plan was rejected. Had it been adopted, the melancholy events of the last Rebellion might not have left an indelible stain upon our national character. The Highlanders, once enlisted in the cause of Government, would have been true to their engagements; and the fidelity of the officers, when serving abroad, would have been a guarantee for the good conduct of their relations at home. It was not, however, deemed practicable; and the energies of a determined and unemployed people were again brought into active force. It is said to have met with the decided approbation of Sir Robert Walpole, but it was negatived by the Cabinet. [51]

The year 1739 witnessed the revival of the Jacobite Association, which had been annihilated by the attainders and exiles of its members after the last Rebellion. The declaration of war between Spain and England, induced a belief that hostilities with France would follow; and accordingly, in 1740, seven persons of distinction met at Edinburgh, and signed an association, which was to be carried to the Chevalier St. George at Rome, together with a list of those chiefs and chieftains who were ready to join the association, if a body of French troops should land in Scotland. This was the commencement of the second Rebellion; and it was seconded with as pure a spirit of devotion to the cause, as exalted an enthusiasm, as if none had bled on the scaffold in the previous reign, or attainders and forfeitures had never visited with poverty and ruin the adherents of James Stuart.

The Marquis of Tullibardine was selected as one of the attendants of Charles Edward, in the perilous enterprise of the invasion. He was the person of the highest rank among those who accompanied the gallant and unfortunate adventurer in his voyage from the mouth of the Loire to Scotland, in a little vessel, La Doutelle, with its escort of a ship of seven hundred tons, the Elizabeth. During this voyage the strictest incognito was preserved by the Prince, who was dressed in the habit of the Scotch College, at Paris, and who suffered his beard to grow, in order still better to disguise himself. At night the ship sailed without a light, except that which proceeded from the compass, and which was closely covered, the more effectually to defy pursuit. As it tracked the ocean, with its guardian, the Elizabeth, the sight of a British man-of-war off Lizard Point excited the ardour of the youthful hero on board of La Doutelle. Captain D'Eau, the commander of the Elizabeth, determined to attack the English ship, and requested the aid of Mr. Walsh, who commanded the Doutelle. His request was denied, probably from the responsibility which would have been incurred by Walsh, if he had endangered the safety of the vessel in which the Prince sailed. The attack was therefore made by the brave D'Eau alone. It was succeeded by a fight of two hours, during which the Doutelle looked on, while the Prince vainly solicited Walsh to engage in the action. The commander refused, and threatened the royal youth to send him to his cabin if he persisted. Both ships were severely damaged in the encounter and La Doutelle was obliged to proceed on her way alone, the Elizabeth returning to France to refit.

On the twenty-first of July, La Doutelle approached the remote range of the Hebrides, comprehending Lewes, Uist, and Barra, often called, from being seen together, the Long Island. As the vessel neared the shore, a large Hebridean eagle hovered over the masts. The Marquis of Tullibardine observed it, and attributed to its appearance that importance to which the imagination of his countrymen gives to such incidents; yet, not wishing to appear superstitious, or to show what is called a "Highland freit, " it was not until the bird had followed the ship's course for some time, that he drew the attention of the Prince to the circumstance. As they returned on deck after dinner, he pointed out the bird to Charles Edward, observing at the same time, "Sir, I hope this is a happy omen, and promises good things to us; the king of birds is come to welcome your Royal Highness, on your arrival in Scotland. "

The Prince and his followers landed, on the twenty-third of July, at the island of Eriska, belonging to Clanranald, and situated between the Isles of Barra and of South Uist, their voyage having been accomplished in eighteen days. Here all the party landed, with the exception of the Marquis, who was laid up with the gout, and unable to move. His condition was supposed to be one of peril, for two ships had been espied, and the Prince and his associates hurried off, with all the expedition they could, to shore. The long boat was got out, and sent to procure a pilot, who was discovered in the person of the hereditary piper of Clanranald, who piloted the precious freight safely to shore. The two vessels which had produced so much alarm, proved afterwards to be only merchant-vessels.

In these "malignant regions, " as Dr. Johnson describes them, referring to the severity of the climate and the poverty of the soil, Prince Charles and his adherents were lodged in a small country house, with a hole in the roof for a chimney, and a fire in the middle of the room. The young adventurer, reared among the delicacies of the palace at Albano, was often obliged to go to the door for fresh air. "What a plague is the matter with that fellow, " exclaimed Angus Macdonald, the landlord, "that he can neither sit nor stand still, nor keep within nor without doors? " The night, it must be observed, was unusually wet and stormy, so that the Prince had no alternative between smoke and rain. The pride of the Scotch, in this remote region, was exemplified in another trifling occurrence: The Prince, who was less fatigued than the rest of the party, with that consideration for others, and disregard of his own personal comfort, which formed at this period so beautiful a part of his character, insisted that his attendants should retire to rest. He took a particular care of Sir Thomas Sheridan, his tutor, and examined closely the bed appropriated to him, in order to see that it was well aired. The landlord, indignant at this investigation, called out to him, "That the bed was so good, and the sheets were so good, that a prince might sleep in them. "[52]

The farm-house in which this little incident took place, and which first received the Prince, who was destined to occupy so great a variety of dwellings in Scotland, was situated in Borrodale, a wild, mountainous tract of country, which forms a tongue of land between two bays. Borrodale, being difficult of access, was well-chosen as the landing-place of Charles; whilst around, in most directions, were the well-wishers to his cause.

The Marquis of Tullibardine accompanied Charles in his progress until the Prince landed at Glenfinnin, [53] which is situated about twenty miles from Fort William, and forms the outlet from Moidart to Lochaber; here the standard of Charles Edward was unfurled. The scene in which this ill-omened ceremonial took place is a deep and narrow valley, in which the river Finnin runs between high and craggy mountains, which are inaccessible to every species of carriage, and only to be surmounted by travellers on foot. At each end of the vale is a lake of about twelve miles in length, and behind the stern mountains which enclose the glen, are salt-water lakes, one of them an arm of the sea. The river Finnin empties itself into the Lake of Glenshiel, at the extremity of the glen. On the eighteenth of August Prince Charles crossed this lake, slept at Glensiarick, and on the nineteenth proceeded to Glenfinnin.

When Charles landed in the glen, he gazed around anxiously for Cameron of Lochiel, the younger, whom he expected to have joined him. He looked for some time in vain; that faithful adherent was not then in sight, nor was the glen, as the Prince had expected, peopled by any of the clansmen whose gathering he had expected. A few poor people from the little knot of hovels, which was called the village, alone greeted the ill-starred adventurer. Disconcerted, Prince Charles entered one of the hovels, which are still standing, and waited there for about two hours. At the end of that time, the notes of the pibroch were heard, and presently, descending from the summit of a hill, appeared the Camerons, advancing in two lines, each of them three men deep. Between the lines walked the prisoners of war, who had been taken some days previously near Loch Lochiel.

The Prince, exhilarated by the sight of six or seven hundred brave Highlanders, immediately gave orders for the standard to be unfurled.

The office of honour was entrusted to the Marquis of Tullibardine, on account of his high rank and importance to the cause. The spot chosen for the ceremony was a knoll in the centre of the vale. Upon this little eminence the Marquis stood, supported on either side by men, for his health was infirm, and what we should now call a premature old age was fast approaching. The banner which it was his lot to unfurl displayed no motto, nor was there inscribed upon it the coffin and the crown which the vulgar notion in England assigned to it. It was simply a large banner of red silk, with a white space in the middle. The Marquis held the staff until the Manifesto of the Chevalier and the Commission of Regency had been read. In a few hours the glen in which this solemnity had been performed, was filled not only with Highlanders, but with ladies and gentlemen to admire the spectacle. Among them was the celebrated Miss, or, more properly, Mrs. Jeanie Cameron, whose passionate attachment for the Prince rendered her so conspicuous in the troublous period of 1745. The description given of her in Bishop Forbes's Jacobite Memoirs destroys much of the romance of the story commonly related of her. "She is a widow, " he declares, "nearer fifty than forty years of age. She is a genteel, well-looking, handsome woman, with a pair of pretty eyes, and hair black as jet. She is of a very sprightly genius, and is very agreeable in conversation. She was so far from accompanying the Prince's army, that she went off with the rest of the spectators as soon as the army marched; neither did she ever follow the camp, nor ever was with the Prince in private, except when he was in Edinburgh. "[54]

Soon after the unfurling of the standard, we find the Marquis of Tullibardine writing to Mrs. Robertson of Lude, a daughter of Lord Nairn, and desiring her to put the Castle of Blair into some order, and to do honours of the place when the Prince should come there. The Marquis, it is here proper to mention, was regarded by all the Jacobites as still the head of his house, and uniformly styled by that party the "Duke of Athole, " yet he seldom adopted the title himself; and in only one or two instances in his correspondence does the signature of Athole occur. [55]

On the thirty-first of August the Prince visited the famous Blair Athole, or Field of Athole, the word *Blair* signifying a pleasant land,

and being descriptive of that beautiful vale situated in the midst of wild and mountainous scenery.

After riding along a black moor, in sight of vast mountains, the castle, a plain massive white house, appears in view. It is seated on an eminence above a plain watered by the Gary, called, by Pennant, "an outrageous stream, which laves and rushes along vast beds of gravel on the valley below. "

The approach to Blair Castle winds up a very steep and high hill, and through a great birch wood, forming a most picturesque scene, from the pendent form of the boughs waving with the wind from the bottom to the utmost summits of the mountains. On attaining the top, a view of the beautiful little Straith, fertile and wooded, with the river in the middle, delights the beholder. The stream, after meandering in various circles, suddenly swells into a lake that fills the vale from side to side; this lake is about three miles long, and retains the name of the river.

When Prince Charles visited Blair, it was a fortified house, and capable of holding out a siege afterwards against his adherents. Its height was consequently lowered, but the inside has been finished with care by the ducal owner. The environs of this beautiful place are thus described by the graphic pen of Pennant, [56] whose description of them, having been written in 1769, is more likely to apply to the state in which it was when Prince Charles beheld it, than that of any more modern traveller.

"The Duke of Athoel's estate is very extensive, and the country populous; while vassalage existed, the chieftain could raise two or three thousand fighting-men, and leave sufficient at home to take care of the ground. The forests, or rather chases, (for they are quite naked,) are very extensive, and feed vast numbers of stags, which range at certain times of the year in herds of five hundred. Some grow to a great size. The hunting of these animals was formerly after the manner of an Eastern monarch. Thousands of vassals surrounded a great tract of country, and drove the deer to the spot where the chieftains were stationed, who shot them at their leisure.

"Near the house is a fine walk surrounding a very deep glen, finely wooded, but in dry weather deficient in water at the bottom; but on the side of the walk on the rock is a small crystalline fountain, inhabited at that time by a pair of Naiads, in the form of golden fish.

"In a spruce-fir was a hang-nest of some unknown bird, suspended at the four corners to the boughs; it was open at top an inch and a half in diameter, and two deep; the sides and bottom thick, the materials moss, worsted, and birch-bark, lined with hair and feathers. The stream affords the parr, [57] a small species of trout seldom exceeding eight inches in length, marked on the sides with nine large bluish spots, and on the lateral line with small red ones. No traveller should omit visiting Yorke Cascade, a magnificent cataract, amidst most suitable scenery, about a mile distant from the house. This country is very mountainous, has no natural woods, except of birch; but the vast plantations that begin to cloath the hills will amply supply these defects. "[58]

With what sensations must the Marquis of Tullibardine have approached this beautiful and princely territory, from which he had been excluded, his vassals becoming the vassals of a younger brother, and he a proscribed and aged man, visiting as an alien the home of his youth!

Sanguine hopes, however, perhaps mitigated the bitterness of the reflections with which the faithful and disinterested Marquis of Tullibardine once more found himself within the precincts of his proud domain.

Several anecdotes are told of Prince Charles at Blair; among others, "that when the Prince was at the Castle, he went into the garden, and taking a walk upon the bowling-green, he said he had never seen a bowling-green before; upon which Mrs. Robertson of Lude called for some bowls that he might see them, but he told her that he had had a present of bowls sent him, as a curiosity, to Rome from England."[59]

On the second of September, the Prince left Blair and went to the house of Lude, where he was very cheerful, and took his share in several dances, such as minuets and Highland reels; the first reel the Prince called for was, "This is no' mine ain House; " he afterwards commanded a Strathspey minuet to be danced.

On the following day, while dining at Dunkeld, some of the company happened to observe what a thoughtful state his father would now be in from the consideration of those dangers and difficulties which he had to encounter, and remarked that upon this account he was much to be pitied, because his mind must be much upon the rack. The Prince replied, that he did not half so much pity his father as his brother; [60] "for, " (he said) "the King has been inured to disappointments and distresses, and has learnt to bear up easily under the misfortunes of life; but, poor Harry! —his young and tender years make him much to be pitied, for few brothers love as we do. "

On the fourth of September, Prince Charles entered Perth; the Marquis of Tullibardine, as it appears from several letters addressed to him by Lord George Murray, who wrote from Perth, remained at Blair, but only, as it is evident from the following extract from a letter by Lord George Murray, whilst awaiting the arrangement of active operations. On the twenty-second of September he received a commission from the Prince, constituting and appointing him Commander-in-Chief of the forces north of the Forth; the active duties of the post were, however, fulfilled by Lord George Murray, who writes in the character of a general: [61]

"Dear Brother,

"Things vary so much from time to time, that I can say nothing certain as yet, but refer you to the enclosed letter; but depend upon having another express from me with you before Monday night. But in the meantime you must resolve to be ready to march on Tuesday morning, by Keinacan and Tay Bridge, so as to be at Crieff on Wednesday, and even that way, if you do your best, you will be half a mark behind; but you will be able to make that up on Thursday, when I reckon we may meet at Dumblane, or Doun; but of this more fully in my next. It is believed for certain, that Cope will embark at Aberdeen.

"I hope the meal was with you this day, thirty-five bolls, —for it was at Invar last night. It shall be my study to have more meal with you on Monday night, for you must distribute a peck a man; and cost what it will, there must be frocks made to each man to contain a peck or two for the men to have always with them.

"Buy linen, yarn, or anything, for these frocks are of absolute necessity—nothing can be done without them. His Royal Highness desires you to acquaint Glenmoriston and Glenco, if they come your way of this intended march, so that they may go by Taybridge (if you please, with you), and what meal you can spare let them have.

You may please tell your own people that there is a project to get arms for them. Yours. Adieu.

"George Murray. "

From his age and infirmities, the Marquis was precluded from taking an active part in the long course of events which succeeded the unfurling of the standard at Glenfinnin. He appears to have exercised a gentle, but certain sway over the conduct of others, and especially to have possessed a control over the high-spirited Lord George Murray, whose conduct he did not always approve. [62]

Whilst at Blair, the Marquis was saluted as Duke of Athole by all who entered his house; but the honour was accompanied by some mortifications. His younger brother, the Duke of Athole, had taken care to carry away everything that could be conveyed, and to drive off every animal that could be driven from his territory. The Marquis had therefore great difficulty in providing even a moderate entertainment for the Prince; whilst the army, now grown numerous, were almost starving. "The priests, " writes a contemptuous opponent, "never had a fitter opportunity to proclaim a general fast than the present. No bull of the Pope's would ever have been more certain of finding a most exact and punctual obedience. "

After the battle of Culloden had sealed the fate of the Jacobites, the Marquis of Tullibardine was forced, a second time, to seek a place of refuge. He threw himself, unhappily, upon the mercy of one who little deserved the confidence which was reposed in his honour, or merited the privilege of succouring the unfortunate. The following are the particulars of his fate: —

About three weeks after the battle of Culloden the Marquis of Tullibardine traversed the moors and mountains through Strathane in search of a place of safety and repose: he had become a very infirm old man, and so unfit for travelling on horseback, that he had a saddle made on purpose, somewhat like a chair, in which he rode in the manner ladies usually do.

On arriving in the vicinity of Loch Lomond he was quite worn out, and recollecting that a daughter of the family of Polmain (who were connected with his own) was married to Buchanan of Drumakiln, who lived in a detached peninsula, running out into the lake, the fainting fugitive thought, on these accounts, that the place might be suitable for a temporary refuge. The Marquis was attended by a French secretary, two servants of that nation, and two or three Highlanders, who had guided him through the solitary passes of the mountains. Against the judgment of these faithful attendants, he bent his course to the Ross, for so the house of Drumakiln is called, where the Laird of Drumakiln was living with his son. The Marquis, after alighting, begged to have a private interview with his cousin, the wife of Drumakiln; he told this lady he was come to put his life into her hands, and what, in some sense, he valued more than life, a small casket, [63] which he delivered to her, intreating her, whatever became of him, that she would keep that carefully till demanded in his name, as it contained papers of consequence to the honour and safety of many other persons. Whilst he was thus talking, the younger Drumakiln rudely broke in upon him, and snatching away the casket, he said he would secure it in a safe place, and went out. Meantime the French secretary and the servants were watchful and alarmed at seeing the father and son walking in earnest consultation, and observing horses saddled and dispatched with an air of mystery, whilst every one appeared to regard them with compassion. All this time the Marquis was treated with seeming kindness; but his attendants suspected some snare. They burst into loud lamentations, and were described by some children, who observed them, to be 'greeting and roaring like women. ' This incident the lady of Drumakiln (who was a person of some capacity) afterwards told her neighbours as a strange instance of effeminacy in these faithful adherents.

At night the secretary went secretly to his master's bedside, and assured him there was treachery. The Marquis answered he could believe no gentleman capable of such baseness, and at any rate he was incapable of escaping through such defiles as they had passed; he told him in that case it could only aggravate his sorrow to see him also betrayed; and advised him to go off immediately, which he did. Early in the morning a party from Dumbarton, summoned for that purpose, arrived to carry the Marquis away prisoner. He bore his fate with calm magnanimity. The fine horses which he brought with him were detained, and he and one attendant who remained were mounted on some horses belonging to Drumakiln. Such was the general sentiment of disgust with Drumakiln, that the officer who commanded the party taunted that gentleman in the bitterest manner, and the commander of Dumbarton Castle, who treated his noble prisoner with the utmost respect and compassion, regarded

Drumakiln with the coldest disdain. The following anecdotes of the odium which Drumakiln incurred, are related by Mrs. Grant. [64]

"Very soon after the Marquis had departed, young Drumakiln mounted the Marquis's horse, (the servant riding another which had belonged to that nobleman,) and set out to a visit to his father-in-law Polmaise.

"When he alighted, he gave his horse to a groom who, knowing the Marquis well, recognised him—'Come in poor beast (said he); times are changed with you since you carried a noble Marquis, but you shall always be treated well here for his sake. ' Drumakiln ran in to his father-in-law, complaining that his servant insulted him. Polmaise made no answer, but turning on his heel, rang the bell for the servant, saying, 'That gentleman's horses. '

"After this and several other rebuffs the father and son began to shrink from the infamy attached to this proceeding. There was at that time only one newspaper published at Edinburgh, conducted by the well-known Ruddiman; to this person the elder Drumakiln addressed a letter or paragraph to be inserted in his paper, bearing that on such a day the Marquis surrendered to him at his house. This was regularly dated at Ross: very soon after the father and son went together to Edinburgh, and waiting on the person appointed to make payments for affairs of this nature, demanded their reward. It should have been before observed, that the Government were at this time not at all desirous to apprehend the Marquis, though his name was the first inserted in the proclamation. This capture indeed greatly embarrassed them, as it would be cruel to punish, and partial to pardon him. The special officer desired Drumakiln to return the next day for the money. Meanwhile he sent privately to Ruddiman and examined him about the paragraph already mentioned. They found it on his file, in the old Laird's handwriting, and delivered it to the commissioner. The commissioner delivered the paragraph, in his own handwriting, up to the elder, saying, '*There* is an order to the Treasury, which ought to satisfy you, ' and turned away from him with marked contempt. "

"Soon after the younger laird was found dead in his bed, to which he had retired in usual health. Of five children which he left, it would shock humanity to relate the wretched lives, and singular, and untimely deaths, of whom, indeed, it might be said,

"On all the line a sudden vengeance waits,
And frequent hearses shall besiege their gates."

And they were literally considered by all the neighbourhood as caitiffs,

"Whose breasts the furies steel'd
And curst with hearts unknowing how to yield."—POPE.

The blasting influence of more than dramatic justice, or of corroding infamy, seemed to reach every branch of this devoted family. After the extinction of the direct male heirs, a brother, who was a captain in the army, came home to take possession of the property. He was a person well-respected in life, and possessed some talent, and much amenity of manners. The country gentlemen, however, shunned and disliked him, on account of the existing prejudice. This person, thus shunned and slighted, seemed to grow desperate, and plunged into the lowest and most abandoned profligacy. It is needless to enter into a detail of crimes which are hastening to desired oblivion. It is enough to observe that the signal miseries of this family have done more to impress the people of that district with a horror of treachery, and a sense of retributive justice, than volumes of the most eloquent instruction could effect. On the dark question relative to temporal judgments it becomes us not to decide. Yet it is of some consequence, in a moral view, to remark how much all generous emulation, all hope of future excellence, is quenched in the human mind by the dreadful blot of imputed infamy. "[65]

This account of the retributive justice of public opinion which was visited upon Drumakiln, is confirmed by other authority. [66] It is consolatory to reflect that the Marquis of Tullibardine, after a life spent in an honest devotion to the cause which he believed to be just, was spared, by a merciful release, from the horrors of a public trial, and of a condemnation to the scaffold, which age and ill-health were not sufficient pleas to avert. After remaining some weeks in confinement at Dumbarton, he was carried to Edinburgh, where he remained until the thirteenth of May, 1746. He was then put on board the Eltham man-of-war, lying in the Leith Roads, bound for London. His health all this time was declining, yet he had the inconvenience of a long sea voyage to sustain, for the Eltham went north for other prisoners before it sailed for London. But at length the Marquis reached his last home, the Tower, where he arrived on the twenty-first of June. He survived only until the ninth of July.

Little is known of this unfortunate nobleman, except what is honourable, consistent, and amiable. He had almost ceased to be Scotch, except in his attachments, and could scarcely write his own language. He seems to have been generally respected; and he bore his reverses of fortune with calmness and fortitude. In his last moments he is said to have declared, that although he had been as much attached to the cause of James Stuart as any of his adherents, if he might now advise his countrymen, it should be never more to enter into rebellious measures, for, having failed in the last attempt, every future one would be hopeless. [68]

The Marquis died in the fifty-eighth year of his age, and was buried in the chapel in the Tower, which has received few more honest men, or public characters more true to the principles which they have professed.

The following letter, written in March, 1746, during the siege of Blair Castle, when it was commanded by a garrison under Sir Andrew Agnew, and addressed to Lord George Murray, shows the strong sense which the Marquis entertained of what was due to his country and his cause.

"Brother George,

"Since, contrary to the rules of right reason, you was pleased to tell me a sham story about the expedition to Blair, without further ceremony for me, you may now do what the gentlemen of the country think fit with the castle: I am in no concern about it. Our great-great-grandfather, grandfather, and father's pictures will be an irreparable loss on blowing up the house; but there is no comparison to be made with these faint images of our forefathers and the more necessary publick service, which requires we should sacrifice everything that can valuably contribute towards the country's safety, as well as materially advancing the royal cause. Pray give my kind service to all valuable friends, to which I can add nothing but that, in all events, you may be assured I shall ever be found with just regard, dear brother, your most affectionate brother and humble servant. "

"Inverness, "March 26, 1746. "

"PS. At the upper end of the door of the old stable, there was formerly a gate which had a portcullis into the castle; it is half built up and boarded over on the stable side, large enough to hold a horse at hack and manger. People that don't know the place imagine it may be much easier dug through than any other part of the wall, so as to make a convenient passage into the vaulted room, which is called the servants' hall. "

Of the fate of this princely territory, and upon the fortunes of the family of which the Marquis of Tullibardine was so respectable a member, much remains to be related; but it appertains more properly to the life of the warlike and ambitious brother of the Marquis, the celebrated Lord George Murray.

FOOTNOTES:

[44] Lord Lovat's Memoirs, p. 39.

[45] Wood's Peerage.

[46] Reay, p. 78.

[47] Wood's Peerage.

[48] See Brown's History of the Highlands. But Home, in his History of the Rebellion, speaks of Lords Tullibardine and Seaforth as coming from a different quarter. "Most of these persons, " he says, "came privately from France. "

[49] Athol Correspondence. Printed for the Abbotsford Club. App. 229.

[50] Home's History of the Rebellion, p. 19.

[51] Home, pp. 22, 23.

[52] Jacobite Memoirs.

[53] Glenfinnin is in the shire of Inverness, and the parish of Glenelg. It is situated at the head of Loch Shiel.

[54] Jacobite Memoirs, p. 23.

[55] Introductory Notice, Athol Correspondence, p. ix.

[56] Pennant's Scotland, vol. i. p. 118.

[57] It has lately been proved, beyond doubt, that the parr is a young salmon, not a distinct fish.

[58] Pennant, p. 119.

[59] Jacobite Memoirs, pp. 26, 27.

[60] Henry Benedict, afterwards Cardinal York.

[61] Jacobite Memoirs, p. 31.

[62] See Forbes's Jacobite Memoirs, p. 51.

[63] This casket was never more seen. It was supposed to contain family jewels.

[64] Mrs. Grant's MS. For which I am indebted for the whole of this account.

[65] Mrs. Grant's MS.

[66] Note in Forbes's Jacobite Memoirs, p. 3.

[67] Wood's Peerage.

[68] Athole Correspondence. Introductory Notice.

SIR JOHN MACLEAN.

The name Maclean, abbreviated from Mac Gillean, is derived from the founder of the clan, "Gillean n'a Tuaidh, " Gillean of the Battle-axe, so called from his carrying with him as his ordinary weapon, a battle-axe. From this hero are descended the three principal families who compose the clan Maclean, who was also designated Gillean of Duart.

It is related of Gillean that, being one day engaged in a stag-hunt on the mountain of Bein't Sheala, and having wandered away from the rest of his party, the mountain became suddenly enveloped in a deep mist, and that he lost his track. For three days he wandered about; and, at length exhausted, threw himself under the shelter of a cranberry bush, previously fixing the handle of his battle-axe in the earth. He was discovered by his party, who had been vainly endeavouring to find him, insensible on the ground, with his arm round the handle of the battle-axe, whilst the head of the weapon rose above the bush. Hence, probably, the origin of the crest used by the clan Maclean, the battle-axe surrounded by a laurel-branch. [69]

To Gillean of the Battle-axe various origins have been ascribed; truly is it observed, that "there is little wisdom in attempting to thread the mazes of fanciful and traditionary genealogies. "[70] Like other families of importance, in feudal times, the Macleans had their seneachie, or historian; and, by the last of these, Dr. John Beaton, the descent, in regular order, from Aonaglius Turmi Teanebrach, a powerful monarch of Ireland, to Fergus the First, of Scotland, is traced.

A tradition had indeed prevailed, that the founder, of the house of Maclean was a son of Fitzgerald, an Earl of Kildare, —a supposition which is contemptuously rejected by the historian of this ancient race. "In fact, " he remarks, "from various sources, Gillean can be proved to have been in his grave, long before such a title as Earl of Kildare was known, and nearly two hundred years before the name of Fitzgerald existed. "[71] It appears, indeed, undoubted, from ancient records and well-authenticated sources, that the origin of Gillean was derived from the source which has been stated.

When the lordship of the Isles was forfeited, the clan Maclean was divided into four branches, each of which held of the Lords of the

Isles; these branches were the Macleans of Duart, the Macleans of Lochbuy, the Macleans of Coll, and the Macleans of Ardgour. Of these, the most important branch was the family of Duart, founded by Lachlan Maclean, surnamed Lubanich. This powerful chief obtained such an ascendant at the court of the Lord of the Isles, as to provoke the enmity of the Chief of Mackinnon, who, on the occasion of a stag-hunt, formed a plot to cut off Lachlan and his brother, Hector Maclean. But the conspiracy was discovered by its objects; Mackinnon suffered death at the hands of the two brothers for his design; and the Lord of the Isles, sailing in his galley towards his Castle of Ardtorinsh in Morven, was captured, and carried to Icolumb-kill, where he was obliged, sitting on the famous black rock of Iona, held sacred in those days, to swear that he would bestow in marriage upon Lachlan Lubanich his daughter Margaret, granddaughter, by her mother's side, of Robert the Second, King of Scotland: and with her, as a dowry, to give to the Lord of Duart, Eriska, with all its isles. The dowry demanded consisted of a towering rock, commanding an extensive view of the islands by which it is surrounded, and occupying a central situation among those tributaries. [72] From the bold and aspiring chief was Sir John Maclean of Duart descended. The marriage of Lachlan Lubanich with Margaret of the Isles took place in the year 1366. [73]

Between the time of Lachlan Lubanich and the birth of Sir John Maclean, the house of Duart encountered various reverses of fortune. It has been shown how the chief added the rock of Eriska to his possessions; in the course of the following century, a great part of the Isles of Mull and Tirey, with detached lands in Isla, Jura, Scarba, and in the districts of Morven, Lochaber, and Knapdale, were included in the estates of the chiefs of Duart, who rose, in the time of James the Sixth, to be among the most powerful of the families of the Hebrides. The principal seats of the chiefs of the Macleans were Duart and Aros Castles in Mull, Castle Gillean in Kerrara, on the coast of Lorn, and Ardtornish Castle in Morven. In 1632, on occasion of the visit of one of the chiefs, Lachlan, to the Court of Charles the First, he was created a Baronet of Nova Scotia, by the title of Sir Lachlan Maclean of Morven. But various circumstances, and more especially the enmity of the Argyle family, and the adherence of Maclean to the Stuarts, had contributed to the decline of their pre-eminence before the young chief, whose destiny it was to make his name known and feared at the court of England, had seen the light.

The family of Maclean in all its numerous and complicated branches, had been distinguished for loyalty and independence during the intervening centuries between the career of Gillean and the birth of that chieftain whose devotion to the Jacobite cause proved eventually the ruin of the house of Duart. Throughout the period of the Great Rebellion, and of the Protectorate, the chief of the Macleans had made immense sacrifices to support the interests of the King, and to bring his clan into the field. In the disgraceful transactions, by which it was agreed that Scotland should withdraw her troops from England upon the payment of four hundred thousand pounds, in full of all demands, the faithful Highland clans of the north and west, the Grahams, Macleans, Camerons, and many others, had no participation. One main actor in that bargain, by which a monarch was bought and sold, was the Marquis of Argyle, the enemy and terror of his Highland neighbours, the Macleans of Duart. Upon the suppression of the royal authority, domestic feuds were ripened into hostilities during the general anarchy; and few of the oppressed and harassed clans suffered more severely, or more permanently than the Macleans of Duart.

Archibald, the first Marquis of Argyle, fixed an indelible stain upon his memory by acts of unbridled licence and aggression, in relation to his Highland neighbours; the unfortunate Macleans of Duart especially experienced the effects of his wrath, and suffered from his manoeuvres. [74]

In the time of Cromwell, Argyle having procured from the Lords of the Treasury, a grant of the tithes of Argyleshire, with a commission to collect several arrears of the feu-duty, cesses, taxation, and supply, and some new contributions laid on the subject by Parliament, under the names of ammunition and contribution money, the power which such an authority bestowed, in days when the standard of right was measured by the amount of force, may readily be conceived. On the part of Argyle, long-cherished views on the territories of his neighbour, Maclean of Duart, were now brought into co-operation with the most remorseless abuse of authority.

Sir Lachlan Maclean of Duart, the great-grandfather of Sir John Maclean, was then chief of the clan. The Marquis of Argyle directed that application should be made to this unfortunate man for his quota of these arrears, and also for some small sums for which he had himself been security for the chief. Sir Lachlan was in no condition to comply with this demand; for he had suffered more deeply in the royal cause than any of his predecessors. During the rule of Argyle and Leslie in Scotland, a rule which might aptly be denominated a reign of terror, the possessions of the chief in Mull had been ravaged by the parliamentary troops, without any resistance from the harmless inhabitants, who had been instructed by their lord to offer no retaliation that could furnish a plea for future oppression. The castle of Duart had been besieged, and surrendered to Argyle and Leslie, upon condition that the defenceless garrison, and eight Irish gentlemen, inmates of the hospitable Highlander's home, should be spared. Still more, the infant son of Sir Lachlan had been kidnapped from his school at Dumbarton by Argyle, and was paraded by the side of the Marquis to intimidate the chief, who was made to understand that any resistance from him would be fatal to his child, —"an instrument, " observes the seneachie, "which the coward well knew might be used with greater effect upon the noble father of his captive, than all the Campbell swords the craven lord could muster. " Under these circumstances, Sir Lachlan Maclean was neither in the temper nor the condition to comply with the exactions of those whom he also regarded as having usurped the sovereign authority. He refused; and his refusal was exactly what his enemy desired.

The next step which Argyle took was to claim the amount due to him from the chief, which, by buying up all the debts, public and private, of Maclean, he swelled to thirty thousand pounds, before a court of law. Such was the state of Scottish judicial proceedings in those days, that the process was ended before Sir Lachlan had even heard of its commencement. He hastened, when informed of it, to Edinburgh, in order to make known his case before the "Committee of Estates, " then acting with sovereign authority in Scotland. But he was intercepted at Inverary, cast into prison upon a writ of attachment, issued and signed by Argyle himself, and immured in Argyle's castle of Carrick, for a debt due to Archibald, Marquis of Argyle. It was there required of him that he should grant a bond for fourteen thousand pounds Scots, and sign a doqueted account for sixteen thousand pounds more, bearing interest.

For a time the unhappy chief refused to sign the bond thus demanded; for a year he resisted the oppression of his enemy, and bore his imprisonment, with the aggravation of declining health. At last his friends, alarmed at his sinking condition, entreated him, as the only means of release, to comply with the demand of Argyle. Sir Lachlan signed the document, was set free, and returned to Duart, where he expired in April, 1649. To his family he bequeathed a legacy of contention and misfortune.

His successor, Sir Hector Maclean, the young hostage who had been kidnapped from Dumbarton, was a youth of a warlike and determined spirit, who resisted the depredations of the plundering clan of Campbells in Lorn and Ardnamuchan, and, on one occasion, hung up two of the invaders at his castle of Dunnin Morvern. Such, in spite of this summary mode of proceeding, were Sir Hector's ideas of honour, that, notwithstanding his doubts of the validity of the bond obtained from his father, he conceived that the superscription of his father's name to it rendered it his duty to comply with its conditions as he could. He is declared by one authority to have paid ten thousand pounds of the demand; by another that fact is doubted, since, when Sir John Maclean's guardians investigated it, no receipts for sums alleged to have been paid on account were to be found. [75] But this is again accounted for by the seneachie or family historian.

Sir Hector Maclean fell in the battle of Inverkeithing, where, out of eight hundred of his clan who fought against General Lambert, only forty escaped. He was succeeded by his brother Allan, a child, subject to the management of guardians. By their good care, a great portion of the debt to Argyle was paid, but there still remained sufficient to afford the insatiable enemy of his house a fair pretext of aggression. The case was again brought before the Scottish Council; it was even referred to Charles the Second; but, by the representations of the Duke of Lauderdale, the Argyle influence prevailed. The famous Marquis of Argyle was, indeed, no longer in existence; he had perished on the scaffold: but his son still grasped at the possessions of his neighbour; and, although King Charles desired that Lauderdale "should see that Maclean had justice, " the Duke, who was then Scottish Lord Commissioner, on his return to Scotland, decided that the rents of the estates should be made payable to Argyle on account of the bond, a certain portion of them being reserved for the maintenance of the chief.

Sir Allan died a little more than a year after this decision had been made, ignorant of the decree; and left, to bear the buffeting of the storm, his son, Sir John Maclean, a child only four years of age, who succeeded his father in 1677. [76] His estates had been placed under the care of two of his nearest kinsmen, Lachlan Maclean of Brolas, and Lachlan Maclean of Torloisk, men of profound judgment and of firm character, from whose guardianship much was expected by the clan. But the minor possessed a friend as true as any kinsman could be, and one of undoubted influence and sagacity, in the celebrated Sir Ewan Cameron of Lochiel. Against his interest, in despite of Argyle, that brave and noble man espoused the cause of the weak and of the fatherless, notwithstanding that he was himself a debtor to Argyle, of whose power and will to injure he had shortly a proof. Finding that Lochiel was resolved to protect and assist the young Maclean, the Earl of Argyle[77] sent to demand from Sir Ewan the payment of the debt he owed, assuring him that it was his intention to follow out the law with the greatest rigour. Sir Ewan answered that he had not the money to pay, neither would he act against his friends. This threat, however, obliged Sir Ewan to continue in arms, contrary to proclamation, and also to obtain a protection from the Privy Council in Edinburgh, against the vengeance of Argyle.

But that which occasioned the greatest vexation to Sir Ewan, was an opportunity which he conceived that the tutors or guardians of the young Maclean had lost the power of emancipating their ward from the clutches of Argyle's power. This, he thought, might have been effected upon the forfeiture of the Marquis of Argyle to the Crown, when he considered that an opportunity might have been afforded to Maclean's guardians to release their ward from Argyle's hands, by a transaction with certain creditors of that nobleman, to whom the sum claimed by Argyle from Maclean had been promised, but never paid. Thus, by an unaccountable oversight, the power of the Argyle family over the fortunes of the Macleans was continued.

Under these adverse circumstances, Sir John Maclean succeeded to his inheritance. His principal guardian, although bearing a high reputation among the clan, was esteemed by Sir Ewan as "a person who seems to have been absolutely unfitt for manageing his affairs att such a juncture; "[78] and soon proved to be far too easy and credulous to contest with the crafty Campbells. Full of compassion for the helpless infant chief, Sir Ewan now resolved never to abandon the Macleans until matters were adjusted between them. He passed the winter of the year in Edinburgh, where he was, at one time, so much incensed against the Earl of Argyle for his cruelty to the Macleans, and so indignant at his conduct to himself, that the valiant chief of the Camerons was with difficulty restrained by his servant from shooting Argyle as he stepped into his coach to attend the council. [79]

Whilst the counsels of Sir Ewan Cameron prevailed with the guardians, the Macleans remained merely on the defensive; but when the insinuations of Lord Macdonald, who had much influence with one of the young heir's guardians, were listened to, the Macleans were incited to reprisals and plunder, to which it was at all times no difficult matter to stimulate Highlanders.

At length the powerful and mortal foe succeeded to his heart's content in his scheme of oppression. Argyle, in his capacity of Hereditary Justiciary of the Isles, summoned the clan Maclean to appear and stand their trials for treasonable convocations, garrisoning their houses and castles, &c. ; the unfortunate clansmen, knowing their enemy to be both judge and evidence, did not obey. Immediately they were declared rebels and outlaws, and a commission of fire and sword was issued against them. All communication between them and the Privy Council, who might have redressed their wrongs, was cut off: those who happened to fall into the hands of the Campbells, were cruelly treated; and those who styled themselves Maclean were blockaded in the Islands, and almost starved for want of provisions. Reduced in strength by the battle of Inverkeithing, the clan was but ill-prepared to resist so formidable a foe as Argyle, whose men, therefore, landed without opposition, the people flying to their mountains as the enemy approached. The young chief was sent, for protection, first to the fortified island of Thernburg, and afterwards to Kintail, under the care of the Earl of Seaforth, who had, not long previously, acted as a sort of arbitrator in the affairs of the family. [80]

While Sir John Maclean was thus, probably, unconscious of his wrongs and dangers, secured from personal injury, the strong old Castle of Duart was taken possession of by Argyle, who, finding it garrisoned, was obliged to publish an indemnity, which he had obtained on purpose, remitting all crimes committed by the Macleans since the eighteenth of September, 1674, on condition that the castle should be delivered to him, —a demand with which the islanders were forced to comply. But in vain did Argyle endeavour to prevail upon the honest and simple clansmen to renounce their allegiance to their chief, and to become his vassals. [81] Every species of indignity and of plunder was inflicted upon these hapless, but faithful Highlanders in vain; a "monster, " as he is termed, "bearing the stamp of human appearance, named Sir Neill Campbell, " in vain chased the poor inhabitants to the hills, and there exhibited acts of cruelty too shocking to be related. A promise, however, of payment of rents was at last obtained by Argyle, and he left the island, after garrisoning the castles. But this tribute was never paid. The Macleans could neither bear to see the halls of Duart and of Aros Castle tenanted by their foes, nor would they submit to pay to them their rents. A league of defence was again formed; letters of fire and sword were, in consequence, issued; but Argyle was baffled by a hurricane in his second invasion of Duart. Nature conspired with the injured in their protection; and, after some time, the guardians of Sir John Maclean, accompanied by Lord Macdonald, proceeded to London in order to appeal to the Privy Council. The appeal thus made was prolonged until the year 1680, when it was at last settled by the Scottish Council; and the island of Tyrie was given to the Earl of Argyle, in full payment of his claim upon the estates of Sir John Maclean.

The character of the young chief was, meantime, formed under the influence of these events, of which, when he grew up, whilst yet the storm raged, he could not be ignorant. One principle he inherited from his ancestors—a determined fidelity to the Stuart cause. When he was fifteen years of age, the death of his guardians threw the management of his affairs into his own hands; this was in the years 1686 and 1687, one of the most critical periods in English history. Having appointed certain gentlemen his agents, or factors, the young chief went, according to the fashion of his times, to travel. He first repaired to the Court of England, at that time under the sway of James the Second; he then crossed to France, and returned not to the British dominions until he accompanied James into Ireland.

The character of Sir John Maclean, as he attained manhood, and entered into the active business of life, has been drawn with great felicity by the author of "The Memoirs of Lochiel. "[82]

"He was, " says this writer, "of a person and disposition more turned for the court and the camp, than for the business of a private life. There was a natural vivacity and politeness in his manner, which he afterwards much improved by a courtly education; and, as his person was well-made and gracefull, so he took care to sett it off by all the ornaments and luxury of dress. He was of a sweet temper, and good-natured. His witt lively and sparkeling, and his humour pleasant and facetious. He loved books, and acquired the languages with great facility, whereby he cultivated and enriched his understanding with all manner of learning, but especially the belles lettres; add to this, a natural elegancy of expression, and ane inexhaustible fancy, which, on all occasions, furnished him with such a copious variety of matter, as rendered his conversation allways new and entertaining. But with all these shining qualitys, the natural indolence of his temper, and ane immoderate love of pleasure, made him unsuiteable to the circumstances of his family. No persons talked of affairs, private or publick, with a better grace, or more to the purpose, but he could not prevail with himself to be att the least trouble in the execution. He seemed to know everything, and from the smallest hint so penetrated into the circumstances of other people's buisiness, that he often did great services by his excellent advice; and he was of a temper so kind and obligeing, that he was fond of every occasion or doeing good to his friends, while he neglected many inviteing opportunities of serveing himself. "

The first hostilities between France and England, after the Revolution, broke out in Ireland, whence it was the design of James the Second to incite his English and Scottish subjects to his cause. And there was, apparently, ample grounds for hope; England was rent with factions, Lord Dundee was raising a civil war in Scotland, and half Europe was in contention with the other, whether the late King of England should be supported.

"I will recover my own dominions with my own subjects, " was the boast of James, "or perish in the attempt. " Unhappily, like his son, his magnanimity ended in expressions.

Sir John Maclean accompanied James when he landed, on the twelfth of March, 1689, in Ireland; after the siege of Derry, the chief returned to Scotland, accompanied by Sir Alexander Maclean of Otter, and there very soon showed his determination in favour of the insurrection raised by Dundee.

Sir John Maclean's first step was to send Maclean of Lochbuy as his lieutenant with three hundred men to join Dundee. His party encountered a major of General Mackay's army at Knockbreak in Badenoch; a conflict ensued, and Mackay's men were put to flight. This was the first blood that was shed for James the Second in Scotland.

Sir John Maclean soon afterwards joined Dundee in person, leaving his castle of Duart well defended. This fort, which had witnessed so many invasions, was besieged during the absence of the chief by Sir George Rooke, who cannonaded it several days without effect. Its owner, meantime, had joined Dundee, and was appointed to the command of the right wing of the army.

At the battle of Killicrankie, Sir John Maclean distinguished himself, as became the descendant of a brave and loyal race, at the head of his clan; he probably witnessed the death of Dundee. Few events in Scottish history could have affected those who followed a General to the field so severely. Lord Dundee had been foremost on foot during the action; he was foremost on horseback, when the enemy retreated, in the pursuit. He pressed on to the mouth of the Pass of Killicrankie to cut off the escape. In a short time he perceived that he had overrun his men: he stopped short: he waved his arm in the air to make them hasten their speed. Conspicuous in his person he was observed; a musket-ball was aimed at that extended arm; it struck him, and found entrance through an opening in his armour. The brave General was wounded in the arm-pit. He rode off the field, desiring that the mischance might not be disclosed, and fainting, dropped from his horse. As soon as he was revived, he desired to be raised, and looking towards the field of battle asked how things went. "Well, " was the reply. "Then, " he said, "I am well, " and expired.

William the Third understood the merits of his brave opponent. An express was sent to Edinburgh with an account of the action. "Dundee, " said the King (and the *soldier* spoke), "must be dead, or he would have been at Edinburgh before the express. " When urged to send troops to Scotland, "It is needless, " he answered; "the war ended with Dundee's life. " And the observation was just: a peace was soon afterwards concluded. [83]

Sir John Maclean, nevertheless, continued in arms under the command of Colonel Cannon, and lost several brave officers by the incapacity of this commander. After the peace was signed, he returned to live upon his estates, until Argyle, having procured a commission from William to reduce the Macleans by fire or sword, invaded the island of Mull with two thousand five hundred men. Sir John being unprepared to resist him, after advising his vassals to accept protection from Argyle, again retired to the island of Thernburg, whence he captured several of King William's vessels which were going to supply the army in Ireland. [84]

The massacre of Glencoe operated in some respects favourably, after the tragedy had been completed, upon the circumstances of the

Jacobites. Terrified at the odium incurred, a more lenient spirit was henceforth shown to them by Government. Many persons were exempted from taking the oaths, and were allowed to remain in their houses. Early in the year 1792, Sir John Maclean took advantage of this favourable turn of affairs, and, after obtaining permission through the influence of Argyle, and placing the castle of Duart under that nobleman's control, he went to England.

He soon became a favourite at the Court of one who, if we except the massacre of Glencoe, evinced few dispositions of cruelty to the Scottish Jacobites. King William is said, nevertheless, to have had a real antipathy to the Highlanders; and Queen Mary, whose heart turned to the adherents of her forefathers, was obliged to conceal her partiality for her Northern subjects. It had appeared, however, on several occasions, during the absence of her consort, and was now evinced in her good offices to the chief of the clan Maclean. That the chief was of a deportment to confirm the kind sentiments thus shown towards him, the character which has been given of him amply proves.

Sir John Maclean was, as the author of Sir Ewan Cameron's life relates, "the only person of his party that went to Court, which no doubt contributed much to his being so particularly observed by the Queen, who received him most graciously, honoured him frequently with her conversation, and said many kind and obliging things to him. Sir John on his part acquitted himself with so much politeness and address, that her Majesty soon began to esteem him. He took the proper occasions to inform her of the misfortunes of his family, and artfully insinuated that he and his predecessors had drawn them all upon themselves by the services they had rendered to her grandfather, father, and uncle. She answered, that the antiquity and merit of his family were no strangers to her ears; and that, though she had taken a resolution never to interpose betwixt her father's friends and the King her husband, yet, she would distinguish him so far as to recommend his services to his Majesty by a letter under her own hand; and that she doubted not but that it would have some influence, since it was the first favour of that nature which she had ever demanded. "

Sir John is, however, declared by another authority to have declined the commission thus offered to him. Although he had received King James's permission to reconcile himself with the Government, he did not, it appears, choose to bear arms in its defence. Such is the statement of one historian. [86] By another it is said that "Sir John was much caressed while he continued in the army, "[87]—a sentence which certainly seems to imply that he had assented to King William's offer. At all events, he managed to engage the confidence of the King so far, that William "not only honoured him with his countenance, but told Argyle that he must part with Sir John's estate, and that he himself would be the purchaser. "

The nobleman to whom William addressed this injunction was of a very different temper from his father and grandfather, who had both died on the scaffold. Archibald, afterwards created by William Duke of Argyle, had in 1685 become the head of that powerful family; he was of a frank, noble, and generous disposition. "He loved, " says the same writer, "his pleasures, affected magnificence, and valued money no further than as it contributed to support the expence which the gallantry of his temper daily put him to. He several times offered very easy terms to Sir John; and particularly he made one overture of quitting all his pretentions to that estate, on condition of submitting to be the Earl's vassall for the greatest part of it, and paying him two thousand pounds sterling, which he had then by him in ready money; but the expensive gayety of Sir John's temper made him unwilling to part with the money, and the name of a vassall suited as ill with his vanity, which occasioned that and several other proposals to be refused. However, as the generous Earl was noways uneasy to part with the estate, so he, with his usewall frankness, answered King William that his Majesty might always command him and his fortunes; and that he submitted his claim upon Sir John's estate, as he did everything else, to his royal pleasure. "

A tradition exists in the family, that when Argyle sent messengers with his proposals to the Castle of Duart, Sir John pushed away the boat, as it neared the shore, with his own hands. This was worthy the pride of a Highland chieftain.

To such a height, in short, did William's favour amount, and so far did he in this instance carry his usual policy of conciliating his enemies by courtesy and aid, that he ordered Maclean to go as a volunteer in his service, assuring him that he would see that no harm was done to his property in his absence. Sir John, previous to his intended departure from England, went to Scotland to put his affairs in order. On his return he was told by Queen Mary that there were reports to his prejudice; he denied them, and satisfied the Queen that all suspicions of his fidelity were unfounded. Upon the strength of this assurance the Queen wrote in Maclean's favour to the King, in Holland, whither Sir John then proceeded to join his Majesty. But this profession of fidelity to one monarch soon proved to be hollow. Maclean was truly one of the politicians of the day, swayed by every turn of fortune, and cherishing a deep regard for his own interest in his heart. To inspire dislike and distrust wherever he desired to secure allegiance was the lot of William, of whom it has been bitterly said, that in return for having delivered three kingdoms from popery and slavery, he was, before having been a year on the throne, repaid "with faction in one of them, with rebellion in the other, and with both in the third. " How expressive was the exclamation wrung from him, "that he wished he had never been King of Scotland. " Sir John Maclean was one of those who added another proof to the King's conviction, "that the flame of party once raised, it was in vain to expect that truth, justice, or public interest could extinguish it. "[88]

On arriving at Bruges, Maclean heard of the battle of Landau, in which the French army had proved victorious against the Confederates; and at the same time a report prevailed that a counter revolution had taken place in England, and that William was already dethroned. Sir John changed his course upon this intelligence, and hastened to St. Germains, where he was, as might be expected, coldly received. He remained there until the death of William, and then he married the daughter of Sir Enæas Macpherson of Skye.

Upon the accession of Anne, Sir John took advantage of the general indemnity offered to those who had gone abroad with James the Second, and resolved to avail himself of this opportunity of returning home; but, unluckily, he was detained until a day after the act had specified, by the confinement of his wife, who was taken ill at Paris, and there, in November 1703, gave birth to a son, who afterwards succeeded to the baronetcy. Although there was some risk in proceeding, yet Sir John, trusting to the Queen's favourable disposition to the Jacobites, embarked, and with his wife and child reached London. There he was immediately committed to the Tower, but his imprisonment had a deeper source than the mere delay of a few weeks. The Queensbury plot at that time agitated the public, and produced considerable embarrassment in the counsels of state. [89]

It appears that Sir John Maclean had taken no part in this obscure transaction which could affect his honour, or impair his chance of favour from Queen Anne; for, so soon as he was liberated, she bestowed upon him a pension of five hundred pounds a-year, which he enjoyed during the remainder of his life.

For some years Sir John Maclean continued to divide his time between London and the Highlands, where he frequently visited his firm friend Sir Ewan Cameron of Lochiel, at his Castle of Achnacarry. His estates had not been materially benefited by the brief sunshine of King William's favour. Upon finding that Maclean had gone to St. Germains, that monarch had confirmed to the Duke of Argyle the former grant of the island of Tyrie, which the successors of the Duke have since uninterruptedly enjoyed until the present day. Its value was, at the time of its passing into the hands of the Campbells, about three hundred pounds sterling per annum. [90] The chief of the clan Maclean was certain never to escape the suspicions of the Government, after the death of Anne, during whose reign the Highlanders experienced an unwonted degree of tranquillity. Upon her demise the whole state of affairs was changed; and none experienced greater inconveniences from the vigilance of Government than Sir Ewan Cameron and his friend Maclean. Lochiel, as his biographer observes, "drank deeply of this bitter cup."[91]

It was during one of Maclean's visits to Achnacarry, when in company with his now venerable friend, that the Governor of Fort William attempted to take him and Sir Ewan prisoners, but they made their escape. During the night of their flight, however, Sir Maclean caught a severe cold, which ended afterwards fatally.

When the Earl of Mar raised the standard of the Chevalier in Scotland, Sir John joined him at Achterarder, some days before the battle of Sherriff Muir. In that engagement the clan Maclean distinguished themselves, and some of their brave chieftains were killed in the battle. After the day was over, Sir John retired to Keith, where he parted from his followers, never to rejoin them. A consumption, incurred from the cold caught in his escape, was then far advanced. He declined an offer made to receive him on board the Chevalier's ship, bound for France, and went to Gordon Castle, where, on the twelfth of March, 1716, he expired.

Thus ended a life characterized by no ordinary share of vicissitude and misfortune. If the fate of Sir John Maclean be less tragical than that of other distinguished Jacobites, it was, it must be acknowledged, one replete with anxiety and disappointment. He may be said to have been peculiarly "born to trouble. " To our modern notions of honour and consistency, his conduct in becoming a courtier of William the Third, appears to betray that unsoundness and hollowness of political principle which, more or less, was the prevalent moral disease of the period, and which was attributable to some of the most celebrated men of the day. It undoubtedly forms an unfavourable contrast to the stern independence of Sir Ewan Cameron of Lochiel, and of other Highland chieftains, and too greatly resembles the code of politics adopted by the Earl of Mar. But those who knew Sir John Maclean intimately, considered him a man of straightforward integrity; they deemed him above dissimulation, and have placed his name among those who despised every worldly advantage for the sake of principle, and who loved the cause which he had espoused for its own sake. The broken towers of Duart and of Aros, the ruins of those once proud lords of the soil, attest the sacrifices which they made, and form a melancholy commentary upon their history.

The castle of Aros, in the Island of Mull, "is interesting, " says Macculloch, [92] "from the picturesque object which it affords to the artist; the more so, as the country is so devoid of scenes on which his pencil can be exerted. Still more striking, from its greater magnitude and more elevated position, is Duart Castle, once the stronghold of the Macleans, and till lately garrisoned by a detachment from Fort William. It is fast falling into ruin since it was abandoned as a barrack. When a few years shall have passed, the almost roofless tenant will surrender his spacious apartments to the bat and the owl, and seek shelter, like his neighbours, in the thatched hovel which rises near him. But the walls, of formidable thickness, may long bid defiance even to the storms of this region; remaining to mark to future times the barbarous splendour of the ancient Highland chieftains, and, with the opposite fortress of Ardtornish, serving to throw a gleam of historical interest over the passage of the Sound of Mull. "

Hitherto Iona had received the last remains of the Lords of Duart; but Sir John Maclean was not carried to the resting-place of his forefathers. He was buried in the church of Raffin in Bamffshire, in the family vault of the Gordons of Buckie. In Iona, that former "light of the western world, " are the tombs of the brave and unfortunate Macleans. Their bones are interred in the vaults of the cathedral, which, after coasting the barren rocks of Mull, buffeted by the waves, the traveller beholds rising out of the sea, "giving, " as it is finely expressed, "to this desolate region an air of civilization, and recalling the consciousness of that human society which, presenting elsewhere no visible traces, seems to have abandoned these rocky shores to the cormorant and the gull. " On the tombs of the Highland warriors who repose within St. Mary's Church in Iona, are sculptured ships, swords, armorial bearings, appropriate memorials to the island lords, or, as the Chevalier not inaptly called them, "little kings; " and, undistinguishable from the graves of the chiefs, are the funereal allotments of the Kings of Scotland, Iceland, and Norway. [93]

Sir John Maclean left one son and six daughters. His son Hector was born in France, but brought to Scotland at the age of four, and placed under the care of his kinsman, Maclean of Coll, where he remained until he was eighteen years of age; when he repaired to Edinburgh, and in the college made considerable progress in the usual course of studies in that institution. After various journeys abroad, chiefly to Paris, Sir Hector Maclean returned in 1745 to Edinburgh, intending again to lead his clansmen to the standard of Prince Charles; but a temporary imprisonment, occasioned by the treachery of a man in whose house he lodged, prevented his appearance in the field. He was detained in confinement until released as a subject of the King of France. He died at Rome in the year 1758, in the forty-seventh year of his age. At his death the title of Baronet devolved upon Allan of Brolas, great-grandson of Donald, first Maclean of Brolas, and younger brother of the first baronet.

Although the chief was thus prevented from following Prince Charles to the field of Culloden, many of his clan distinguished themselves there; Charles Maclean of Drimnin appeared at the head of five hundred of the clan, and his regiment, which was under the command of the Duke of Perth, was among those that broke forward with drawn swords from the lines, and routed the left wing of the Duke of Cumberland's army. The whole of the front line of this gallant regiment was swept away as they presented themselves before their foes. They were afterwards overpowered by numbers, and obliged to retire. Their leader, as he retreated, inquired for one of his sons, who was missing. "I fear, " said an attendant to whom the inquiry was addressed, "that he has fallen. " The fate of the father is well told in these few words, [94] "If he has, it shall not be for naught, " was his reply; and he rushed forward to avenge him.

Many of the clan fell in the massacre after the battle of Culloden Muir. Hundreds of the Highlanders who escaped the inhumanity of their conquerors, died of their wounds or of hunger, in the hills, at twelve or fourteen miles' distance from the field of battle. "Their misery, " says a contemporary writer, "was inexpressible. " While the cannon was sounding, and bells were pealing in the capital cities of England and Ireland, for the united events of the Duke of Cumberland's birth and the battle of Culloden Moor, fires were seen blazing in Morvern, in which numerous villages were burned by order of the victorious Cumberland. The Macleans who came from Mull, seem generally to have escaped; they made off in one of the long boats for their island, the night after the engagement, and were fortunate enough to carry with them a cargo of brandy and some money. [95]

A calmer, though less interesting career has, since 1745, been the fate of the chiefs of the clan Maclean. [96] Sir Allan, respected and beloved, became a colonel in the British army. He retired eventually to the sacred Isle of Inch Kenneth, in Mull, where he exercised the hospitality characteristic, in ancient times, of the Lords of Duart. Dr. Johnson has handed down the memory of the venerable chief, not only in a few descriptive pages of a Tour to the Hebrides, but in a Latin poem, translated by Sir Daniel Sandford. [97] In the lines he refers to Sir Allan in these terms.

"O'er glassy tides I thither flew,
The wonders of the spot to view;
In lowly cottage great Maclean
Held there his high ancestral reign."[98]

Sir Allan Maclean died in 1783: he was succeeded by his nearest male relation, Sir Hector Maclean, of the family of Brolas. The brother of Sir Hector, Sir Fitzroy Grafton Maclean, a distinguished officer, and formerly Governor of the island of St. Thomas, is now chief of the clan Maclean. Two sons continue the line. Of these, the eldest, Colonel Charles Fitzroy Maclean, has chosen, like his father, the profession of arms. He commands the eighty-first foot: and has, by his marriage with a daughter of the Hon. and Rev. Dr. Marsham, an heir to the ancestral honours of the house. The youngest son of Sir Fitzroy Maclean is Donald Maclean, of Witton Castle, Durham, the member for Oxford, married to Harriet, daughter of General Frederick Maitland, a descendant of the Duke of Lauderdale, whose former injustice to the clan Maclean has been noticed in this work. It is remarkable, that the same fidelity, the same loyalty, that sacrificed every possession to the cause of James Stuart, has been, since the extinction of that cause, worthily employed, with distinguished talent and success, in the service of Government. Such instances are not uncommon in the history of the Jacobites.

FOOTNOTES:

[69] Historical and Genealogical Account of the Clan Maclean, by a Seneachie.

[70] Brown's Highlands.

[71] Historical Account of the Clan Maclean, p. 4.

[72] "Eriska is interesting as having been the first place where Charles Edward landed in Scotland. It is the boundary of Ottervore toward the north, and is separated from South Uist by a narrow rocky sound. Upon a detached and high rock at its southern end are to be seen the remains of a square tower, the abode of some ancient chieftain. "—*Macculloch,* vol. i. p. 87.

[73] Hist. Account.

[74] Memoirs of Lochiel, p. 193. This account is preferable to that given by the historian of the house of Maclean, as it is of course a more dispassionate statement, although the facts stated are nearly the same. See Hist. and Gen. Acct. pp. 140, 141.

[75] Memoir of Lochiel, p. 194.

[76] According to the Memoirs of Lochiel, it appears that Sir Allan must have died in 1673 or 1674; since the author speaks, in 1674, of the "late Sir Allan. "

[77] Archibald, ninth Earl, was only restored to the Earldom.

[78] Memoirs of Lochiel, p. 196.

[79] Id. p. 198.

[80] Mem. of Lochiel, p. 195. Hist. Acct. of the Clan, p. 174.

[81] Memoirs of Lochiel.

[82] Supposed to be John Drummond of Balhaldy.

[83] Dalrymple's Memorials, p. 358.

[84] Hist. Acct. p. 198.

[85] Memoirs of Lochiel, p. 326.

[86] Hist. Account of the Maclean Family, p. 198.

[87] Memoirs of Lochiel, p. 326.

[88] Dalrymple, p. 383.

[89] Dalrymple's Memorials. See Collection of Original Papers, p. 31. Sir John Maclean's Discovery, Part II. p. 4.

[90] Mem. of Locheil, p. 352.

[91] Id. p. 204.

[92] Macculloch's Western Islands of Scotland, vol. i. p. 535.

[93] Macculloch, vol. i. p. 13.

[94] Hist. Notices of the Macleans, p. 206.

[95] Hist. of the Rebellion, p. 199. From the Scots' Magazine. Aberdeen, 1745.

[96] An accomplished descendant of the Macleans of Lochbuy, Miss Moss, of Edinburgh, has left a beautiful tribute to the valour of her clan in a ballad of the forty-five. The following passage occurs in Dr. Brown's History of the Highlands, vol. iv. part II. p. 493, relative to the Macleans of Lochbuy, Coll, and Ardgour: —"Their estates being afterwards restored, they listened to the persuasions of Professor Forbes, and remained quiet until the subsequent insurrection of 1745, when a general rising of the clans would most probably have placed the crown upon the head of the descendant of their ancient line of kings. " This reproach rests only on the three houses just mentioned, and not on the Macleans of Brolas, nor of Mull, who were at the battle of Culloden.

For a portion of the materials of the foregoing narrative I am greatly indebted to the Historical and Genealogical Account of the Clan Maclean, by a Seneachie. The work is compiled chiefly from the Duart Manuscripts.

[97] Hist. Notices, p. 209.

[98] See History of Iona by Lachlan Maclean, Esq., Glasgow.

ROB ROY MACGREGOR CAMPBELL.

"The Clan Gregiour, " according to an anonymous writer of the seventeenth century, "is a race of men so utterly infamous for thieving, depredation, and murder, that after many Acts of the Council of Scotland against them, at length in the reign of King Charles the First, the Parliament made a strict Act suppressing the very name. " Upon the Restoration, when, as the same writer declares, "the reins were given to all licentiousness, and loyalty, as it was called, was thought sufficient to compound for all wickedness, the Act was rescinded. But, upon the late happy Revolution, when the nation began to recover her senses, some horrid barbarities having been committed by that execrable crew, under the leading of one Robert Roy Macgregiour, yet living, the Parliament under King William and Queen Mary annulled the said Act rescissory, and revived the former penal statute against them. "[99]

Such is the summary account of one who is evidently adverse to the political creed, no less than to the daring violence, of the clan Macgregor. Little can, it is true, be offered in palliation for the extraordinary career of spoliation and outrage which the history of this race of Highlanders presents; and which terminated only with the existence of the clan itself.

The clan Gregor, anciently known by the name of clan Albin, dated their origin from the ninth century, and assumed to be the descendants of King Alpin, who flourished in the year 787: so great is its antiquity, that an old chronicle asserts, speaking of the clan Macarthur, "that none are older than that clan, except the hills, the rivers, and the clan Albin. "

Among the conflicts which for centuries rendered the Highlands the theatre of perpetual strife, the clan Albin, or, as in process of time it was called, the clan Gregor, was marked as the most turbulent members of the state. It was never safe to dispute with them, and was deemed idle to inquire whether the lands which they occupied were theirs by legal titles, or by the right of the sword. Situate on the confines of Scotland, and protected by the inaccessible mountains which surrounded them, they could defy even their most powerful neighbours, who were always desirous of conciliating allies so dangerous in times of peace, so prompt in war. The boundaries which they occupied stretched along the wilds of the Trosaëhs and

Balquhidder, to the northern and western heights of Mannach and Glenurely, comprehending portions of the counties of Argyle, Perth, Dumbarton, and Stirling, which regions obtained the name of the country of the Mac Gregors. A part of these domains being held by the *coir à glaive*, or right of the sword, exposed the clan Gregor to the enmity of their formidable neighbours, the Earls of Argyle and Breadalbane, who, obtaining royal grants of such lands, lost no opportunity of annoying and despoiling their neighbours, under legal pretexts. Hence many of the contests which procured for the Macgregors a character of ferocity, and brought upon them 'letters of fire and sword. ' A commission was granted first in the reign of Queen Mary, in 1563, to the most powerful clansmen and nobles, to pursue, and exterminate the clan Gregor, and prohibiting, at the same time, that her Majesty's liege subjects should receive or assist any of the clan, or give them meat, drink, or clothes. The effect which such an edict was likely to produce upon a bold, determined, desperate people may readily be conceived. Hitherto the clan Gregor had been a loyal clan. From the house of Alpin had descended the royal family of Stewart, with whom the Macgregors claimed kindred, bearing upon their shields, in Gaelic, the words, 'My tribe is royal. ' They had been also in favour with the early Scottish monarchs, one of whom had ennobled the Macgregors of Glenurely, who could cope with the most elevated families in Scotland, in possessions and importance. But, after the edict of Mary, a palpable decline in the fortunes of the clan Gregor was manifest, until it was for ever extinguished in modern days. Henceforth the Macgregors exhibited a contempt for those laws which had never afforded them protection. They became, in consequence of the cruel proclamation against them, dependent for subsistence upon their system of predatory warfare. They grew accustomed to bloodshed, and could easily be '*hounded out*, ' as Sir Walter Scott expresses it, to commit deeds of violence. Hence they were incessantly engaged in desperate feuds, in which the vengeance of an injured and persecuted people was poured out mercilessly upon the defenceless. Hence they became objects of hatred to the community, until the famous contest of Glenfruin, between the Macgregors and the Colquhouns of Luss, brought once more the royal displeasure upon them in the reign of James the Sixth.

The sequestered valley, which obtained, from the memorable and tragical events of the combat, the name of the Glen of Sorrow, is situated about six miles from Loch Lomond, and is watered by the river Fruin which empties itself into that lake. In the spring of the year 1603, Alexander of Glenstrae, chief of the Macgregors, went from the country of Lennox to Balquhidder, for the express purpose of conciliating the feuds which subsisted between his brother and Sir Humphrey Colquhoun of Luss. After a conference, apparently pacific, but well understood by the Macgregors to augur no friendly intentions, the assembled members of that clan prepared to return to their homes. They were followed by the Laird of Luss, who was resolved to surprise them on their route. But his treachery was secretly known by those whom he pursued.

The right bank of Loch Lomond is so steep and woody that before the formation of roads, the Highlanders found it impossible to pass that way. The way to Argyleshire, therefore, ran along the vale of Fruin in a circuitous direction to the head of Loch Long, and again turned eastward towards Loch Lomond. In the middle of the glen the Macgregors, who were peacefully returning home, were attacked by the Colquhouns. The assailants were four to one; but the valour of the Macgregors prevailed, and two hundred Colquhouns were left dead on the field. The very name of Colquhoun was nearly annihilated. The account of the battle was transmitted by the Laird of Luss to James the Sixth, at Edinburgh; and the message was accompanied by two hundred and twenty shirts, stained with blood, which were presented to the King by sixty women, widows of those slain in the Glen of Sorrow. These ladies rode on white poneys, and carried in their hands long poles, on which were extended the stained garments. But the shirts, it is said, were soiled by the way, and the widows were hireling mourners, who comforted themselves with the loved beverages of their country on their return, and were in many instances obliged to be carried to their homes. [100]

The indignation of James the Sixth, unmitigated by any friendly representations on behalf of the Macgregors, burst forth fatally for the clan. The Macgregors were formally outlawed by Act of Parliament; they were pursued with blood-hounds, and when seized, were put to death without trial. Their chief, the unfortunate Alexander of Glenstrae surrendered to his enemy the Earl of Argyle, with eighteen of his followers, on condition that he might be taken safely out of Scotland. But the severity of Government stopped not here. The very name of Gregor was blotted out, by an order in Council, from the names of Scotland. Those who had hitherto borne it were commanded to change it under pain of death, and were forbidden to retain the appellations which they had been accustomed from their infancy to cherish. Those who had been at

Glenfruin were also deprived of their weapons, excepting a pointless knife to cut their victuals. They were never to assemble in any number exceeding four; and by an Act of Parliament passed in 1617, these laws were extended to the rising generation, lest as the children of the proscribed parents grew up, the strength of the clan should be restored.

For these severe acts, the only apology that can be offered is the unbridled fury and cruelty of the Macgregors, when irritated; of which it is necessary to mention one instance, as an example of the many left on record, of which the clan were convicted.

In the battle of Glenfruin, which James had visited so rigorously upon the Macgregors, the greater part of those who bore the name of Colquhoun were exterminated. Yet a still more savage act was perpetrated after the day was won.

The town of Dumbarton contained, at that time, a seminary famous for learning, where many of the Colquhouns, as well as the sons of the neighbouring gentry, were sent for education. Upon hearing of the encounter at Glenfruin, eighty of these high-spirited boys set off to join their relatives; but the Colquhouns, anxious for the safety of their young kinsfolk, would not permit them to join in the fight, but locked them up in a barn for safety. Here they remained, until the event of the day left the Macgregors masters of what might well be called "the Glen of Sorrow. " The boys, growing impatient for their release, became noisy; when the Macgregors, discovering their hiding-place, and thirsting for vengeance, set fire to the barn, and the young inmates were consumed. According to another account, they were all put to the sword by one of the guard, a Macgregor, whose distinctive appellation was Ciar Mohr, "the mouse-coloured man. " When the chief of the Macgregor's clan repaired to the barn, and, knowing that the boys were the sons of gentlemen, was desirous of ensuring their safety, he asked their guards where they were. When told of what had occurred, Macgregor broke out into the exclamation, that "his clan was ruined. " The sad event was commemorated, until the year 1757, by an annual procession of the Dumbarton youths, to a field at some distance from their school, where they enacted the melancholy ceremonial of a mock funeral, over which they set up a loud lamentation. The site of the farm where this scene was enacted is still pointed out; and near it runs a rivulet, the Gaelic name of which signifies "the burn of the young ghosts: " so deep was the memory of this horrible deed. [101]

A fearful retribution followed the clan for years. They had no friend at Court to plead their cause; and the most cruel hardships became the lot of the innocent, as well as the guilty, of their clan. The country was filled with troops ready to destroy them, so that all who were able, were forced to fly to rocks, caverns, and to hide themselves among the woods. Few of the Macgregors, at this period of the Scottish history, were permitted to die a natural death.

As an inducement to the murder of these wretched people, a reward was offered for every head of a Macgregor that was conveyed to the Privy Council at Edinburgh. Those who died a natural death were buried in silence and secrecy by their kinsfolk, for the graves of the persecuted clan were not respected; the bodies of the dead being exhumed, and the heads cut off, to be sent to the Council. Never has there been, in the history of mankind, a more signal instance of national odium than that which pursued this brave, though violent race. The spirit in which they were denounced has in it little of the character of justice, and reminds us of the vengeance of the Jewish people upon the different hostile tribes to whom they were opposed.

In process of time, the last remnant of the lands pertaining to the Macgregors was bestowed upon Archibald, seventh Earl of Argyle, whose family had profited largely by the destruction of the clan: for every Macgregor whom they had destroyed, they had received a reward. In 1611, the Earl was commanded to root out this thievish and barbarous race; a commission which he executed remorselessly, dragging the parents to death, and leaving their offspring to misery and to revenge; for the deep consciousness of their wrongs grew up with the young, and prepared them for deeds of violence and vengeance.

Notwithstanding the severities of the Stuarts towards the Macgregors, the loyalty of the clan continued unimpeachable. It was appreciated by one who is not celebrated for remembering benefits. Charles the Second had, in 1663, the grace to remove the proscription from the Macgregors, by an Act which was passed in the first Scottish Parliament after his Restoration. He permitted them the use of their family name, and other privileges of his liege subjects, assigning as a reason for this act of favour, that the loyalty and affection of those who were once called Macgregors, during the late troubles, might justly wipe off all former reproach from their clan. This act of grace, according to the anonymous writer quoted in the commencement of this memoir, was to be accounted for by the prevalent licentiousness of that monarch's reign. It gave, indeed, but little satisfaction to the nonconforming Presbyterians, who saw with resentment that the penalties unjustly imposed upon themselves were relaxed in favour of the Macgregors. But this dissatisfaction was of short duration. After the Revolution, "an influence, " says Sir Walter Scott, "inimical to this unfortunate clan, said to be the same with that which afterwards dictated the massacre of Glencoe, occasioned the reaction of the penal statutes against the Macgregors. "[102] It is, however, consolatory to find that the proscription was not acted upon during the reign of William. The name of Macgregor was again heard in public halls, in parliament, and courts of justice. Still, however, whilst the statutes remained, it could not legally be borne. Attempts were made to restore the appellation of clan Alb, but nothing was decided; when, at length, all necessity for such an alteration was done away by an Act of Parliament abolishing forever the penal statutes against the clan.

Whilst the Macgregors were still a proscribed race, Robert Macgregor Campbell, or Robert Roy, so called among his kindred, in the adoption of a Celtic phrase, expressive of his ruddy complexion and red hair, appeared as their champion. At the time of his birth, to bear the name of Macgregor was felony; and the descendant of King Alpin adopted the maiden name of his mother, a daughter of Campbell of Fanieagle, in order to escape the penalty of disobedience. His father, Donald Macgregor of Glengyle, was a lieutenant-colonel in the King's service: his ancestry was deduced from Ciar Mohr, "the mouse-coloured man, " who had slain the young students at the battle of Glenfruin.

After the death of Allaster Macgregor of Glenstrae, the last chieftain, the office of chief had ceased to be held by any representative of the scattered remnant of this hunted tribe. Various families had ranged themselves under the guidance of chieftains, which, among Highlanders, signifies the head of a branch of a tribe, in contradistinction to that of chief, who is the leader of the whole name. [103] The chieftain of Glengyle lived in the mountainous region between Loch Lomond and Loch Katrine; his right to his territories there might or might not be legal; it was far more convenient to his neighbours to waive the question with any member of this fierce race, than to inquire too rigidly into the tenure by which the lands were held.

Rob Roy, though he deduced his origin from a younger son of the Laird of Macgregor, was one of a family who had, within the preceding century, been of humble fortunes. His great-grandfather had been a cotter; from his grandfather he inherited the generous temper and the daring spirit which, more or less, characterized the clan. Callum, or Malcolm, had been outlawed for an attempt to carry off an heiress, but obtained his pardon for saving the life of his enemy, the Duke of Argyle. The date of Rob Roy's birth is uncertain, but is supposed to have taken place about the middle of the seventeenth century; consequently, after the period when his clan had endured every variety of fortune, from the cruel edicts of James the Sixth to the consolatory acts of Charles the Second.

The education of this extraordinary man was limited; and he is said not to have exhibited in his youth any striking traits of the intrepidity which distinguished him in after life. But he was endowed with a vigorous intellect, and with an enthusiasm which had been deepened by the peculiar circumstances of his clan and kinsfolk. It is impossible to comprehend the character of Rob Roy, unless we look into the history of his race, as we have briefly done, and consider how strong must have been the impressions which hereditary feuds, and wrongs visited upon father and child, had made upon a mind of no common order.

His youth was occupied in acquiring the rude accomplishments of the age. In the management of the broadsword the ardent and daring boy soon acquired proficiency; his frame was robust and muscular, and his arm of unusual length. At an early age he is said by tradition to have tried his powers in a predatory excursion, of which he was the leader. This was in the year 1691, and it was called the herdship, or devastation of Kippen, in the Lennox. No lives were sacrificed, but the marauding system was carried to its extent.

The young Macgregor was educated in the Presbyterian faith. "He was not, " says his biographer, [104] "free from those superstitious notions so prevalent in his country; and, although few men possessed more strength of mind in resisting the operation of false and gloomy tenets, he was sometimes led away from the principles he had adopted, to a belief in supernatural appearances. " Nor was it likely that it should be otherwise; for the wildest dreams of fancy were cherished in the seclusion of the region, then inconceivably retired and remote, in which Rob Roy is said to have passed days in silent admiration of Nature in her grandest aspects; for the man who afterwards appeared so stern and rugged to his enemies, was accessible to the tenderest feelings, and to the most generous sympathies. [105]

Although his father had succeeded in military life, Rob Roy was destined to a far more humble occupation. The discrepancy between the Scottish pride of ancestry and the lowly tracks which are occasionally chalked out for persons of the loftiest pretensions to origin, is manifest in the destination of Rob Roy. He became a dealer in cattle. It was, it is true, the custom for landed proprietors, as well as their tenantry, to deal in the trade of grazing and selling cattle. In those days, no Lowlanders, nor any English drovers, had the audacity to enter the Highlands.

"The cattle, " says Sir Walter Scott, "which were the staple commodity of the mountains, were escorted down to fairs, on the borders of the Lowlands, by a party of Highlanders, with their arms rattling round them; and who dealt, however, in all faith and honour with their southern customers. " After describing the nature of the affrays which were the result of such collision, Sir Walter remarks, "A slash or two, or a broken head, was easily accommodated, and as the trade was of benefit to both parties, trifling skirmishes were not allowed to interrupt its harmony. "

For some time, the speculations in which Rob Roy engaged were profitable; he took a tract of land in Balquhidder for the purpose of grazing, and his success soon raised him in the estimation of the county. But his cattle were often carried away by hordes of big robbers from Inverness, Ross, and Sutherland, and he was obliged, in defence, to maintain a party of men to repel these incursions. Hence the warlike tastes which were afterwards more fully displayed.

The death of his father placed Rob Roy in an important situation in his county; he became, moreover, guardian to his nephew, Gregor of Macgregor of Glengyle, —a position which gave him great influence with the clan. He had now become the proprietor of Craig Royston; but his ordinary dwelling was at Inversnaid, from which place he took his appellation, Macgregor of Inversnaid. These estates were of considerable extent, but of small value: they extended from the head of Loch Lomond twelve miles along its eastern border, and stretched into the interior of the country, partly around the base of Ben Lomond. From these estates Rob Roy assumed sometimes the title of

Craig Royston, sometimes that of Baron of Inversnaid, —a term long applied in Scotland to puisne lairds. [106]

The influence of an energetic and powerful mind was now plainly exhibited in the celebrity which Rob Roy soon acquired in the neighbouring counties. The Macgregors had a peculiar constitution in their clanship, which rendered them compact and formidable as a body. In all the forays so common at that period, Rob Roy took little or no part; yet the terror of his name caused him to receive all the credit of much that occurred in the vicinity.

Three great noblemen, bitter enemies, sought his alliance; of these one was James the first Duke of Montrose, and Archibald tenth Earl of Argyle, who were opposed to each other not only in political opinions, but from personal dislike. Montrose deemed it essential to conciliate Rob Roy as a matter of speculation, and entered into a sort of partnership with the far-famed drover in the buying and selling of cattle, of which Rob Roy was considered an excellent judge. Argyle, on the other hand, was conscious of the injuries which his ancestors had inflicted on the Macgregors, and was inclined to befriend Rob Roy from compassion, and a sense of justice. The Earl was also flattered by the Laird's having assumed the name of Campbell, which he regarded as a compliment to himself. But the overtures of Argyle were at first spurned by Rob Roy, whose alliance with the Marquis of Montrose increased his hatred of Argyle. He was afterwards won over to more moderate sentiments, and a lasting friendship was eventually formed between him and Argyle.

The friendship and patronage of Montrose were secure until money transactions, the usual source of alienations and bickerings, produced distrust on the one hand, and bitterness on the other. Montrose had advanced Rob Roy certain sums to carry on his speculations: they were successful until the defalcation of a third and inferior partner prevented Rob Roy from repaying the Marquis the money due to him. He was required to give up his lands to satisfy the demands upon him. For a time he refused, but ultimately he was compelled by a law-suit to mortgage his estates to Montrose with an understanding that they were to be restored to him whenever he could pay the money. Some time afterwards he made an attempt to recover his estate by the payment of his debts; but he was at first amused by excuses, and afterwards deprived of his property. Such is the simple statement of his partial biographer; but Sir Walter Scott gives the story a darker colouring. In his preface to Rob Roy he mentions that Rob Roy absconded, taking with him the sum of one thousand pounds which he had obtained from different gentlemen in Scotland for the purpose of buying cattle. In 1712 an advertisement to that effect was put into the daily papers repeatedly; but the active Highlander was beyond the reach of law. To this period we must assign a total change in the habits and characteristics of Rob Roy, who now began a lawless and marauding course of life. He went up into the Highlands where he was followed by one whose character has been variously represented—Mary Macgregor of Comar, his wife. According to one account, she was by no means the masculine and cruel being whom Scott has so powerfully described; yet, from several traits, it is obvious that she was one of the most determined of her sex, and that her natural boldness of spirit was exaggerated by an insult which was never forgiven, either by herself or by her husband. This was the forcible expulsion of herself and her family from their home at Inversnaid by Graham of Killearn, one of Montrose's agents; and the cruel act was accompanied by circumstances which nothing but death could blot from the memory of the outraged and injured Macgregor. The loss of property was nothing when compared with that one galling recollection.

The kind and once honourable Rob Roy was now driven to desperation. His natural capacity for warlike affairs had been improved in the collection of the black mail, or protection fees; a service of danger, in which many a bloody conflict with freebooters had shown the Macgregors of what materials their leader was composed. The black mail was a private contribution, often compulsatory, for the maintenance of the famous black watch, an independent corps of provincial militia, and so called from the colour of their dress, in contradistinction to the red soldiers, or *leidar dearag*. "From the time they were first embodied, " writes General Stewart, "till they were regimented, the Highlanders continued to wear the dress of their country. This, as it consisted so much of the black, green, and blue tartan, gave them a dark and sombre appearance in comparison with the bright uniform of the regulars, who, at that time, had coats waistcoats, and breeches of scarlet cloth. Hence the term *dhu*, or black, as applied to this corps. "[107]

In collecting both the imposts laid on for the maintenance of this corps, and in enforcing the black mail, Rob Roy had already gained the confidence of the better classes, whilst, by his exploits, he had taught the freebooter to tremble at his name. His journeys to

England had not, either, been unprofitable to him in gaining friends. By a strict regard to his word, a true Highland quality, he had gained confidence; whilst his open and engaging demeanour had procured him friends.

Soon after his expulsion from his property, Rob Roy travelled into England to collect a sum of money which was due to him. On returning through Moffat, his generous indignation was aroused by seeing the penalty of the law inflicted upon a young girl for fanaticism: two of her kinsmen had already suffered. As a party of soldiers were preparing to carry the girl, bound hand and foot, to a river, Rob Roy interposed; and, receiving an insolent reply, he sprang upon the soldiers and in an instant released the young woman, by plunging eight of her guards into the water. He then drew his claymore, and cut the cords which bound the intended victim. A short skirmish left him master of the field.

Rob Roy now prepared to remove from his dwelling at Inversnaid, into one more remote, and protected by its natural position. This was Craig Royston, or, as it is sometimes spelt, Craigrostan, whither Rob Roy removed his furniture and other effects. A tract, entitled "The Highland Rogue, " published during the lifetime of Rob Roy, contains a striking description of this almost inaccessible retreat. It is situated on the borders of Loch Lomond, and is surrounded with stupendous rocks and mountains. The passages along these heights are so narrow, that two men cannot walk abreast; "It is a place, " adds the same writer, "of such strength and safety, that one person well acquainted with it, and supplied with ammunition, might easily destroy a considerable army if they came to attack him, and he, at the same time, need not so much as be seen by them. " For this romantic scene, Rob Roy quitted Inversnaid; henceforth his occupation as a grazier and drover, and his character as a country gentleman, were lost in that of a freebooter. Many anecdotes have been related of his feats in the dangerous course which he henceforth adopted: but of these, some are so extraordinary, as to be incredible; others are perfectly consistent with the daring spirit of a man who had vowed to avenge his wrongs.

The Duke of Montrose was the first object of his wrath; accordingly, hearing that the tenantry of the Duke had notice to pay their rents, he mustered his men, and visiting these gentlemen, compelled them to pay him the money, giving them, nevertheless receipts, which discharged them of any future call from Montrose. This practice he carried on with impunity for several years, until a more flagrant outrage drew down the anger of his enemy.

This was no less than the abduction of the Duke's factor, Killearn, who had formerly expelled the family of Rob Roy from Inversnaid. Killearn had gone to Chapellaroch in Stirlingshire, for the purpose of collecting rents; he anticipated, on this occasion, no interruption to his office, because Rob Roy had caused it to be given out, by proclamation, some days before, that he had gone to Ireland. Towards evening, nevertheless, he made his appearance before the inn at Chapellaroch, his piper playing before him; his followers were stationed in a neighbouring wood. The rents had just been collected, when the sound of the bagpipes announced to Killearn the approach of his enemy. The factor sprang up, and threw the bags, full of money, into a loft. Rob Roy entered, with the usual salutations, laid down his sword, and sat down to partake of the entertainment. No sooner was the repast ended, than he desired his piper to strike up a tune. In a few minutes, by this signal, six armed men entered the room; when Rob Roy, taking hold of his sword, asked the factor, "How he had prospered in his collection of the rents? " "I have got nothing yet, " replied the trembling Killearn; "I have not begun to collect. " "No, no, Chamberlain, " cried Rob Roy, "falsehood will not do for me. I demand your book. " The book was produced, the money was found and delivered to Rob Roy, who gave his usual receipt. After this, the unfortunate factor was carried off to an island near the east of Loch Katrine, where he was confined a considerable time; and when he was released, was warned not to collect the rents of the country in future, as Rob Roy intended to do so himself, —the more especially as the lands had originally belonged to the Macgregors, and he was, therefore, only reclaiming his own. [108]

This predatory war against the Duke of Montrose was carried on for a considerable time. It was favoured by the nature of the country over which the freebooter ruled triumphant, and by the secret good wishes of the Highlanders who resided in the neighbourhood. No roads were at that time formed in this region of singular beauty. Narrow valleys, thinly inhabited, and surrounded by forests and wilds, and guarded by rocks, passes, and other features of natural strength, afforded to Rob Roy all those advantages which he, who knew every defence which Nature gave to marauders in those retired haunts, could well appreciate.

The habits of the Highlanders were also, at this time, essentially warlike. "The use of arms, " to borrow a description from an anonymous writer, "formed their common occupation, and the affairs of war their ordinary pursuit. They appeared on all public occasions, at market, and even at church, with their broadswords and their dirks; and, more recently, when the use of fire-arms became general, they seldom travelled without a musket and pistol. " The clan Macgregor possessed these military tastes in an inordinate degree; and the wars of the foregoing century had accustomed them to a degree of union and discipline not, at that period, common among the Highlanders, who were considered, in those respects, as superior to their Lowland brethren. [109] The vicinity of the rich districts of the Lowlands gave a rich stimulus to the appetite for plunder natural to a martial and impoverished people. Above all, their energies were inspired by an undying sense of ancient and present injuries, and the remembrance of their sufferings was never erased from their minds. At this time, the most disturbed districts in Scotland were those nearest to the Lowlands; the bitterness of political feelings was added to the sense of injustice, and the loss of lands. Rob Roy knew well how to avail himself of this additional incentive to violence; he avowed his determination to molest all who were not of Jacobite principles; and he put that resolution into active practice.

The character of the individual who exercised so singular a control over his followers, and over the district in which he lived, had changed since his early, dreamy days, or since the period of his honest exertions as a drover. Rob Roy had become in repute with Robin Hood of the Lowlands. His personal appearance added greatly to the impression of his singular qualities. The author of "the Highland Rogue" describes him as a man of prodigious strength, and of such uncommon stature as to approach almost to a gigantic size. He wore a beard above a foot long, and his face as well as his body was covered with dark red hair, from which his nick-name originated. The description given by Sir Walter Scott does not entirely correspond with this portraiture. "His stature, " says that writer, "was not of the tallest, but his person was uncommonly strong and compact. " The great peculiarity of his frame was the great length of his arms, owing to which he could, without stooping, tie the garters of his Highland hose, which are placed two inches below the knee. His countenance was sternly expressive in the hour of peril; but, at calmer moments, it wore that frank and kindly aspect which wins upon the affections of our species. His frame was so muscular, that his knee was described as resembling that of a Highland bull, evincing strength similar to that animal. His exercise of the broadsword was, even in those days, superlative; and his intimate knowledge of the wild country over which he may be said to have ruled, gave him as great an advantage as his personal prowess. To these qualifications may be added another, perhaps more important still, —that quick perception of character, and that penetration into human motives, without which no mind can obtain a mastery over another.

To these characteristics were added a fearless and generous spirit, a hatred of oppression, and compassion for the oppressed. Although descended from the dark murderer of the young students, Rob Roy had none of the ferocity of his race in his composition. He was never the cause of unnecessary bloodshed, nor the contriver of any act of cruel revenge. "Like Robin Hood, " says Scott, "he was a kind and gentle robber, and while he took from the rich, he was liberal to the poor. This might in part be policy, but the universal tradition of the country speaks it to have arisen from a better motive. All whom I have conversed with, and I have in my youth seen some who knew Rob Roy personally, gave him the character of a benevolent, humane man, in his way. "

That "way" was certainly not followed out on the most approved principles of morality, and he is well described as resembling in his code of morals an "Arab chief. " But if ever man may be excused for a predatory course of life, the chieftain, as he was now called, of the Macgregors may be pardoned for actions which, in those who had suffered less from wrong and oppression, would be deemed unpardonable.

The revival of that latent affection for the Stuarts which ever existed in the Highlands, greatly favoured the success of Rob Roy in his unsettled and exciting career. Many of the chieftains were now arraying their people to follow them to the field upon a summons from their rightful Prince; and even the Duke of Argyle, who had at first attached himself to the Prince of Orange, was wavering in his resolutions, never having been restored to his property and jurisdiction since the attainder and death of his father. Under these circumstances the assistance of Rob Roy became of infinite importance to Argyle. The most deadly feuds raged between him and Montrose, who, upon hearing that Roy was on friendly terms with Argyle, had sent to offer to the freebooter not only that he would withdraw his claims on his estate, but also that he would give him a sum of money if he would go to Edinburgh and give information against Argyle for treasonable practices. But this base overture was indignantly rejected by Rob Roy, who deigned not even to reply to the letter, but contented himself with forwarding it to Argyle. Hence the bitter enmity of Montrose towards the Macgregors, during the whole course of his future life. [110]

From this time Rob Roy kept no measures with his enemies, and his incursions were so frequent and so dreaded, that in 1713 a garrison was established at Inversnaid to check the irruptions of his party. But Rob Roy was too subtle and too powerful for his enemies. He bribed an old woman of his clan, who lived within the garrison, to distribute whiskey to the soldiers. Whilst they were in a state of intoxication, he set fire to the fort. He was suspected of this outrage, but still it passed with impunity, for no one dared to attack him; the affair was passed over in silence, and the Government re-established the fort of Inversnaid.

Numbers of the desperate and vagrant part of his clansmen now crowded around Rob Roy at Craig Royston, and swore obedience to him as their chieftain. The country was kept in continual awe by these marauders, who broke into houses and carried off the inmates to Craig Royston, there to remain until heavy ransoms were paid. Their chieftain, meantime, laughed at justice, and defied even the great Montrose. He had spies in every direction, who brought him intelligence of all that was going on. No person could travel near the abode of this mountain bandit without risk of being captured and carried to Craig Royston. In many instances the treatment of the prisoners is said to have been harsh; in some it was tempered by the relentings of Rob Roy. On one occasion, having seized upon a gentleman whose means had been reduced by great losses, he not only set him at liberty, but gave him money to pay his travelling expenses, and sent him in one of his own boats as far as he could travel by water.

The incursions of this Scottish Robin Hood were contrived with the utmost caution and secrecy, and executed with almost incredible rapidity. No one knew when he would appear, nor in what direction he would turn his dreaded attention. He is even said to have threatened the Duke of Montrose in his own residence at Buchanan. His enterprises were, however, not always contrived for a serious end, but sometimes partook of the love of a practical joke, which is a feature in the Scottish character.

"The Highland Rogue" gives the following account of one of his exploits: —[111]

"Rob Roy's creditors now grew almost past hopes of recovering their money. They offered a large reward to any that should attempt it successfully; but not an officer could be found who was willing to run such a hazard of his life; till at length a bailiff, who had no small opinion of his own courage and conduct, undertook the affair.

"Having provided a good horse and equipt himself for the journey, he set out without any attendance, and in a few hours arrived at Craigroiston, where, meeting with some of Rob Roy's men, he told them he had business of great importance to deliver to their master in private. Rob Roy having notice of it, ordered them to give him admittance. As soon as he came in, the Captain demanded his business. 'Sir, ' (says the other) 'tho' you have had misfortunes in the world, yet knowing you to be in your nature an honourable gentleman, I made bold to visit you upon account of a small debt, which I don't doubt but you will discharge if it lies in your power. ' 'Honest friend, ' (says M'Gregor) 'I am sorry that at present I cannot answer your demand; but if your affairs will permit you to lodge at my house to-night, I hope by to-morrow I shall be better provided. ' The bailiff complied, and was overjoyed at the success he had met with. He was entertained with abundance of civility, and went to bed at a seasonable time.

"Rob Roy then ordered an old suit of clothes to be stuffed full of straw, not wholly unlike one of the Taffies that the mob dress up and expose upon the 1st of March, in ridicule of the Welshmen; only, instead of a hat with a leek in it, they bound his head with a napkin. The ghastly figure being completely formed, they hung it upon the arm of a tree directly opposite to the window where the officer lay: he rising in the morning and finding his door locked, steps back to the window and opens the casement, in expectation of finding some of the servants, when, to his great astonishment, he cast his eye upon the dreary object before him: he knew not what to make of it; he began to curse his enterprise, and wished himself safe in his own house again. In the midst of his consternation, he spied one of the servants, and calling to him, desired him to open the door. The fellow seemed surprised at finding it locked, begged his pardon, and protested it was done by mistake. As soon as the bailiff got out, 'Prithee friend, ' (says he) 'what is it that hangs upon yonder tree? ' 'O sir, ' (says the other) ''tis a bailiff, a cursed rogue that has the impudence to come hither to my master, and dun him for an old debt; and therefore he ordered him to be hanged there for a warning to all his fraternity. I think the impudent dog deserved it, and in troth, we have been commended by all his neighbours for so doing. ' The catchpole was strangely terrified at this account, but hoping that the servant did not know him to be one of the same profession, he walked away with a seeming carelessness, till he thought himself out of sight, and then looking round and finding the way clear, he threw off his coat and ran for his life, not resting, nor so much as looking behind him, till he came to a village about three or four miles off; where, when he had recovered breath, he told the story of his danger and escape, just as he apprehended it to be. Rob Roy was so pleased with the success of his frolic, that the next day he sent home the bailiff's coat and horse, and withal let his neighbours know that it was only a contrivance to frighten him away; by which means the poor rogue became the common subject of the people's diversion. "

This adventure was immediately recounted to the Governor of Stirling Castle by the messenger, who hastened to that fortress. A party of soldiers was ordered out to seize Rob Roy; but the chieftain gained intelligence of their approach, and Rob Roy retreated to the hills; whilst the country of the Macgregors was roused, and put into a state of defence. The soldiers, meantime, worn out with their search among the hills, took possession of an empty house and filled it with heath for beds. The Macgregors, always active and watchful, set fire to the house, and drove their enemies from their post. Thus Rob Roy escaped the pursuit of justice, the troopers being obliged to return to Stirling Castle. He was not always so fortunate as to avoid imminent danger; yet he had a faithful friend who watched over his safety, and who would have willingly sacrificed his life for that of Macgregor. This was the chieftain's lieutenant, Fletcher, or Macanaleister, "the *Little John* of his band, " and an excellent marksman. "It happened, " writes Sir W. Scott, "that MacGregor and his party had been surprised and dispersed by a superior force of horse and foot, and the word was given to 'split and squander. ' Jack shifted for himself; but a bold dragoon attached himself to pursuit of Rob Roy, and overtaking him, struck at him with his broadsword. A plate of iron in his bonnet saved Mac Gregor from being cut down to the teeth; but the blow was heavy enough to bear him to the ground, crying as he fell, 'O Macanaleister, there is naething in her, ' (*i. e.* in the gun:) the trooper at the same time exclaiming, 'D—n ye, your mother never brought your nightcap; ' had his arm raised for a second blow, when Macanaleister fired, and the ball pierced the dragoon. "

His feats had, however, in most instances, the character of an unwarrantable oppression, notwithstanding that they were sometimes accompanied by traits of a generous and chivalric spirit. Very few of those who lived in his neighbourhood could depend upon an hour's security, without paying the tax of black mail, which he audaciously demanded; and the licentiousness of his reckless troop was the theme of just reprobation, and the cause of terror to many innocent and peaceable inhabitants in the west of Perth and Stirlingshire. On one occasion Campbell, of Abernchile, who had found it convenient to submit to the assessment of the black mail, neglected the regular payment of the tax. Rob Roy, angry at his disobedience, rode up to his house, knocked at the door, and demanded admittance. A party of friends was at dinner with the host, and the door was closed against Macgregor. Rob Roy sounded his horn; instantly his followers appeared in view. Rob Roy ordered them to drive off the cattle from the estate: Abernchile was forced to make an humble apology in order to avert his wrath, and to pay the exaction.

Another enterprise of Rob Roy's was directed to the welfare of his ward and relative, Macgregor of Glengyle. The estates of Glengyle were pledged, or, as it is called in Scotland, "under a contract of wadset. " The creditor was a man of influence and fortune; but, like most other Scottish proprietors who were enabled to take advantage of the wadset rights, he was grasping and merciless. It was not uncommon, in those times, for men to whom estates had been pledged, to take the most unfair advantages of small and needy proprietors; and from the great superiority which a superior claimed over his vassals, it became almost impossible for his inferiors to resist his rapacity, or to defeat his cunning.

Some months before the period of redemption had expired, Rob Roy, aware of the danger to which his ward was exposed, raised a sum of money in order to redeem the pledge. It was pretended by the creditor, that the bond securing the power of redemption was lost; and since a few months only of the period remained, a plan was formed by him for protracting the settlement of the affair. Rob Roy, unhappily, was elsewhere occupied: the period expired; the young

Macgregor ceased, therefore, to be the proprietor of his estate; he was ordered to leave it, and to remove his attendants, cattle, and tenants within eight days. "But law, " as Dr. Johnson observes, "is nothing without power. " Before those eight days had elapsed, Rob Roy had assembled his *gillies,* had followed his creditor into Argyleshire, had met him, nevertheless, in Strathfillan, and had carried him prisoner to an inn. There the unjust creditor was desired to give up the bond, and told to send for it from his castle. The affrighted man promised all that could be required of him; Rob Roy would not trust him, but sent two of his followers for the bond, which was brought at the end of two days. When it was delivered to Macgregor, he refused to pay the sum of redemption, telling the creditor that the money was too small a fine for the wrong which he had inflicted; and that he might be thankful to escape as well as he might.

Against all acts of oppression, except those which he thought proper to commit himself, Rob Roy waged war. He was the avenger of the injured, and the protector of the humble; and lest his own resources should prove insufficient for these purposes, a contract was entered into with several neighbouring proprietors to combine, for the purposes of defence, and protection to others.

The Duke of Montrose and his agent, Graham of Killearn, were still the especial objects of Macgregor's hatred. When a widow was persecuted by the merciless factor, and distrained for rent, Rob Roy intercepted the officers who went out against her, and gave them a severe chastisement; and a similar excursion was made in favour of any poor man who was obliged to pay a sum of money for rent. The collectors of the rent were disarmed, and obliged to refund what they had received. Upon the same principle of might against right, Rob Roy supported his family and retainers upon the contents of a meal-store which Montrose kept at a place called Moulin; and when any poor family in the neighbourhood were in want of meat, Rob Roy went to the store-keeper, ordered the quantity which he wanted, and directed the tenants to carry it away. There was no power either of resistance or complaint. If the parks of Montrose were cleared of their cattle, the Duke was obliged to bear the loss in silence. At length, harassed by constant depredations, Montrose applied to the Privy Council for redress, and obtained the power of pursuing and repressing robbers, and of recovering the goods stolen by them. But, in this act, such was the dread of Rob Roy's power, that his name was intentionally omitted in the order in Council.

The retreat into which Rob Roy retired, in times of danger, was a cave at the base of Ben Lomond, and on the borders of the Loch. The entrance to this celebrated recess is extremely difficult from the precipitous heights which surround it. Mighty fragments of rock, partially overgrown with brushwood and heather, guard the approach. Here Robert de Bruce sheltered himself from his enemies; and here Rob Roy, who had an enthusiastic veneration for that monarch, believed that he was securing to himself an appropriate retirement. It was, indeed, inaccessible to all but those who knew the rugged entrance; and here, had it not been for the projects which brought the Chevalier St. George to England, Rob Roy might have defied, during his whole lifetime, the vengeance of Montrose. From this spot Macgregor could almost command the whole country around Loch Lomond; a passionate affection to the spot became the feeling, not only of his mind, but of that of his wife, who, upon being compelled to quit the banks of Loch Lomond, gave way to her grief in a strain which obtained the name of "Rob Roy's Lament. "

Of the exquisite beauty, and of the grandeur and interest of the scene of Rob Roy's seclusion, thousands can now form an estimate. Dr. Johnson was no enthusiast when he thus coldly and briefly adverted to the characteristics of Loch Lomond. "Had Loch Lomond been in a happier climate, it would have been the boast of wealth and vanity to own one of the little spots which it incloses, and to have employed upon it all the arts of embellishment. But as it is, the islets which court the gazer at a distance, disgust him at his approach, when he finds instead of soft lawns and shady thickets, nothing more than uncultivated ruggedness. "[112]

From this retreat Rob Roy frequently emerged upon some mission of destruction, or some errand of redress. His name was a terror to all who had ever incurred his wrath; his depredations were soon extended to the Lowlands. One night a report prevailed in Dumbarton, that Rob Roy intended to surprise the militia and to fire the town. It was resolved to anticipate this attack, and accordingly the militia made their way to Craig Royston; and having secured the boats on Loch Lomond, which belonged to the Macgregors, they proceeded to seek for Rob Roy. But the chieftain had collected his followers, and, retreating into his cave, he laughed at his enemies, who were forced to retire without encountering him, the object of their search.

It is indeed remarkable, that outrages so audacious, and a power so imperative as that of Rob Roy, should have defied all control within forty miles of the city of Glasgow, an important and commercial city. "Thus, " as Sir Walter Scott observes, "a character like his, blending the wild virtues, the subtle policy, and unconstrained licence of an American Indian, was flourishing in Scotland during the Augustan age of Queen Anne and George the First. Addison, it is probable, and Pope, would have been considerably surprised if they had known that there existed, in the same island with them, a personage of Rob Roy's peculiar habits and profession. "

To the various other traits in the character of Rob Roy, there was added that tenacity of purpose, that obstinate and indefatigable hatred, which were common to the Highlanders. Their feuds were, it is true, hereditary, and were implanted in their minds before the reason could calm the passions. The fierce, implacable temper of the Macgregors had been aggravated by long-standing injuries and insults; among those who might be considered the chief foes of their race were the heads of the house of Athole. An uncontrolled, vehement spirit of revenge against that family burned in the breast of Rob Roy Macgregor; nor did he lose any opportunity of proving the sincerity of his professions of hatred.

Hitherto the wild feats of the marauder had met with continual success; no reverse had lessened his control over his followers, nor lowered his individual pride. But at length his enemy, the Earl of Athole, had a brief, but signal triumph over the dreaded chief. The circumstances under which it occurred are the following: —

Emboldened by his continued success, Rob Roy had descended into the plains, and headed an enterprise which was attended with the direst consequences: so desolating were its effects, that it is known by the name of the "Herriship of Kilrane. " The outrage was severely taken up by Government, and a reward was offered for the head of the freebooter. It was even resolved to explore his cave. One day, when on the banks of Lochearn, attended by two of his followers, Rob Roy encountered seven men, who required him to surrender; but the freebooter darted from their view, and climbed a neighbouring hill, whence he shot three of the troopers, and dispersed the rest. This occurrence drove him, for some time, from his stronghold on Loch Lomond.

The Earl of Athole had deeply felt the insults of Rob Roy, and he now took advantage of this temporary change of fortune to ensnare him. On a former occasion he had made an ineffectual attempt to overcome Macgregor. The scene had taken place on the day of the funeral of Rob Roy's mother. This was at Balquhidder: when Rob Roy had beheld the party of the Earl's friends approaching, he grasped his sword, yet met the Earl with a smile, and affected to thank him for the honour of his company. The Earl replied, that his was not a visit of compliment: and that Rob Roy must accompany him to Perth. Remonstrance was vain, and Rob Roy pretended compliance; but, whilst his friends looked on indignant and amazed, Macgregor drew his sword; the Earl instantly discharged a pistol at him: it missed its mark, and, during a momentary pause, the sister of Rob Roy, and the wife of Glenfalloch, grasped Athole by the throat and brought him to the ground. The clan meantime assembled in numbers, and the Earl was thankful to be released from the fierce amazon who held him, and to retire from the country of the Macgregors.

The Earl of Athole now judged force to be unavailing, and he resolved to try stratagem. After wandering, in consequence of the proclamation of Government, from place to place, Rob Roy was greeted by a friendly message from the Earl of Athole, inviting him to Blair Athole. Macgregor had not forgotten the day of his mother's funeral. He acted, on this occasion, with the frankness of an honest and unsuspecting nature. He doubted the Earl's sincerity; and he wrote to him, freely stating that he did so. He was answered by the most solemn assurances of protection, notwithstanding that all this time Athole was employed by Government to bring Rob Roy to justice. Macgregor was, however, deceived: he rode to Blair, attended only by one servant, and was received with the utmost professions of regard, but was requested to lay aside his dirk and sword, as the Countess of Athole would not suffer any armed man to enter the castle. Rob Roy complied with Lord Athole's entreaty. What was his surprise when the first remark made by Lady Athole was her surprise at his appearing unarmed; Rob Roy then felt that he was betrayed. Angry words, followed by a scuffle, ensued: the freebooter was overpowered; for sixty men, armed, entered before he could strike a blow.

Rob Roy was carried towards Edinburgh. He had proceeded as far as Logierait, under a strong guard, when he contrived, with his usual address and good luck, to make his escape. But the dangers which attended his eventful career were not at an end. He was surprised as he retired to the farm of Portnellan, near the head of Loch Katrine, by his old enemy, the factor of Montrose, with a party of men, who surrounded the house in which Rob Roy slept before he was out of bed; yet, the moment that he appeared, sword in hand, they fled in dismay. These, and many other incidents, rest so much upon tradition, and are so little supported by authority, that they belong rather to romance than to history. It is with the part which Rob Roy took in the actual concerns of his country that his biographer has most concern.

This brave but reckless individual was exactly the man to adopt a dangerous cause, and to play a desperate game. Proscribed, hunted, surrounded by enemies, burning under the consciousness of wrong, and unable to retrace his path to a peaceable mode of life, Rob Roy was a ready partisan of the Jacobite cause.

In 1713, he had transactions with two emissaries of the house of Stuart, and was called to account for that negotiation before the commander-in-chief in Edinburgh. He escaped punishment; and prepared, in 1715, to lead his clans to the field, headed by Macgregor of Glengyle, his nephew. [113] Upon Michaelmas day, having made themselves masters of the boats in Loch Lomond, seventy of the Macgregors possessed themselves of Inch-murrain, a large island on the lake. About midnight they went ashore at Bonhill, about three miles above Dumbarton. Meantime the alarm was spread over the country; bells were rung, and cannon fired from Dumbarton Castle. The Macgregors, therefore, thought fit to scamper away to their boats, and to return to the island. Here they indulged themselves in their usual marauding practices, "carrying off deer, slaughtering cows, and other depredations. " Soon afterwards they all hurried away to the Earl of Mar's encampment at Perth; here they did not long remain, but returned to Loch Lomond on the tenth of October. [114]

They now mustered their forces. Such was the terror of their name, that both parties appear to have been afraid of the Macgregors, and to think "it would be their wisdom to part peaceably with them, because, if they should make any resistance, and shed the blood of so much as one Macgregiour, they would set no bounds to their fury, but burn and slay without mercy. " This was the opinion held by some; by others resistance was thought the more discreet as well as the more honourable part. A body of volunteers was brought from

Paisley, and it was resolved, if possible, to retake the boats captured by the Macgregors, who could now make a descent wherever they pleased. A singular spectacle was beheld on the bosom of Loch Lomond: four pinnaces and seven boats, which had been drawn by the strength of horses up the river Levin, which, next to the Spey, is the most rapid stream in Scotland, were beheld, their sails spread, cleaving the dark waters which reflected in their mirror a sight of armed men, who were marching along the side of the loch, in order to scour the coast. Never had anything been seen of the kind on Loch Lomond before. "The men on the shore, " writes an eyewitness, "marched with the greatest ardour and alacrity. The pinnaces on the water discharging their patararoes, and the men their small arms, made so very dreadful a noise thro' the multiply'd rebounding echoes of the vast mountains on both sides the loch, that perhaps there never was a more lively resemblance of thunder. " This little fleet was joined in the evening by the enemy of the Macgregors, Sir Humphrey Colquhoun of Luss, followed by "fourty or fifty stately fellows, in their short hose and belted plaids, armed each of 'em with a well-fixed gun on his shoulder. " At Luss a report prevailed that the Macgregors were reinforced by Macdonald of Glengarry, and had amounted to fifteen hundred strong: but this proved to be an idle rumour; their numbers were only four hundred.

This falsehood did not dishearten the men of Paisley. "They knew, " says the chronicler of their feats, "that the Macgregiours and the devil are to be dealt with after the same way; and that if they be resisted, they will flee. "

On the following morning the party from Paisley went on their expedition, and arrived at Inversnaid. Here, in order to "arouse those thieves and rebels from their dens, " they fired a gun through the roof of a house on the declivity of a mountain; upon which an old woman or two came crawling out, and scrambled up the hill; but no other persons appeared. "Whereupon, " adds the narrator, [115] "the Paisley men, under the command of Captain Finlason, assisted by Captain Scot, a half-pay officer, of late a lieutenant of Colonel Kerr's regiment of dragoons, who is indeed an officer, wise, stout, and honest; the Dumbarton men, under the command of David Colquhoun and James Duncanson, of Garshark, magistrates of the burgh, with several of the other companies, to the number of an hundred men in all, with the greatest intrepidity leapt on shore, got up to the top of the mountain, and drew up in order, and stood about an hour, their drums beating all the while: but no enemie appearing, they thereupon went in quest of the boats which the rebels had seized; and having casually lighted on some ropes, anchors, and oars hid among the shrubs, at length they found the boats drawn up a good way on the land, which they hurled down to the loch. Such of them as were not damaged, they carried off with them; and such as were, they sunk or hewed in pieces. And that same night they return'd to Luss, and thence next day, without the loss or hurt of so much as one man, to Dumbarton, whence they had first set out altogether, bringing along with them the whole boats they found in their way on either side the loch, and in creeks of the isles, and moored them under the cannon of the castle. And thus in a short time, and with little expense, the M'Greigours were towed, and a way pointed how the Government might easily keep them in awe."

The historian remarks, as a good augury, that a violent storm had raged for three days before. In the morning, notwithstanding this much magnified triumph on the part of his enemies, neither Rob Roy nor his followers were in the least daunted, but went about "proclaiming the Pretender, " and carrying off plunder. "Yesternight, [116] about seven, " writes the same historian, "we had ane accountt from one of our townsmen, who had been five miles in the country, in the paroch of Baldernock, that three or four hundred of the clans, forerunners of the body coming, had at Drummen, near Dunkeld, proclaimed the Pretender; but no accountt to us from these places, nor from Sterling. Our magistrates sent fitt men at eight yesternight for information, and can hardly return till afternoon, if they have access to the three garrisons, of which they are I hear ordered to goe to to-day. I hear by report, without sufficient authority, that it's the M'Grigors come with a party, proclaimed the Pretender, tore the exciseman's book, and went away.

H. E."

*****

In a letter from Leslie, dated the twentieth of January, 1716, it is stated that the country did not oppose the incursions of Rob Roy, being mostly in his interest, or indifferent. Emboldened by this passive conduct, Rob Roy marched to Falkland on the fourth of January, 1716, and took possession of the palace for a garrison. He afterwards joined the Earl of Mar's forces at Perth, yet, whether from indolence or caution, took but little share in the signal events of the day. He hovered sometimes in the Lowlands, uncertain whether to proclaim peace, or to embark with his Macgregors in the war: some said he declined fighting under Lord Mar, from the fear of offending the Duke of Argyle; at all events he had the wiliness to make the belligerent powers each conceive him as of their respective parties.

At the battle of Sherriff Muir, Macgregor had the address to make both the Jacobites and Hanoverians conceive, that, had he joined them, the glory of the day would have been secured.

The inhabitants of Leslie, who had heard, with dismay, the news of the burning of Auchterarder and Blackford, were now affrighted by a rumour that Rob Roy had a commission to burn Leslie, and all between that place and Perth. But, whilst the burgesses of Leslie were daily looking for this dreaded event, Rob Roy was forced to retreat to Dundee, by the approach of the King's troops. He left behind him a character of reckless rapacity, and of a determined will, notwithstanding some generous and humane actions. He was, nevertheless, esteemed to be among the fairest and discreetest of the party to whom he was attached, notwithstanding his favourite speech, "that he desired no better breakfast than to see a Whig's house burning. " The people could not, indeed, trust any man's assurances after the recent and cruel devastation at Auchterarder.

When the fortune of the battle was decided, he was heard to say, in answer to demands that he should send his forces to the attack, "If they cannot do it without me, they cannot do it with me, " and he immediately left the field. Such is the popular account of his conduct on that occasion.

The partizans of Rob Roy have, however, given a very different version of his conduct. The Duke of Argyle was the patron and friend of Macgregor; and he could neither, therefore, openly adopt a course which the Duke disapproved, nor would he altogether retire from a cause to which he was disposed to be favourable. With the true Gaelic caution Rob Roy waited to see which side prevailed, and then hastened to avail himself of an opportunity of that which had become the darling pursuit of his existence—plunder.

He retired from Sherriff Muir to Falkland, carrying terror wherever he passed.

The following letter, descriptive of his progress affords a curious picture of the state of that harassed and wretched country: —

"D. B.

"I received yours this evening, but I find you have been quit mistaken about our condition. You datt our freedom and libertie from the rebels long befor its commencement, and for profe take the folowing accompt of what past heir these last ten days. Upon the fourth instant Rob Roey, with one hundred and fifty men, com to Falkland, and took possession of the place for a garrison, from which they came through the countrey side and robs and plunder, taking cloaths and victuals, and every thing that maks for them, nor to oposs them till this day eight days. The sixth instant there coms thirty-two Highland men (I had almost said devils) to Leslie; we saw them at Formand Hills and resolved to resist, and so man, wife, and child drew out.

"The men went to the east end of the town, and met them in the green with drawn swords in the hands, and we askt them what they were for; they said they wanted cloaths and money; we answeared they should get neither of them heir, at which they stormed and swore terribly, and we told them if they were come for mischeif they should have thee fill of it; at which ther were some blows. But they seeing us so bold, they began to feear that we should fall upon them, and so they askt libertie to march through the town, which we granted, but withall told them if they went upon the least house in the town, ther should never a man go back to Fackland to tell the news, though we should die on the spot, and so they marsht through the town and got not so much as the rise of a cap. And they were so afraid that they did not return, but went down over the Hank Hill, and east to the minister's land; and their they faced about and fired twenty shots in upon the peple that were looking at them, but, glory to God, without doing the least hurt. And so they went off to the Formand Hils, and plundred all the could carry or drive, and threatned dreadfully they should be avenged on Leslie and burn it. "

The pursuit of plunder was considered by Rob Roy as a far more venial offence than if he had fought against Lord Mar, or offended Argyle, with whom he continued on such convenient terms, that he did not leave Perth until after the arrival of that General. He then retired with the spoils he had acquired, and continued for some years in the practice of the same marauding incursions which had already proved so troublesome and distressing to his neighbours.

In the subsequent indemnity, or free pardon, the tribe of Macgregor was specially excepted; and their leader, Robert Campbell, alias Macgregor, commonly called Robert Roy, was attainted.

The severities which followed the Rebellion of 1715, drove Rob Roy to a remote retreat in the Highlands, where he lived in a solitary hut, half covered with copsewood, and seated under the brow of a barren mountain. Here he resided in poverty, and what was worse to his restless spirit, in idleness. Here he was in frequent dread of pursuit from the agents of the law; and several anecdotes are told with what veracity it is difficult to judge, of his dexterity in evading justice. Attainted, disappointed, aged, and poor, he had one grievous addition to his sorrows, which it required a cheerful and energetic mind to sustain, —that of a family devoid of principle.

Among the five sons of Macgregor, Coll, James, Robert, Duncan, and Ronald, four were known to be but too worthy of the name given by the enemies of the Macgregors to the individuals of that tribe—"devils. " Of Coll, the eldest, little is ascertained. Robert, or Robbiq, or the younger, as the Gaelic word signifies, inherited all the fierceness, without the generosity, of his race. At sixteen years of age, he deliberately shot at a man of the name of Maclaren, and wounded him so severely that he died. His brothers were implicated in this murder. On their trials, they were charged with being not only murderers, but notorious thieves and receivers of stolen goods. Robert was proved to have boasted of having drawn the first blood of the Maclarens; and the brothers were all accused of having followed this murder by houghing and killing forty head of young cattle belonging to a kinsman of the deceased.

Robert Roy, the principal party in the crime, did not appear before the High Court of Justiciary, to which he was summoned: he was therefore outlawed. The other brothers were tried, and the prosecution was conducted by the celebrated Duncan Forbes, of Culloden. The prisoners were acquitted of being accessory to the murder of Maclaren; but the jury were unanimous in thinking that the charge of being reputed thieves was made out, and they were ordered to find caution for their good behaviour.

Robert Roy was advised to retire to France: his brother James remained in Scotland, and took an active part in the Rebellion of 1745; when, with the assistance of his cousin Glengyle, he surprised the fort of Inversnaid; he afterwards led to the battle of Preston Pans six companies of his clan. His thigh-bone was broken in that battle; yet he appeared again at Culloden, and was subsequently attainted.

The life of James Macgregor was spared only to present a tissue of guilty schemes, and to end in infamy and exile. That of Rob Roy was dyed yet deeper in crimes, of which a second trial and an ignominious death were the dreadful result. He was hung in the Grass Market in Edinburgh, in the year 1754. James, his brother, being reduced to the most humiliating condition, died in France, after exhibiting in his conduct, whilst in Scotland, if possible, almost a deeper shade of depravity than that displayed by his brother.

Their father was, however, released from his existence before these desperate men had sullied the name which he transmitted to them by their transgressions.

As he declined in strength, Rob Roy became more peaceable in disposition; and his nephew, the head of the clan, renounced the enmity which had subsisted between the Macgregors and the Duke of Montrose. The time of this celebrated freebooter's death is uncertain, but is generally supposed to have occurred after the year 1738. "When he found himself approaching his final change, " says Sir Walter Scott, "he expressed some contrition for particular parts of his life. His wife laughed at these scruples of conscience, and exhorted him to die like a man, as he had lived. In reply, he rebuked her for her violent passions and the counsels she had given him. "You have put strife, " he said, "betwixt me and the best men of my country, and now you would place enmity between me and my God.""

Although he had been educated in the Protestant faith, Rob Roy had become a Catholic long before his death. "It was a convenient religion, " he used to say, "which for a little money could put asleep the conscience, and clear the soul from sin. " The time and causes of his conversion are only surmised; but when he had resolved on this important step, the freebooter left his lovely residence in the Highlands, and repairing to Drummond Castle, in Perthshire, sought an old Catholic priest, by name Alexander Drummond. His confessions were stated by himself to have been received by groans from the aged man to whom he unburthened his heart, and who frequently crossed himself whilst listening to the recital.

Even after this manifestation of penitence, Rob Roy returned to his old practices, and accompanying his nephew to the Northern Highlands, he is stated to have so greatly enriched himself, that he returned to the Braes of Balquhidder, and began farming.

He is said in the decline of life to have visited London, and to have been pointed out to George the Second by the Duke of Argyle, whilst walking in the front of St. James's Palace. He still had an imposing and youthful appearance, and the King is said to have declared that he had never seen a handsomer man in the Highland garb. [117] But this, and other anecdotes, rest on no better authority than tradition. His strength, always prodigious, continued until a very late period; but at last it was extinguished even before the spirit which had stimulated it had died away. He is acknowledged, even by his partial biographer, to have declined one duel, and to have been worsted in another; but impaired eyesight, and decayed faculties are pleaded in defence of a weakness which cast dishonour on Macgregor.

His deathbed was in character with his life: when confined to bed, a person with whom he was at enmity proposed to visit him. "Raise me up, " said Rob Roy to his attendants, "dress me in my best clothes, tie on my arms, place me in my chair. It shall never be said that Rob Roy Macgregor was seen defenceless and unarmed by an enemy. " His wishes were executed; and he received his guest with haughty courtesy. When he had departed, the dying chief exclaimed: "It is all over now—put me to bed—call in the piper; let him play *'Ha til mi tulidh'* (we return no more) as long as I breathe. " He was obeyed, —he died, it is said, before the dirge was finished. His tempestuous life was closed at the farm of Inverlochlarigbeg, (the scene, afterwards, of his son's frightful crimes,) in the Braes of Balquhidder. He died in 1735, and his remains repose in the parish churchyard, beneath a stone upon which some admirer of this extraordinary man has carved a sword. His funeral is said to have been attended by all ranks of people, and a deep regret was expressed for one whose character had much to recommend it to the regard of Highlanders.

He left behind him the memory of a character by nature singularly noble, humane, and honourable, but corrupted by the indulgence of predatory habits. That he had ever very deep religious impressions is doubted; and his conversion to popery has been conjectured to have succeeded a wavering and unsettled faith. When dying, he showed that he entertained a sense of the practical part of Christianity, very consistent with his Highland notions. He was exhorted by the clergyman who attended him to forgive his enemies; and that clause in the Lord's prayer which enjoins such a state of mind was quoted. Rob Roy replied: "Ay, now ye hae gien me baith law and gospel for it. It's a hard law, but I ken it's gospel. " "Rob, " he said, turning to his son, "my sword and dirk lie there: never draw them without reason, nor put them up without honour. I forgive my enemies; but see you to them, —or may"—the words died away, and he expired.

Reason may disapprove of such a character as that of Rob Roy, but the imagination and the feelings are carried away by so much generosity, such dauntless exertion in behalf of the friendless, as were displayed by the outlawed and attainted freebooter. He was true to his word, faithful to his friends, and honourable in the fulfilment of his pecuniary obligations. How many are there, who abide in the sunshine of the world's good opinion, who have little claim to similar virtues!

FOOTNOTES:

[99] From the Wodrow MS. in the Advocate's Library.

[100] Macleay's History of the Macgregors, p. 110.

[101] Historical Memoir of the Clan Macgregor, by Dr. Macleay, p.109.

[102] Preface to Rob Roy. Waverley Novels.

[103] Sir W. Scott.

[104] Macleay.

[105] Id.

[106] Macleay.

[107] Stewart's Sketches, vol. i. p. 224.

[108] Macleay, p. 188.

[109] Trials of the Macgregors, xxiv.

[110] Macleay, p. 181.

[111] See Trials, &c. p. 76.

[112] Tour to the Hebrides.

[113] Macleay.

[114] This account of what is called in history the "Loch Lomond Expedition, " is taken from the Wodrow MSS. in the Advocate's Library in Edinburgh. Extracts from these MSS. have been printed by James Dennistoun, Esq., to whose work I am indebted for this narrative of Rob Roy's martial career.

[115] The Loch Lomond Expedition, p. 9.

[116] Loch Lomond Expedition. Wodrow Correspondence, p. 30. Also Reay's History of the Rebellion, p. 286.

[117] Macleay, p. 279.

SIMON FRASER, LORD LOVAT.

SIMON FRASER,
LORD LOVAT, CHIEF OF THE CLAN FRASER.

The memoirs of Simon Fraser, Lord Lovat, have been written in various forms, and with a great diversity of opinions. Some have composed accounts of this singular, depraved, and unfortunate man, with the evident determination to give to every action the darkest possible tinge; others have waived all discussion on his demerits by insisting largely upon the fame and antiquity of his family. He has himself bequeathed to posterity an apology for his life, and from his word we are bound to take so much, but only so much, as may accord with the statements of others in mitigation of the heinous facts which blast his memory with eternal opprobrium.

As far as the researches into the remote antiquity of Scotland may be relied upon, it appears that the name of Fraser was amongst the first of those which Scotland derived from Normandy, and the origin of this name has been referred to the remote age of Charles the Simple. A nobleman of Bourbon—such is the fable, —presented that monarch with a dish of strawberries. The loyal subject, who bore the name of Julius De Berry, was knighted on the spot, and the sirname of Fraize was given him in lieu of that which he had borne. Hence the ancient armorial bearing of the Frasers, a field azure, semé with strawberries: and hence the widely-spreading connection of the Frasers with the noble family of Frezeau, or Frezel, in France, a race connected with many of the royal families in Europe. For a considerable period after the elevation of Julius de Berry, the name was written Frezeau, or Frisil.

The period at which the Frasers left Normandy for Scotland has been assigned to the days of Malcolm Canmore, where John, the eldest of three brothers of the house, founded the fortunes of the Frasers of Oliver Castle in Tweedale, by marrying Eupheme Sloan, heiress of Tweedale: whilst another brother settled beyond the Forth, and became possessed of the lands of Inverkeithing. Eventually those members of this Norman race who had at first settled in Tweedale, branched off to Aberdeenshire, and to Inverness-shire; [118] and it was in this latter county, at Beaufort, a property which had been long held by his family, that the famous Lord Lovat was born.

Such is the account generally received. According to others, the family of Fraser is of Scandinavian origin. When the Scandinavians invaded the eastern coast of Britain, and the northern coast of France, one branch of the family of Frizell, or Fryzell, settled in Scotland; another in Normandy, where the name has retained its original pronunciation. [119]

The castle of Beaufort, anciently a royal fortress, had been bestowed upon the Frasers, in the year 1367. It is situated in the beautiful neighbourhood of Inverness, in the district of the Aird; it was besieged by the army of Edward the First during the invasion of Scotland by the usual method of throwing stones from catapultæ, at a distance of seven hundred yards. A subsidiary fortress, Lovat, heretofore inhabited by one of the constables of the Crown, whom the lawlessness of the wild inhabitants and the turbulence of their chieftains had rendered it necessary to establish in the west of Scotland, also fell into the possession of the Frasers.

The present seat of the family of Lovat, still called Beaufort, is built on a part of the ground originally occupied by a fortress. It lies on a beautiful eminence near the Beauly, and is surrounded by extensive plantations.

The race, thus engrafted upon a Scottish stock, continued to acquire from time to time fresh honours. It was distinguished by bravery and fidelity. When Edward the First determined to subdue Scotland, he found three Powers refuse to acknowledge his pretensions. These were, Sir William Wallace, Sir Simon Fraser, commonly called the Patriot, and the garrison of Stirling. When Bruce, with an inconsiderable force fought the English army at Methven, near Perth, and was thrice dismounted, Sir Simon Fraser thrice replaced him on his saddle; he was himself taken prisoner and ordered to be executed. And then might be witnessed one of those romantic instances of Highland devotion, which appear almost incredible to the calmer notions of a modern era. A rumour went abroad that the stay of the country, the gallant Fraser, was to suffer for his fidelity to his country's interests. Herbert de Norham, one of his followers, and Thomas de Boys, his armour-bearer, swore, that if the report were true, they would not survive their master. They died voluntarily on the day of his execution.

In 1431, the Frasers were ennobled; the head of the house was created a Lord of Parliament by James the First, and the title was preserved in regular succession, until, by the death of Hugh, the eleventh Lord Lovat, it reverted, together with all the family estates, now of considerable value and extent, to Thomas Fraser, of Beaufort, great uncle of the last nobleman. This destination of the property and honours was settled by a deed, executed by Hugh, Lord Lovat, in order to preserve the male succession in the family. It was the cause of endless heart-burnings and feuds. Hugh had married the Lady Emelia Murray, daughter of John, Marquis of Athole, and had daughters by that marriage. He had, in the first instance, settled upon the eldest of them the succession, on condition of her marrying a gentleman of the name of Fraser. But this arrangement agreed ill with the Highland pride; and upon a plea of his having been prevailed on to give this bond, contrary to the old rights and investments of the family, he being of an easy temper, having been imposed on to grant this bond, he set it aside by a subsequent will in favour of his great uncle, dated March 26th, 1696. [120]

The families of Murray and Fraser were, at the time that the title of Lovat descended upon Thomas Fraser, united in what outwardly appeared to be an alliance of friendship. Their politics, indeed, at times differed. The late Lord Lovat had persisted in his adherence to James the Second of England after his abdication, and had marshalled his own troops under the banners of the brave Dundee. The Marquis of Athole, then Lord Tullibardine, on the other hand, had adopted the principles of the Revolution, and had received a commission of Colonel from William the Third, to raise a regiment of infantry for the reigning monarch. [121] Thus were the seeds of estrangement between these families, so nearly united in blood, sown; and they were aggravated by private and jarring interests, and by manoeuvres and intrigues, of which Lord Lovat, who has left a recital of them, was, from his own innate taste for cabals, and aptitude to dissimulation, calculated to be an incomparable judge.

Of the character of Thomas of Beaufort, the father of Simon, little idea can be formed, except that he seems to have been chiefly guided by the subtle spirit of his son Simon. The loss of an elder son, Alexander, after whose death Simon was considered as the acknowledged heir of the Frasers, may have increased the influence which a young, ardent temper naturally exercises over a parent advanced in years. Of his father, Simon, in his various memoirs and letters, always speaks with respect; and he refers with pride and pleasure to his mother's lineage.

"His mother, " he remarks, writing in the third person, "was Dame Sybilla Macleod, daughter of the chief of the clan of the Macleods, so famous for its inviolable loyalty to its princes. "[122]

During his life-time his great nephew, Thomas Fraser of Beaufort, had borne the title of Laird of Beaufort. "He now took possession, " says his biographer, "without opposition, of the honours and titles which had descended to him, and enjoyed them until his death. " According to other authorities, however, Thomas Fraser never assumed the rank of a nobleman, but retired to the Isle of Sky, where he died in 1699, three years after his accession to the disputed honours and estates.

The family of Thomas of Beaufort was numerous. Of fourteen children, six died in infancy; of the eight who survived, Simon Fraser only mentions two, —his elder brother, Alexander, and his younger, John. Alexander, who died in 1692, was of a violent and daring temper. A determined adherent of James the Second, he joined Viscount Dundee in 1689, when the standard was raised in favour of the abdicated monarch. During a funeral which had assembled at Beauly, near Inverness, Alexander received some affront, which, in a fit of passion, he avenged. He killed his antagonist, and instantly fled to Wales, in order to escape the effects of his crime. He died in Wales, without issue. John became a brigadier in the Dutch service, and was known by the name of Le Chevalier Fraser. He died in 1716, "when, " says his brother, Lord Lovat, in his Memoirs, "I lost my only brother, a fine young fellow. "[123]

Simon Fraser, afterwards Lord Lovat, was born at Inverness, —according to some accounts in 1668, to others in 1670: he fixes the date himself at 1676. He was educated at the University of Aberdeen, where he distinguished himself, and took the degree of Master of Arts. During his boyhood he shewed his hereditary affection to the Stuarts, —an affection which was probably sincere at that early age: and he was even imprisoned for his open avowal of that cause, at the time when his elder brother repaired to the standard of Dundee. Deserting the study of the civil law, to which he had been originally destined, Simon Fraser entered a company in the regiment of Lord Tullibardine, his relation; nevertheless, he twice attempted to benefit the Jacobite cause, —once, by joining the insurrection promoted by General Buchan, and a second time by forming a plan, which was rendered abortive by the famous victory at La Hogue, for surprising the Castle of Edinburgh, and proclaiming King James in that capital.

This plot escaped detection; and the young soldier pursued his military duties, until the death of Hugh Lord Lovat drew him from the routine of his daily life into intrigues which better suited his restless and dauntless character.

Although his father, it is clearly understood, never bore the title of Lord Lovat, Simon, immediately upon the death of Lord Hugh, took upon himself the dignity and the offices of Master of Lovat. He seems, indeed, to have assumed all the importance, and to have exercised all the authority, which properly belonged to Lord Lovat. He was at this time nearly thirty years of age, and he had passed his life, not in mere amusement, but in acquiring a knowledge of the world in prosecuting his own interests. It is true, his leisure hours might have been more innocently bestowed even in the most desultory pursuits, than in the debasing schemes and scandalous society in which his existence was passed: it is true, that in studying his own interests, he forgot his true interest, and failed lamentably; still, he had not been idle in his vocation.

He is said, on tradition, to have been one of the most frightful men ever seen; and the portrait which Hogarth took of him, corroborates that report. He inherited the courage natural to his family, and his character, in that single respect, shone out at the last with a radiancy that one almost regrets, since it seemed so inconsistent that a career of the blackest vice and perfidy should close with something little less than dignity of virtue. He seems to have been endowed with a capacity worthy of a better employment than waiting upon a noble and wealthy relative, or inflaming discords between Highland clans. If we may adduce the Latin quotations which Lovat parades in his Memoirs, and which he uttered during his last hours, we must allow him to have cultivated the classics. His letters are skilful, even masterly, cajoling, yet characteristic. It is affirmed that in spite of a physiognomy vulgar in feature, and coarse and malignant in expression, he could, like Richard of Gloucester, obliterate the impression produced by his countenance, and charm those whom it was his interest to please. His effrontery was unconquerable: whilst conscious of the most venal motives, and even after he had displayed to the world a shameless tergiversation, he had the assurance always to claim for himself the merit of patriotism. "For my part, " he said on one occasion, in conversation with his friends, "I die a martyr to my country. "[124]

In after life, Lovat is described by a contemporary writer, "to have had a fine comely head to grace Temple Bar. " He was a man of lofty stature, and large proportion; and in the later portion of his life, he grew so corpulent, that "I imagined, " says the same writer, "the doors of the Tower must be altered to get him in. "[125]

"Lord Lovat, " says another writer, "makes an odd figure, being generally more loaded with clothes than a Dutchman: he is tall, walks very upright, considering his great age, and is tolerably well shaped; he has a large mouth and short nose, with eyes very much contracted and down-looking; a very small forehead, covered with a large periwig, —this gives him a grim aspect, but on addressing any one, he puts on a smiling countenance: he is near-sighted, and affects to be much more so than he really is. "

"His natural abilities, " remarks the editor of the Culloden Papers, "were excellent, and his address, accomplishments, and learning far above the usual lot of his countrymen, even of equal rank. With the civilized, he was the modern perfect fine gentleman; and in the North, among his people, the feudal baron of the tenth century."[126]

It seems absurd to talk of the religious principles of a man who violated every principle which religion inculcates; yet the mind is naturally curious to know whether any bonds of faith, or suggestion of conscience ever checked, even for an instant, the career of this base, unprincipled man. After much deception, much shuffling, and perhaps much self-delusion, Lord Lovat was, by his own declaration, a Roman Catholic: his sincerity, even in this avowal, has been questioned. In politics, he was in heart (if he had a heart) a Jacobite; and yet, on his trial, he insisted strongly upon his affection for the reigning family.

Such were the characteristics of Simon Fraser, when, by the death of Hugh Lord Lovat, his father and himself were raised from the subservience of clansmen to the dignity of chieftains. To these traits may be added a virtue rare in those days, and, until a long time afterwards, rare in Highland districts; —he was temperate: when others lost themselves by excesses, he preserved the superiority of sobriety; and perhaps his crafty character, his never-ending designs, his remorseless selfishness, were rendered more fatal and potent by this singular feature in his deportment. There was another circumstance, less rare in his country, the advantage of an admirable constitution. It was this, coupled with his original want of feeling, which sustained him in the imprisonment in the Tower, and enabled him to display, at eighty, the elasticity of youth. Lord Lovat was never known to have had the headache, and to the hour of his death he read without spectacles. A very short time after the death of Hugh Lord Lovat elapsed, before those relatives to whom he had bequeathed his estates were involved in the deadliest quarrel with the family of Lord Tullibardine.

The family of Lord Tullibardine, at that time called Lord Murray, furnish one of those numerous instances which occur in the reign of William the Third, of an open avowal of Whig principles, joined to a secret inclination to favour the Jacobite party. The Marquis of Athole, the father of Lord Tullibardine, had been a powerful Royalist in the time of Charles the First; but had, nevertheless, promoted the Revolution, and had hastened, in 1689, to court the favour of the Prince of Orange, with whom his lady claimed kindred.

Disappointed in his hopes of distinction, the Marquis returned to his former views upon the subject of legitimacy; and finally retired into private life, leaving the pursuit of fortune to his son, Lord John, afterwards Earl Tullibardine, and Marquis of Athole. The disgust of the old Marquis towards the government of William the Third, and the evident determination which his son soon manifested to ingratiate himself with that monarch, had, at the time when the death of Hugh Lord Lovat took place, completely alienated the Marquis from his son, and produced an entire separation of their interests. [127]

In his zeal for the King's service, Lord Tullibardine had endeavoured to raise a regiment of infantry; and it happened, that at this time Simon Fraser, as he expresses it, "by a most extraordinary stroke of Providence, held a commission in that regiment. " This commission had been procured for him by his cousin, Lord Lovat, who looked upon it as the best means of "bringing him out in the world, " as he expressed himself. The mode in which Simon was induced by Lord Murray to accept of this commission, and the manner in which he was, according to his own statement, induced to support a scheme which was adverse to the interests of King James, is narrated in his own Memoirs. If we may believe his account, he opposed the formation of this regiment by every exertion in his power: he aided the Stewarts and Robinsons of Athole, devoted Jacobites, and determined opposers of Lord Murray, whose claims on them as their chieftain they refused to admit; and when Lord Murray, on being appointed one of the Secretaries of State, resolved to give up the colonelcy of the troop, he tried every means in his power to dissuade his cousin, Hugh Lord Lovat, to whom it was offered, from accepting the honour which it was inconsistent with his principles to bear. This conduct, according to the hero of the tale, was highly applauded by the old Marquis of Athole, who even engaged his young relative, Simon, to pass the winter in the city of Perth with the younger son of the Marquis, Lord Mungo Murray, in order that they might there prosecute together the study of mathematics.

Simon accepted the invitation; and whilst he was at Perth, he was, according to his own statement, cajoled by Lord Murray into accepting the commission, which "he held by a stroke of Providence; " and which was represented by Lord Murray, as Simon affirms, to be actually a regiment intended for the service of King James, who, it was expected, would make a descent into Scotland in the following summer. And it was observed that since the Laird of Beaufort was so zealous in his service, he could not do his Majesty a greater benefit than in accepting this commission.

Influenced by these declarations, Simon had not only accepted the commission, but had used his influence to make up a complete company from his own clan: nevertheless, the command of the company was long delayed. His pride as a Highlander and a soldier was aggrieved by being obliged to sit down content, for some time, as a lieutenant of grenadiers; and, at last, the company was only given upon the payment of a sum of money to the captain, who made room for the Laird of Beaufort. Nor was this all; for upon the Lord Murray being made one of the Secretaries of State, he insisted upon the regiment taking oath of abjuration, which had never before been tendered to the Scottish army. [128]

Such had been the state of affairs when Hugh Lord Lovat was taken ill, and died at Perth. The manner in which Simon Fraser represents this event, is far more characteristic of his own malignant temper, than derogating to the family upon whom he wreaks all the luxury of vengeance that words could give. Simon, it appears, had persuaded Lord Lovat to go to Dunkeld, to meet his wife, the daughter of the Marquis of Athole, in order to conduct her to Lovat. Lord Lovat, disgusted by the treachery of the Earl of Tullibardine in respect to the regiment, had refused to have anything more to do with "this savage family of Athole, " as he called them, "who would certainly kill him. "[129] According to an account more to be relied on than that of the scheming and perfidious Simon, the aversion which Lord Lovat imbibed during his latter days to his wife's kindred, was implanted in his mind by Simon Fraser, in order to gain his weak-minded relative over to that plot which he had formed in order to secure the estates of Lovat to his own branch of the house. [130] This, however, is the account given by Fraser of his kinsman's last illness: —

"In reality he had been only two days at Dunkeld, when he fell sick, and the Atholes, not willing to be troubled with the care of an invalid, or for some other reasons, sent him to an inn in the city of Perth, hard by the house of Dr. James Murray, a physician, the relation or creature of the Marquis of Athole, upon whom the care of Lord Lovat's person was devolved.

"The moment the Laird of Beaufort heard the news that Lord Lovat had been conducted, very ill, to the town of Perth, he set out to his assistance. But before his arrival, in consequence of the violent remedies that had been administered to him, he lost the use of his reason, and lay in his bed in a manner incapable of motion, — abandoned by his wife and the whole family of Athole, who waited for his dissolution in great tranquillity, at the house of Dr. Murray, their relation. "

Lord Lovat, however, recollected his cousin, and embracing him said, "Did not I tell you, my dear Simon, that these devils would certainly kill me? See in what a condition I am! " Simon could not refrain from tears at this melancholy spectacle. He threw himself on the bed beside Lord Lovat, and did not quit him till he died the next morning in his arms. Meanwhile, not an individual of the Athole family entered his apartment after having once seen him in the desperate condition in which he had been found by the Laird of Beaufort.

Such was the state of family discord when Lord Lovat died; and it was discovered, to the consternation of the Marquis of Athole and his sons, that he had made a will in favour of his relation Thomas of Beaufort, and to the exclusion of his own daughter.

The right of Thomas of Beaufort was deemed incontestable; and not a man, it was presumed, dreamed of disputing it. Yet it was soon obvious that the Earl of Tullibardine, who had now acquired the title of Viceroy of Scotland, was determined to support a claim in behalf of the daughter of Lord Lovat, and to have her declared heiress to her father. This scheme was coupled with a design of marrying the young lady also to one of Lord Tullibardine's own sons, [131] of whom he had five, and, according to Simon Fraser, without fortune to bestow on any of his children.

The Master of Lovat, Simon Fraser, as he rightfully was now, communicated this scheme to his father, and entreated him to resist this claim. Recourse was had to several of the most able lawyers of the kingdom, and their opinion unanimously was, that Lord

Tullibardine had no more right to make his "niece heiress of Lovat than to put her in possession of the throne of Scotland: that the right of Thomas of Beaufort to those honours and estates was incontrovertible, and that the King himself would not deprive him of them, except for high treason. " It appears that Lord Tullibardine was satisfied of the justice of the opinion as far as the title was concerned, but he still considered that the property of the last Lord Lovat ought to descend to his daughter and heiress. The point was warmly viewed between the Earl and the Master of Lovat; but the conference ended with no farther satisfaction to either of the gentlemen than that of having each a full opportunity of reviling the other: such, at least, is the account given by one of the parties; no reasonable person will venture wholly to vouch for its accuracy, yet the dialogue does not appear improbable. This firmness and spirit threw the Lord Commissioner into a violent passion; he exclaimed in a furious tone, "I have always known you for an obstinate, insolent rascal; I don't know what should hinder me from cutting off your ears, or from throwing you into a dungeon, and bringing you to the gallows, as your treasons against the Government so richly deserve. " Simon, having never before been accustomed to such language, immediately stuck his hat on his head, and laying his hand upon the hilt of his sword, was upon the point of drawing it, when he observed that Lord Tullibardine had no sword: upon this he addressed him in the following manner.

"I do not know what hinders me, knave and coward as you are, from running my sword through your body. You are well known for a poltroon, and if you had one grain of courage, you would never have chosen your ground in the midst of your guards, to insult a gentleman of a better house, and of a more honourable birth than your own; but I shall one day have my revenge. As for the paltry company that I hold in your regiment, and which I have bought dearer than ever any company was bought before, —it is the greatest disgrace to which I was ever subject, to be a moment under your command; and now, if you please, you may give it to your footman."[132]

Such was the beginning of a long course of hostilities which were thenceforth carried on between the Murrays and the clan of Fraser, and which was productive of the deepest crimes on the part of the Master of Lovat. That he was fully prepared to enter into any schemes, however desperate, to ensure the succession of the estates of Lovat, cannot be doubted. He prosecuted his designs without remorse or shame. The matter of surprise must be, that he found partisans and followers willing to aid him in crime, and that he possessed an influence over his followers little short, on their part, of infatuation.

The first suggestion that occurred to the mind of this bold and reckless man was, perhaps, a natural and certainly an innocent method of securing tranquillity to the enjoyment of his inheritance. He resolved to engage the affections of the young daughter of the late Lord Lovat, and, by an union with that lady, to satisfy himself that no doubt could arise as to his title to the estates, nor with regard to any children whom he might have in that marriage; nor was the hand of the Master of Lovat, if we put aside the important point of character, a proffer to be despised. The estate of Beaufort had long been in the possession of his father, as an appanage of a younger son; and had only been lent as a residence to Hugh Lord Lovat, on account of the ruinous state of the castle of Lovat. Downie Castle, another important fortress, also accrued to the father of Simon Lovat; and the estate of Lovat itself was one of the finest and best situated in Scotland. [133] In addition to these, the family owned the large domain of Sthratheric, which stretches along the western banks of the Ness, and comprises almost the whole circumference of that extensive and beautiful lake. The pretensions of the Master were, therefore, by no means contemptible; and as he was young, although, according to dates, ten years older than he states himself to be, in his Memoir of his life, he had every reason to augur success.

For a time, this scheme seemed to prosper. The young lady, Amelia Fraser, was not averse to receive the Master of Lovat as her suitor; and the intermediate party, Fraser, of Tenechiel, who acted as interpreter to the wishes of the Master, actually succeeded in persuading the young creature to elope with him, and to fix the very day of her marriage with the Master, to whom Fraser promised to conduct her. But either she repented of this clandestine step, or Fraser of Tenechiel, dreading the power of the Athole family, drew back; for he reconducted her back to her mother at Castle Downie, even after her assurance had been given that she would marry her cousin. [134]

The circumstances of this elopement are obscurely stated by Lord Lovat in his account of the affair; and he does not refer to the treachery or remorse of his emissary Fraser of Tenechiel, nor does he dwell upon a disappointment which must have gratified his mortal enemies of the house of Athole. Yet it appears, from the long and early intimacy to which he alludes as having subsisted between himself and the Dowager Lady Lovat, that he may have had many opportunities of gaining the regard of the young daughter of that lady, —an idea which accounts, in some measure, for her readiness to engage in the scheme of the elopement. At all events, he expresses his rage and contempt, and makes no secret of his determined revenge on those who had, as he conceived, frustrated his project.

The young lady was at first placed under the protection of her mother at Castle Downie, the chief residence of the clan Fraser; but there it was not thought prudent to allow her to abide, and she was therefore carried, under an escort, to Dunkeld, the house of her uncle, the Marquis of Athole. And here another match was very soon provided for her, and again her consent was gained, and again the preliminaries of marriage were arranged for this passive individual. The nobleman whom her relations now proposed to her was William, afterwards eleventh Lord Salton, also a Fraser, whose father was a man of great wealth and influence, although referred to by the Master of Lovat as the "representative of an unconsiderable branch of the Frasers who had settled in the lowlands of the county of Aberdeen. "[135] This match was suggested to the Athole family by one Robert Fraser "an apostate wretch, " as the Master of Lovat calls him, a kinsman, and an advocate; and he advised the Marquis of Athole, not only to marry the young lady to the heir of Lord Salton, but also, by various schemes and manoeuvres, to get Lord Salton declared head of the clan of Frasers. This plot was soon divulged; disappointment, rage, revenge were raised to the height in the breast of the Master of Lovat. His pride was as prominent a feature in this bold and vindictive man, as his duplicity. Throughout life, he could, it is true, bend for a purpose, as low as his designs required him to bend; but the fierce exclusiveness of a Highland chieftain never died away, but rankled in his heart to the last.

It must be admitted that he had just cause of irritation against the Murrays, first for disputing the claim of his father to the Lovat title and estates, a claim indisputably just; nor was their project for constituting Lord Salton the head of the clan Fraser, either a wise or an equitable scheme. It was heard with loud indignation in that part of the country where the original stock of this time-honoured race were, until their name was stained by the crimes of Simon Fraser, held in love and reverence. It was heard by the Master of Lovat perhaps with less expression of his feelings than by his followers; but the meditated affront was avenged, and avenged by a scheme which none but a demon could have devised. It was avenged; but it brought ruin on the head of the avenger.

Perhaps in no other country, at the same period, could the wrongs of an individual have been visited upon an aggressor with the same dispatch and ruthless determination as in the Highlands. Until the year 1748, when the spirit of clanship was broken, never to be restored, those "hereditary monarchies founded on custom, and allowed by general consent rather than established by laws, "[136] existed in their full vigour. The military ranks of the clans was fixed and continual during the rare intervals of local quiet, and every head of a family was captain of his own tribe. [137] The spirit of rivalry between the clans kept up a taste for hostility, and converted rapine into a service of honour. Revenge was considered as a duty, and superstition aided the dictates of a fiery and impetuous spirit. A people naturally humane, naturally forbearing, had thus, by the habits of ages immemorial, become remorseless plunderers and resolute avengers. When any affront was offered to a chieftain, the clan was instantly summoned. They came from their straths and their secluded valleys, wherein there was little intercourse with society in general to tame their native pride, or to weaken the predominant emotion of their hearts, —their pride in their chieftain. They came fearlessly, trusting, not only in the barriers which Nature had given them in their rocks and fastnesses, but in the unanimity of their purpose. Each clan had its stated place of meeting, and when it was summoned upon any emergency, the fiery cross, one end burning, the other wrapt in a piece of linen stained with blood, was sent among the aroused clansmen, traversing those wild moors, and penetrating into the secluded glens of those sublime regions. It was sent, by two messengers, throughout the country, and passed from hand to hand, these messengers shouting, as they went, the war-cry of the clan, which was echoed from rock to rock. And then arose the cry of the coronach, that wail, appropriate to the dead, but uttered also by women, as the fiery cross roused them from their peaceful occupations, and hurried from them their sons and their husbands.

Never was the fiery cross borne throughout the beautiful country of Invernessshire, never was the wail of the coronach heard on a more ignoble occasion, than on the summons of the Master of Lovat, in the September of the year 1698. After some fruitless negotiation, it is true, with Lord Salton, and after availing himself of the power of his father, as chieftain, to imprison Robert Fraser, and several other disaffected clansmen whom that person had seduced from their allegiance, the Master of Lovat prepared for action. The traitors to his cause had escaped death by flight, but the clan were otherwise perfectly faithful to their chieftain. Fear, as well as love, had a part in their allegiance; yet it has been conjectured that the hereditary devotion of the Highlanders must, originally, have had its origin in gratitude for services and for bounty, which it was the interest of every chieftain to bestow.

The Master of Lovat, or, as he was called by his people, the chieftain, first assembled his people at their accustomed place, to the number of sixty and seventy, and bade them be in readiness when called upon. He thanked them for their prompt attendance, and then dismissed them. During the next month, however, he was met, coming from Inverness, by Lord Salton and Lord Mungo Murray, who were returning from Castle Downie. Such was the preparation for the disgraceful scenes which quickly followed. As soon as the Master of Lovat and his father were informed of the flight of their treacherous clansmen, they wrote a letter to Lord Salton, and conjured him, in the name of the clan, to remain at home, and not to disturb their repose nor to interfere with the interests of their chief; and they assured him, that though a Fraser, he should, if he entered their country, pay for that act of audacity by his head. Such is Lord Lovat's account: it is not borne out by the statements of others; yet since the affair must have been generally discussed among the clan, it is probable, that he would not have given this version of it without foundation. Lord Salton, according to the same statement, at first received this letter in good part; and wrote to Lord Lovat and to the Master, giving his word that he would only interfere to make peace; and that, for this reason, he would proceed to the seat of the Dowager Lady Lovat, at Beaufort. [138] Upon afterwards discovering that this courtesy was a mere feint, and that this new claimant to the honours of chief was in close correspondence with the Murrays, who were with him and the Dowager at Beaufort, the Master of Lovat wrote to his father, who was at Sthratheric, to meet him at Lovat, which was only three miles' distance from Beaufort, whilst he should himself proceed to the same place by way of Inverness, where he trusted that Lord Salton would grant him an interview for the purpose of explaining their mutual differences. [139]

No sooner had the Master arrived at Inverness, than he found, as he declares, so much reason to distrust the assurances of Lord Salton, that he wrote him a letter, sent, as he says, "with all diligence by a gentleman of his train, to adhere to his word passed to his father and himself, and to meet him the next day at two in the afternoon, three miles from Beaufort, either like a friend, or with sword and pistol, as he pleased. "[140]

Such is the account transmitted by Lord Lovat, and intended to give the air of an "affair of honour" to a desperate and lawless attack upon Fraser of Salton, and on those friends who supported his pretensions to the hand of the heiress of Lovat.

The real facts of the case were, that Fraser of Salton was to pass through Inverness on his way to Dunkeld, where the espousals between him and the heiress of Lovat were to be celebrated. Whether Simon Fraser purposed merely to prevent the accomplishment of this marriage, or whether he had fully matured another scheme: — whether he was incited by disappointment to rush into unpremeditated deeds of violence, or whether his design had been fostered in the recesses of his own dark mind, cannot be fully ascertained. In some measure his revenge was gratified. He was enabled, by the events which followed, to delay the marriage of Fraser of Salton, and to retard the nuptials, —which, indeed, never took place. "This wild enterprise, " observes Arnot, in his Collection of Criminal Trials in Scotland, "was to be accomplished by such deeds, that the stern contriver of the principal action is less shocking than the abject submission of his accomplices. "[141]

Lord Salton dispatched an answer, saying, that he would meet the Master of Lovat at the appointed time, as his "good friend and servant. " But the bearer of that message distrusted the reply, and informed the Master that he believed it was Fraser of Salton's intention to set out and to pass through Inverness early in the morning, in order to escape the interview. Measures were taken accordingly, by the Master of Lovat. At a very early hour he was seen passing over the bridge of Inverness, attended by six gentlemen, as he himself relates, and two servants, completely armed. This is the Master's statement; but on his subsequent trial, it appeared that the fiery cross and the coronach had been sent throughout all the country; that a body of four or five hundred men in arms were in attendance, and that they had met in the house of one of the clansmen, Fraser of Strichen, where the Master took their oaths of fidelity, and where they swore on their dirks to be faithful to him in his enterprise. [142] "The inhabitants of Inverness, " says

Lord Lovat, "observing their alert and spirited appearance, lifted up their hands to heaven, and prayed God to prosper their enterprise. " These simple and deluded people, doubtless, but partially understood the nature of that undertaking which they thus called on Heaven to bless.

The Master of Lovat and his party had not proceeded more than four or five miles from Inverness, than they observed a large party of "runners issuing out of the wood of Bonshrive, which is crossed by the high road. " "It is a custom, " adds Lord Lovat, "in the north of Scotland, for almost every gentleman to have a servant in livery, who runs before his horse, and who is always at his stirrup when he wishes to mount or to alight; and however swift any horse may be, a good runner is always able to match him. "

The gentlemen who attended the Master of Lovat, were soon able to perceive that Lord Salton was one of the leaders of the party who was quitting the Wood of Bonshrive, and emerging into the high road; and that his Lordship was accompanied by Lord Mungo Murray, a younger son of the Marquis of Athole, and, as the Master of Lovat intimates, an early friend of his own. The account which Lord Lovat's narrative henceforth presents, of that which ensued, is so totally at variance with the evidence on his trial, that it must be disregarded and rejected as unworthy of credit, as well as the boast with which he concludes it, of having generously saved the lives of Lord Salton, and of his own kinsman, Lord Mungo. It appeared afterwards, that his followers had orders to seize them, dead or alive.

These two young noblemen were, it seems, almost instantly overpowered by numbers, notwithstanding the attendance of the "runners, " on whom Lord Lovat so much insists. Lord Mungo was taken prisoner by the Master himself. They were then deprived of their horses, and being mounted on poneys, were conducted to Fanellan, guards surrounding them, with their muskets loaded, and dirks drawn, to a house belonging to Lord Lovat, where they were kept in close confinement, guarded by a hundred clansmen. Gibbets were erected under the windows of the house, to intimidate the prisoners; and at the end of a week they were marched off to Castle Downie, —the Master of Lovat going there in warlike array, with a pair of colours and a body of five hundred men. From Castle Downie, Lord Salton and Lord Mungo were led away into the islands and mountains, and were treated with great indignity.

These adversaries being thus disposed of, the Master of Lovat invested the castle of Downie with an armed force, and soon took possession of a fortress, tenanted only by a defenceless woman, the Dowager Lady Lovat. But that lady was a Murray; one of a resolute family, and descended on her mother's side from a Stanley. She was the grand-daughter of Charlotte de la Tremouille, who defended Latham House against the Parliamentary forces in 1644. Notwithstanding that armed men were placed in the different apartments of the castle, she was undaunted. Attempts were made by the Master of Lovat to compel her to sign certain deeds, securing to him that certainty of the right to the estates, for which he was ready to plunge in the deepest of crimes. She was firm—she refused to subscribe her name. Her refusal was the signal, or the incentive, for the completion of another plot, of a last resource, —a compulsory marriage between the Master of Lovat and herself.

The awful and almost incredible details of that last act of infuriated villany, prove Lady Lovat to have been a woman of strong resolution, and of a deep sensibility. The ceremony of marriage was pronounced by Robert Monro, Minister of Abertaaffe. The unhappy Lady Lovat's resistance and prayers were heard in the very court-yard below, although the sound of bagpipes were intended to drown her screams. Morning found the poor wretched being, to make use of one of the expressions used by an eye-witness, "out of her judgment; she spoke none, but gave the deponent a broad stare. " For several days reason was not restored to her, until, greeted by one of her friends with the epithet "Madam, " she answered, "Call me not Madam, but the most miserable wretch alive. " The scene of this act of diabolical wickedness[143] is razed to the ground: Castle Downie was burned by the royal troops, in the presence of him who had committed such crimes within its walls, and of three hundred of his clansmen, shortly after the battle of Culloden.

It appears from a letter written by Thomas Lovat, the father of the Master, to the Duke of Argyle, that he and his son were shortly "impeached for a convocation, " and for making prisoners of Lord Salton and Lord Mungo Murray, for which they were charged before him, were fined, discharged their fines, and "gave security to keep the peace. "[144] So lightly was that gross invasion of the liberty that threatened the lives of others at first treated! "We have many advertisements, " adds Thomas Lovat, "that Athole is coming here in person, with all the armed men he is able to make, to compel us to duty, and that without delay. If he come, so we are resolved to defend ourselves; the laws of God, of nature, and the laws of all nations, not only allowing, but obliging all men, *vim vi repellere*. And I should wish from my heart, if it were consistent with divine and human laws, that the estates of Athole and Lovat were laid as a prize, depending on the result of a fair day betwixt him and me. "[145] It was, perhaps, an endeavour to avert the impending ruin and devastation that followed, that the Master of Lovat gave their liberty to Lord Saltoun and Lord Mungo Murray, although not until he had threatened them both with hanging for interfering with his inheritance, and compelling Lord Saltoun to promise that he would, on arriving at Inverness, send a formal obligation for eight thousand pounds, never more to concern himself with the affairs of the Lovat estate, and that neither he nor the Marquis of Athole would ever prosecute either Lord Lovat or his son, or their clan in general, for the disgrace they had received in having been made prisoners, for any of the transactions of this affair. [146]

But it was evident that, in spite of this concession, the vengeance of the Marquis of Athole never slept; and that he was resolved to wreak it upon the head of the wretch who had for ever blasted the happiness of his sister.

The Master of Lovat was shortly aware that it would no longer be prudent to remain with his victim in the castle of Downie. His wife, as it was then his pleasure to call her, remained in a condition of the deepest despair. She would neither eat nor drink whilst she was in his power; and her health appears to have suffered greatly from distress and fear. In the dead of night she was summoned to leave Castle Downie, to be removed to a more remote and a wilder region, where the unhappy creature might naturally expect, from the desperate character of her pretended husband, no mitigation of her sorrows. Since rumours were daily increasing of the approach of Lord Athole's troops, the clan of Fraser was again, when Lady Lovat was conveyed from the scene of her anguish, called forth to assist their leader, and the wail of the coronach was again heard in that dismal and portentous night: for portentous it was. This crime, the first signal offence of Simon Fraser, stamped his destiny. Its effects followed him through life: it entailed others: it was the commencement of a catalogue of iniquities almost unprecedented in the career of one man's existence.

Crushed, broken-spirited, afraid of returning to her kindred, whose high fame she seems to have thought would be sullied by her misfortunes, Lady Lovat was conducted by Fraser to the Island of Aigas. They stole thither on horseback, attended by a single servant, and arriving at the sea-shore, they there took a boat, and were carried to the obscure island which Fraser had chosen for his retreat. Thomas Fraser of Beaufort, the father of Simon, thus writes to the Duke of Argyle respecting this singular and revolting union.

"We have gained a considerable advantage by my eldest son's being married to the Dowager of Lovat; and if it please God they live together some years, our circumstances will be very good. Our enemies are so galled at it, that there is nothing malice or cruelty can invent but they design and practice against us; so that we are forced to take to the hills, and keep spies at all parts; by which, among many other difficulties, the greatest is this, —that my daughter-in-law, being a tender creature, fatigue and fear of bloodshed may put an end to her, which would make our condition worse than ever."[147]

And now there took place, in the mind of Lady Lovat, one of those singular revulsions which experience teaches us to explain rather than induces us to believe as neither impossible nor uncommon. Lady Lovat, it is said upon the grave authority of a reverend biographer, became attached to the bonds which held her. "Here, " says Mr. Arbuthnot, in his Life of Lord Lovat, [148] "he continued a month or six weeks, and by this time the captain had found means to work himself so effectually into the good graces of the lady, that, as he reported, 'she doated on him, and was always unhappy at his absence. '" However true or however false this representation may be, the marriage service was again, as it was said, solemnized, at the suggestion of the Master of Lovat, and with the free consent of Lady Lovat. [149] On the twenty-sixth of October, 1697, we find Simon Fraser writing in the following terms to the Laird of Culloden. The answer is not given in the Culloden Papers, but it not improbably contained a recommendation to repeat the marriage ceremonials: —

"Beaufort, the 26th of Oct., 1797.

"Dear Sir,

"Thir Lords att Inverness, with the rest of my implacable enemies, does so confound my wife, that she is uneasy till she see them. I am afraid that they are so madd with this disapointment, that they will propose something to her that is dangerous, her brother having such power with her; so that really, till things be perfectly accommodatt, I do nott desire they should see her, and I know not how to manage her. So I hope you will send all the advice you can to your oblidged humble servant,

SIM. FRASER. "

"I hope you will excuse me for not going your lenth, since I have such a hard task at home. "

FROM SIMON FRASER TO THE LAIRD OF CULLODEN.

"Nov. 23rd, 1697.

"Sir,

"I pray you receive the inclosed acompt of my business, and see if your own conscience, in sight of God, doth not convince you that it is literally true. I hade sent it to you upon Saturday last, but you were not at home; however, I sent it that day to the Laird of Calder, who, I hope, will not sitt down on me, but transmitt it to my best friends; and I beseech you, Sir, for God's sak, that you do the like. I know the Chancellour is a just man, notwithstanding his friendship to my Lord Tilliberdine. I forgive you for betraying of me; but neither you, nor I, nor I hope God himself, will forgive him that deceived you, and caused you to do it. I am very hopeful in my dear wife's constancey, if they do not put her to death. Now I ad no more, but leaves myself to your discretion; and reste, Sir, your faithful friend and servant,

SIM. FRASER. "

Lady Lovat lived to hear her husband deny that he had ever sought her in marriage, and to see him married to two different wives; and he scrupled not to represent the unfortunate Lady Lovat as the last possible object of his regard—as a "widow, old enough to be his mother, dwarfish in her person, and deformed in her shape. "[150] This, as far as related to disparity of years, was untrue; the Dowager was only four years older than the Master of Lovat.

Meantime justice had not slumbered; and one morning, a charge "against Captain Simon Fraser, of Beaufort, and many others, persons mostly of the clan Fraser, for high treason, in forming unlawful associations, collecting an armed force, occupying and fortifying houses and garrisons, &c., " was left by the herald, pursuant to an old Scottish custom, in a cloven stick which was deposited at the river side, opposite to the Isle of Aigas. [151] Of this no notice was taken by Simon, except to renew his addresses to his clan, and to hasten, as far as he could from his secluded retreat, a systematic resistance to the Marquis of Athole, and even to the royal troops, whose approach was expected. But his fears were aroused. Again he sought to avert the coming danger by concession; and he determined, in the first instance, on restoring Lady Lovat to her friends.

It is stated by Mr. Arbuthnot, but still on the authority of the Master of Lovat, that Lady Lovat had now become reluctant to return to her relations. Nor is it improbable that this statement is true, without referring that reluctance to any affection for the wretch with whom her fate was linked. She complied, nevertheless, with the proposal of the Master; and leaving the Island of Aigas, she proceeded first to Castle Downie, and afterwards to Dunkeld, where, according to Arbuthnot, she was obliged by her brother, the Marquis, to join in a prosecution against her husband, for a crime which she had forgiven. According to a letter from the Duke of Argyle, addressed to the Rev. Mr. Carstares, chaplain to King William, she fully exculpated the Master from the charges made against him on her account. [152] This exculpation was doubtless given when the unhappy woman was under the influence of that subtle and powerful mind, which lent its aid to its guilty schemes. Simon Fraser himself, as we have seen, in writing to Duncan Forbes, declared—"I am very hopeful in my dear wife's constancy, if they do not put her to death. " This might be only a part of his usual acting, —a trait of that dissimulation which was the moral taint of his character; or it may have been true that the humiliated being whom he called his wife had really learned to cherish one who seemed born to be distrusted, hated, and shunned.

The return of Lady Lovat to her family was of no avail in mitigating the indignation of the Marquis of Athole. By his influence with the Privy Council, who were, it is said, completely under his control, he procured an order from King William for the march of troops against the clan of Fraser, with instructions, according to Simon Fraser, to overrun the country, to burn, kill, and to destroy the whole clan, without exception; and, without issuing a citation to Thomas Fraser of Beaufort, or to his son, to appear—without examining a single witness—a printed sentence was published against all the Frasers, men and women and children, and their adherents. Even the sanctuary of churches was not to be respected: "in a word, " says Lord Lovat's Manifesto, "history, sacred or profane, cannot produce an order so pregnant with such unexampled cruelty as this sentence, which is carefully preserved in the house of Lovat, to the eternal confusion and infamy of those who signed it. "[153] The Government which sanctioned the massacre of Glencoe was perfectly capable of issuing a proclamation which confounded the innocent with the guilty, and punished before trial.

The Master of Lovat assembled his clan. That simple and faithful people, trusting in the worth and honour of their leader, swore that they would never desert him, that they would leave their wives, their children, and all that they most valued, to live and die with him. An organized resistance was planned; and the Master of Lovat intreated his father, as he himself expressed it, with tears, "to retire into the country of his kinsmen, the Macleods of Rye. " The proposal was accepted, and Thomas of Beaufort, for he never assumed the disputed title of Lord Lovat, took refuge among that powerful and friendly clan.

The prosecution against the Master of Lovat was, in the mean time, commenced in the Court of Justiciary; "the only case, " so it has been called, "since the Revolution, in which a person was tried in absence, before the Court of Justiciary, a proof led, a jury inclosed, a verdict returned, and sentence pronounced; forfeiting life, estate, honours, fame, and posterity. "[154] None of the parties who were summoned, appeared. The jury returned a verdict finding the indictment proved, and the Court adjudged Captain Fraser and the other persons accused, to be executed as traitors; "their name, fame, memory, and honours, to be extinct, and their arms to be riven forth and deleted out of the books of arms; so that their posterity may never have place, nor be able hereafter to bruite or enjoy any honours, offices, titles, or dignities; and to have forfeited all their lands, heritages, and possessions whatsoever. "[155]

After this sentence, a severer one than that usually passed in such cases, the Master of Lovat, for the period of four years, led a life of skirmishes, escapes, and hardships of every description. He retired into the remote Highlands, then almost impenetrable; and, followed by a small band of his clansmen, he wandered from mountain to mountain, resolved never to submit, nor yield himself up to justice.

Since his father's estates were forfeited, and he could draw no means of subsistence from them, he was often obliged to the charity of the hospitable Highlanders for some of their coarse fare; and when that resource failed, or when he had lived too long on the bounty of a neighbourhood, he and his companions made nightly incursions into the Lowlands, and, carrying off cattle and provisions, retreated again to their caverns, there to satisfy hunger with the fruits of their incursions. [156]

During the four years of misery and peril in which the Master of Lovat continued to evade justice, his father died, among his relations in the island of Skye. His decease was caused, according to the representation of his son, by a hasty march made to escape the King's troops, who, he heard, were coming to the islands to pursue him. Among the few humane traits in the character of Simon Fraser, the habitual respect and affection borne by the Highlanders to parents appears to have been perceptible. He speaks of Thomas of Beaufort in his Life with regret and regard; but seals those expressions of tenderness with an oath that he "would revenge himself on his own and his father's enemies with their blood, or perish in the attempt. " Such were his notions of filial piety.

The Master of Lovat had now attained the rank for which he had made such sacrifices of safety and of fame; and had the hollow satisfaction of a disputed title, with an attainted estate, and a life over which the sword of destiny was suspended.

A sentence of outlawry followed that of condemnation, and letters of fire and sword were issued against him. He was forbidden all correspondence or intercourse with his fellow subjects: he was cast off and rejected by his friends, and in constant danger either of being captured by the officers of justice, or assassinated by his enemies. The commission for destroying the clan of Fraser was not, indeed, put into execution; but that wild and beautiful district which owned him for its lord, was ravaged by the King's troops stationed at Inverness, or intimidated by the Highland army, commanded by Lord Lovat's early companions, but now deadly foes, —Lord James and Lord Mungo Murray. At length, after gaining a complete victory, according to his own account, at Stratheric, over the tributaries of Lord Athole, and extracting from the prisoners an oath by which they "renounced the claims on our Saviour and their hopes in Heaven if ever they returned to the territories of his enemy, the guilty and unfortunate man grew weary of his life of wandering, penury, and disgrace. "

He was always fertile in expedients, and audacious in proffering his petitions for mercy. During his father's life, a petition in the form of a letter, written by Thomas of Beaufort, and signed by seven Frasers, had been addressed to the Duke of Argyle, appealing to his aid at Court, upon the plea of that "entire friendship which the family of Lovat had with, and dependence upon, that of Argyle, grounded upon an ancient propinquity of blood, and zealously maintained by both through a tract and series of many ages. "[157] The Duke of Argyle had, it was well understood, made some applications on behalf of the Frasers; and Lord Lovat now resolved to push his interest in the same friendly quarter, and to endeavour to obtain a remission of the sentence out against his head.

His efforts were the more successful, because King William had by this time begun to suspect the fidelity of Lord Tullibardine, and to place a strong reliance upon the integrity and abilities of the Duke of Argyle. The Duke represented to his Majesty not only the ancient friendship subsisting between the house of Campbell and that of Fraser, but also that the King might spend "a hundred times the value of the Fraser estate before he could reduce it, on account of its inaccessible situation and its connection with the neighbouring clans. "[158] The Duke's account of his success is given with characteristic good sense in the following letter: —

THE EARL OF ARGYLE TO THE LAIRD OF CULLODEN.

"Edinburgh, Sept. 5, 1700.

"Sir,

"In complyance with your desyre and a great many other gentlemen, with my own inclination to endeavour a piece of justice, I have made it my chief concern to obtain Beaufort's (now I think I may say Lord Lovatt's) pardon, and the other gentlemen concerned with him in the convocation and seizing of prisoners, which are crymes more immediately against his Majesty, which I have at last obtained and have it in my custody. I designe to-morrow for Argyllshire; and, there not being a quorum of Exchequer in town, am oblidged to delay passing the remission till next moneth. We have all had lyes enuf of his Majestie before: his goodness in this will, I hope, return my friend Culloden to his old consistency, and make E. Argyll appear to him as good a Presbiterian and a weel wisher to his country in no lesse a degree then Tullibardine, who plundered my land some tyme agoe, and Culloden's lately. Pray recover the same spiritt you had at the Revolution; let us lay assyde all resentments ill founded, all projects which may shake our foundation; let us follow no more phantasms (I may say rather divells), who, with a specious pretext leading us into the dark, may drownd us. I fynd some honest men's eyes are opened, and I shall be sorie if Culloden's continue dimm. You have been led by Jacobitt generales to fight for Presbiterie and the liberty of the country. Is that consistent? If not speedily remedied, remember I tell you the posteritie of such will curse them. Let me have a plain satisfactorie answer from you, that I may be in perfect charitie with Culloden. Adieu. "

Accordingly, the Duke having obtained his pardon, Lord Lovat was enjoined to lay down his arms, and to go privately to London. That sentence, which had followed the prosecution on the part of Lady Lovat, was not, at that time, remitted, for fear of disobliging the Athole family. Upon arriving in London, Lord Lovat found that Lord Seafield, the colleague of the Earl of Tullibardine, was disinclined to risk incurring the displeasure of the Athole family. He put off the signing of the pardon from time to time. He was even so much in awe of the Earl of Tullibardine, that he endeavoured to get the King to sign the pardon when he was at Loo; that Mr. Pringle, the other Secretary of State, might bear the odium of presenting it for signature. During this delay, Lord Lovat, not being able with safety to return to Scotland, resolved to occupy the interval of suspense by a journey into France.

Whilst Lord Lovat's affairs were in this condition, the Marquis of Athole, resolved for ever to put it out of Lord Lovat's power to gain any ascendancy over the young heiress of Lovat, Amelia Fraser, was employed in arranging a marriage for that lady to the son of Alexander Mackenzie, Lord Prestonhall. It was agreed, by a marriage settlement, that Mr. Mackenzie should take the name and title of Fraserdale, and that the children of that marriage should bear the name of Fraser. The estate of Lovat was settled upon Fraserdale in his life, with remainder to his children by his wife. [159] It indeed appears, that the estate of Lovat was never surrendered to Lord Lovat; that he bore in Scotland, according to some statements, no higher title than that of Lord of Beaufort; and that a regular receiver of the rents was appointed by the guardians of Amelia Fraser: [160]

so completely were the dark designs of Simon Fraser defeated in their object! He was, however, graciously received at St. Germains, whither he went whilst yet, James the Second, in all the glory of a sanctified superstition, lived with his Queen, the faithful partner of his misfortunes. Lord Lovat ascribes this visit to St. Germains to his intention of dissipating the calumnious stories circulated against him by the Marquis of Athole. The flourishing statement which he gives in his memoirs of King James's reception, may, however, be treated as wholly apocryphal. James the Second, with all his errors, was too shrewd a man, too practised in kingcraft, to speak of the "perfidious family of Athole, " or to mention the head of that noble house by the title of that "old traitor. " Lord Lovat's incapacity to write the truth, and his perpetual endeavour to magnify himself in his narrative, cause us equally to distrust the existence of that document, with the royal seal affixed to it, which he says the King signed with his own hand, declaring that he would protect Lord Lovat from "the perfidious and faithless family of Athole. "[161]

The fact is, and it redounds to the credit of James the Second, that monarch, eager as he ever remained to attach partisans to his interests, never received Lord Lovat into his presence. [162] The infamy of the exploits of the former Master of Lovat had preceded his visit to France: the whole account of his own reception at St. Germains, written with astonishing audacity, and most circumstantially worded, was a fabrication.

Lord Lovat's usual readiness in difficulties did not fail him; he was a ruined man, and it was puerile to shrink from expedients. He applied to the Pope's nuncio, and expressed his readiness to become a Roman Catholic. The suit was, of course, encouraged, and the arch hypocrite, making a recantation of all his former errors, professed himself a member of the holy Catholic Church, and acknowledged the Pope as its head. This avowal cost him little, for he was by no means prejudiced in favour of any specific faith; and it gained him for the time, some little popularity in the gay metropolis in which he had taken refuge.

King James, indeed, to his honour, was still resolute in declining his personal homage; but Louis the Fourteenth was less scrupulous, and the Marquis de Torcy, the favourite and Minister of the French King, presented the abjured of England and Scotland at the Palais of Versailles. It is difficult to picture to oneself the savage and merciless Fraser, the pillager, the destroyer, the outlaw, conversing, as he is said to have done, with the saintly and sagacious Madame Maintenon. It is scarcely possible to conceive elegant and refined women of any nation receiving this depraved, impenitent man, with the rumour of his recent crimes still fresh in their memory, into their polished circles. Yet they made no scruple in that dissolute city, to associate with the abandoned wretch who dared not return to Scotland, and who only looked for a pardon for his crimes through the potent workings of a faction.

Lord Lovat well knew the value of female influence. He dressed in the height of fashion—he adapted his language and sentiments to the tone of those around the Court. He was a man of considerable conversational talents; "his deportment, " says his biographer, "was graceful and manly. " When he was first presented to Louis the Fourteenth, who was desirous of asking some questions concerning the invasion of Scotland, he is said to have prepared an elaborate address, which he forgot in the confusion produced by the splendour around him, but to have delivered an able extempore speech, with infinite ease and good taste, upon the spur of the moment, to the great amusement of Louis, who learned from De Torcy the circumstance. [163]

His advancement at the Court of Versailles was interrupted by the necessity of his return to England, in order to obtain at last a final pardon from the King for his offences. It is singular that the instrument by whom he sought to procure this remission was William Carstairs, that extraordinary man, who had suffered in the reign of James the Second the thumb-screw, and had been threatened with the iron boot, for refusing to disclose the correspondence between the friends of the Revolution. Mr. Carstairs was now secretary to King William, and he little knew, when he counselled that monarch to pardon Lovat, what a partisan of the Jacobite cause he was thus restoring to society.

His mediation was effectual, perhaps owing to a dislike which had arisen in the mind of William against the Athole family; and a pardon was procured for Lord Lovat. The affair was concluded at Loo, whither Lovat followed the King from England. "He is a bold man, " the Monarch is said to have observed to Carstairs, "to come so far under sentence of death. " The pardon was unlimited, and that it might comprise the offence against Lady Athole, it was now "a complete and ample pardon for every imaginable crime. " The royal seal was appended to it, and there remained only to get that of Scotland also affixed.

Lovat entrusted the management of that delicate and difficult matter to a cousin, a Simon Fraser also, by whose treachery it was suppressed; and Lord Seafield caused another pardon to pass the great seal, in which the treason against King William was alone specified; and other offences were left unpardoned. Upon this, Lord Lovat cited the Marquis of Athole before the Lords Justiciary in Edinburgh to answer before them for a false accusation: but on the very day of supporting his charge, as the biographer of his family relates, his patron the Duke of Argyle was informed that the judges had been corrupted, and that "certain death would be the result if he appeared. "[164] This statement is taken from Lord Lovat's own complication of falsehoods, his incomparably audacious "Manifesto. " Notwithstanding that Lovat had appeared with a retinue of a hundred armed gentlemen, "as honorable as himself, " with the intention of intimidating the judges; —in spite of the Duke of Argyle's powerful influence, the friends of the outlawed nobleman counselled him again to retreat to England, and to suffer judgment to go by default. The Duke of Argyle, he says, would not lose sight of him till he had seen him on horseback, and had ordered his own best horse to be brought round to the door. There was no remedy for what was called by Lord Lovat's friends, the "rascality" of the judges: —and again this unworthy Highlander was driven from his own country to seek safety in the land wherein his offences had received their pardon. The inflexibility of the justiciary lords, or their known integrity, form a fine incident in history; for the Scottish nation was at this period, ridden by Court faction, and broken down by recent oppression and massacre.

Lord Lovat, meeting the Duke of Argyle on the frontiers, accompanied his Grace to London; and here, notwithstanding his boast, "that after his arrival in London he was at the Duke's house every day, " he appears, about this time, to have been reduced to a state of miserable poverty, and merited desertion.

In the following letter to Mr. Carstairs, he complains that nothing is done for him—he applies to Mr. Carstairs for a little money to carry him home, "having no other door open. "

LORD LOVAT TO MR. CARSTAIRS,

"London, June 20th, 1701.

"Dear Sir,

"I reckon myself very unhappy that my friends here do so much neglect me; and I believe my last journey to England has done me a vast prejudice; for if I had been at home, I would have got something done in my Lord Evelin's business, and would have got money before now, that might serve me to go a volunteer with the King, or maintain me anywhere; but my friend at home must have worse thoughts now of my affairs than ever, having staid so long here, and got nothing done. However, I now resolve to go to Scotland, not being able to subsist longer here. I have sent the inclosed note, that, according to your kind promise, I may have the little money which will carry me home, and it shall be precisely paid before two months; and I must say, it is one of the greatest favours ever was done me, not having any other door open, if you were not so generous as to assist me, which I shall alwise gratefully remember, and continue with all sincerity, Dear Sir, Your faithful and obliged servant,

LOVAT. "

The death of William the Third revived the hopes of the Jacobite party; and to that centre of attraction the ruined and the restless, the aspiring and the profligate, alike turned their regards. Never was so great a variety of character, and so great a diversity of motives displayed in any cause, as in the various attempts which were made to secure the restoration of the Stuarts. On some natures those opinions, those schemes, which were generally known under the name of Jacobitism, acted as an incentive to self-sacrifice—and to a constancy worthy of better fortune. In other minds the poison of faction worked irremediable mischief: many who began with great and generous resolves, sank into intrigue, and ended in infidelity to the cause which that had espoused. But Lord Lovat came under neither of these classes; he knew not the existence of a generous emotion; he was consistent in the undeviating selfishness and baseness of his career.

If he had a sincere predilection, he was disposed to the interest of King James. Hereditary tendencies scarcely ever lose their hold upon the mind entirely: notions on politics are formed at a much earlier age than is generally supposed. The family of Fraser had been, as we have seen, from ages immemorial employed in defence of the Stuart Kings; and early prepossessions were imbibed by the unworthy descendant of a brave race, before his passions had interfered to warp the generous sentiment of loyalty. As he grew up, Lord Lovat learned to accommodate himself to any party; and it was justly observed by Lord Middleton, one of the favourite courtiers at St. Germains, that though he boasted so much of his adherence to his Sovereign, he had never served any sovereign but King William, in whose army he had commanded a regiment. [165]

The period was now, however, approaching, when he whose moral atmosphere was, like his native climate, the tempest and the whirlwind, might hope to glean some benefit from the impending storm which threatened the peace of the British empire.

On the sixth of September, 1701, James the Second of England expired at St. Germains. This event was favourable to those of the Jacobite party who wished to bring forward the interests of the young Prince of Wales. James had long been infirm, and had laid aside all schemes of worldly elevation. He had passed his time between the diversion of hunting and the duties of religion. His widowed Queen retained, on the contrary, an ardent desire to see her son restored to the throne of England. She implanted that wish in his own breast; she nourished it by the society of those whom she placed around him; and she passed her time in constantly forming new schemes for the promotion of that restoration to which her sanguine anticipations were continually directed.

The death of James was succeeded by two events: one, the avowed determination of Louis the Fourteenth to take the exiled family of Stuart under his protection, and the consequent proclamation of the young Prince of Wales as King of England; the other, the bill for the attainder of the pretended Prince of Wales, in the English Parliament, with an additional clause of attainder against the Queen, Mary of Modena, together with an oath of abjuration of the "Pretender. " The debates which impeded the progress of this measure, plainly prove how deeply engrafted in the hearts of many of the higher classes were those rights which they were thus enforced to abjure. [166]

This was one of the last acts of William. His death, in 1702, revived the spirits of the Jacobites, for the partiality of Anne to her brother, the young Prince, was generally understood; and it appears, from the letters which have been published in later days to have been of a far more real and sisterly character than has generally been supposed. The death of the young Duke of Gloucester appeared, naturally, to make way for the restoration of the Stuart family; and there is no doubt but that Anne earnestly desired it; and that on one occasion, when her brother's life was in danger from illness, her anxiety was considerable on his account.

It is, therefore, no matter of reproach to the Jacobites, as an infatuation, although it has frequently been so represented, that they cherished those schemes which were ultimately so unfortunate, but which, had it not been that "popery appeared more dreadful in England than even the prospect of slavery and temporal oppression, " would doubtless have been successful without the disastrous scenes which marked the struggle to bring them to bear.

Lord Lovat was at this time no insignificant instrument in the hands of the Jacobite party. When he found that the sentence of outlawry was not reversed; when he perceived that he must no longer hope for the peaceable enjoyment of the Lovat inheritance, his whole soul turned to the restoration of King James; and, after his death, to that of the young Prince of Wales. Yet he seems, in the course of the extraordinary affairs in which the Queen, Mary of Modena, was rash enough to employ him, to have one eye fixed upon St. James's, another upon St. Germains, and to have been perfectly uncertain as to which power he should eventually dedicate his boasted influence and talents.

Lord Lovat may be regarded as the first promoter of the Insurrection of 1715 in Scotland. Whether his exertions proceeded from a real endeavour to promote the cause of the Jacobites, or whether they were, as it has been supposed, the result of a political scheme of the Duke of Queensbury's, it is difficult to determine, and immaterial to decide; because his perfidy in disclosing the whole to that nobleman has been clearly discovered. It seems, however, more than probable, that he could not go on in the straightforward path; and that he was in the employ of the Duke of Queensbury from the first, has been confidently stated. [167]

Early in 1702, Lord Lovat went to France, and pretending to have authority from some of the Highland clans and Scottish nobility, offered the services of his countrymen to the Court of St. Germains.

This offer was made shortly before the death of James the Second, and a proposal was made in the name of the Scottish Jacobites to raise an army of twelve thousand men, if the King of France would consent to land five thousand men at Dundee, and five hundred at Fort William. His proposals were listened to, but his integrity was suspected. [168]

According to his own account, Lord Lovat, being in full possession of his family honours, upon the death of King William, immediately proclaimed the Prince of Wales in his own province, and acting, as he declares, in accordance with the advice of his friend, the Duke of Argyle, repaired to France, "in order to do the best that he could in that country. "[169]

He immediately, to pursue his own statement, engaged the Earl Lord Marischal, the Earl of Errol, Lord Constable of Scotland, in the cause; and then, passing through England and Holland, in order to go to France through Flanders, he arrived in Paris with this commission about the month of September.

Sir John Maclean, cousin-german of Lord Lovat, had resided ten years at the Court of St. Germains, and to his guidance Lovat confided himself. By Maclean, Lovat was introduced to the Duke of Perth, as he was called, who had been Chancellor of Scotland when James the Second abdicated, and whose influence was now divided at the Court of St. Germains, by the Earl of Middleton. For never was faction more virulent than in the Court of the exiled Monarch, and during the minority of his son. The Duke of Perth represented Lord Middleton as a "faithless traitor, a pensionary of the English Parliament, to give intelligence of all that passes at the Court of St. Germains. " It was therefore agreed that this scheme of the invasion should be carried on unknown to that nobleman, and to this secrecy the Queen, it is said, gave her consent. She hailed the prospect of an insurrection in Scotland with joy, and declared twenty times to Lord Lovat that she had sent her jewels to Paris to be sold, in order to send the twenty thousand crowns, [170] which Lord Lovat represented would be necessary to equip the Highland forces. Hitherto the Court of St. Germains had been contented merely to keep up a correspondence with their friends, retaining them in their principles, though without any expectation of immediate assistance. The offer of Lord Lovat was the first step towards more active exertions in the cause of the Stuarts. It is in this sense that he may almost be considered as the father of the Rebellion of 1715. He first excited those ardent spirits to unanimity and to action; and the project of restoration, which only languished whilst Anne lived, was never afterwards abandoned until after the year 1746.

Either through the indiscretion of Queen Mary of Modena, or through some other channel, the plot of the invasion became known to Lord Middleton. Jealous of the family of Perth, his avowed enemies, Lord Middleton, according to Lord Lovat, was enraged at the project, and determined to ruin the projectors. It is very true that the antipathies between the prevailing factions may have excited Lord Middleton's anger; but it is evident, from his lordship's letters and memoranda, that his dislike had a far deeper source—the profligacy of the agent Lovat; a profligacy which had deterred, as it was afterwards found, many of the Highland chiefs from lending their aid to the cause. Party fury, however, ran high, and before the affair of the insurrection could be settled, Lord Middleton, declaring that the last words of King James had made a powerful impression on his mind, retired into the convent of Benedictines at Paris, to be satisfied of some doubts, and to be instructed in the doctrines of the Roman Catholic Church. But this temporary retirement rather revived than decreased the favour of the Queen towards him. She trusted to his advice; and, as the statement which Lord Lovat gave of the affairs of Scotland appeared too favourable to the excluded family to be believed, Louis the Fourteenth counselled the Court of St. Germains to send with Lord Lovat, or, as he is invariably called in all contemporary documents, Simon Fraser, a person who could be trusted to bring back a genuine account. Accordingly, James Murray of Stanhope, the brother of Sir David Murray, was employed to this effect. "He was, " says Lord Lovat, "a spy of Lord Middleton's, his sworn creature, and a man who had no other means of subsistence. "[171] From other accounts, however, Mr. Murray is shown to have been a man of probity, although in great pecuniary difficulties, as many of the younger members of old families were at that time. [172] Mr. James Murray was sent forward into Scotland six weeks before Lord Lovat set out from France; and the Court had the wisdom to send with the latter another emissary in the person of Mr. John Murray, of Abercairney.

After these arrangements were completed, Lord Lovat received his commission. He set out upon his expedition by way of Brussels, to Calais. Not being furnished with passports, and having no other pass than the orders of the Marquis De Torcy to the commandants of the different forts upon the coast, he was obliged also, to wait for an entire month, the arrival of an English packet for the exchange of prisoners, —the captain of the vessel having been bribed to take him and his companions on board as English prisoners of war, and to put them on shore during the night, in his boat, near Dover.

Through the interest of Louis the Fourteenth, Lovat had received the commission from King James of major-general, with power to raise and command forces in his behalf: [173] and thus provided, he proceeded to Scotland, where he was met by the Duke of Argyle, his friend, and conducted by that nobleman to Edinburgh. Such was the simple statement of Lovat's first steps on this occasion. According to his memorial, which he afterwards presented to Queen Mary, he received assurances of support from the Catholic gentry of Durham, who, "when he showed them the King's picture, fell down on their knees and kissed it. "[174] This flattering statement appeared, however, to resemble the rest of the memorial of his proceedings, and met with little or no credence even in the quarter where it was most likely to be well received.

From the Duke of Queensbury, Lord Lovat received a pass to go into the Highlands, which was procured under feigned names, both for him and his two companions, from Lord Nottingham, then Secretary of State. After this necessary preliminary, Lord Lovat made a tour among some of the principal nobility in the Lowlands. He found them, even according to his own statement, averse to take up arms without an express commission from the King. But he remarks, writing always as he does in the third person, "My Lord Lovat pursued his journey to the Highlands, where they were overjoyed to see him, because they believed him dead, having been fourteen months in France, without writing any word to his country. They came from all quarters to see him. He showed them the King's instructions, and the King of France's great promises. They were ravished to see them, and prayed to God to have their King there, and they should soon put him on the throne. My Lord Lovat told them that they must first fight for him, and beat his enemies in the kingdom. They answered him, that, if they got the assistance he promised them, they would march in three days' advertisement, and beat all the King's enemies in the kingdom. "[175] This statement, though possibly not wholly untrue, must be taken with more than the usual degree of allowance for the exaggeration of a partisan. Many of the Highland noblemen and chieftains were, indeed, well disposed to the cause of which Lord Lovat was the unfortunate and unworthy representative; but all regretted that their young King, as they styled him, should repose trust in so bad a character, and in many instances refused to treat with Lovat. And, indeed, the partial success which he attained might be ascribed to the credit of his companion Captain John Murray, a gentleman of good family, whose brother, Murray of Abercairney, was greatly respected in his county.

The embryo of the two Rebellions may be distinctly traced in the plain and modest memorial which Captain Murray also presented, on his return from Scotland, at the Court of St. Germains. "The Earl and Countess of Errol, " he relates, "with their son Lord Hay, were the first to whom I spoke of the affairs of the King of England. " "Speaking at Edinburgh with the King's friends, about his Majesty's affairs, in a more serious way than I had done before, I found that these affairs had not been mentioned among them a long time before, and that it was to them an agreeable surprise to see some hopes that they were to be revived by my negotiation. "

The greatest families in Scotland were, indeed, [176] ready to come forward upon condition of a certain assistance from France; and a scheme seems even to have been suggested for the invasion of England, and to have formed the main feature in one of those various plots which were as often concerted, and as often defeated, in favour of the excluded family. [177]

In France, these continual schemes, and the various changes in the English Government, were regarded with the utmost contempt. "The people, " writes the Duke of Perth, Chancellor of Scotland, "are kept from amusement, frameing conceits of government and religion, such as our giddy people frame to themselves, and make themselves the scorn and reproach of mankind, for all are now foes under the name of English, and we are said to be so changeable and foolish, that nothing from our parts seems strange. Beheading, dethroning, and banishing of kings, being but children's play with us. "[178]

But all the promise of this plan was defeated, as it is generally and confidently asserted, by the character of Lord Lovat. A general distrust prevailed, of his motives and of his authority, even in that very country where he had once led on his clansmen to crimes for which they had paid dearly in the humiliation and devastation of their clan. He was indeed, prevented from lingering near the home of his youth, from the decrees which had been issued against him, and the risk of discovery. Disappointed in his efforts, unable to raise even fifty men of his own clan, and resolved upon gaining influence and favour in some quarter or another, he determined upon betraying the whole scheme, which has since obtained in history the name of the Scottish Plot, to the Duke of Queensbury.

It was on pretext of obtaining a passport for France, that Lord Lovat now sought an interview with the Duke in London. He there discovered to that able and influential minister, then Secretary of State for Scotland, the entire details of the meditated insurrection, together with the names of the principal Scottish nobility concerned in the conspiracy. The Duke, it appears, perfectly appreciated the character of his informant. He seems to have reflected, that from such materials as those which composed the desperate and hardened character of Lovat, the best instruments of party may be selected. He consented, it is generally believed, —although historians differ greatly according to their particular bias, as to the fact, —to furnish Lovat with a passport, and to employ him as a spy in the French Court, in order to prosecute his discoveries still farther.

When Lovat was afterwards charged with this act of treachery, he declared, that he had told the Duke of Queensbury little more than what had escaped through the folly or malice of the Jacobites; but acknowledged that a mutual compact had passed between him and the Duke of Queensbury. [179]

Somerville, in his history of the reign of Queen Anne, remarks, that it is doubtful whether Fraser of Lovat had ever any intention of performing effectual service to the Chevalier. "No sooner had he set foot in England, " adds the same historian, "than he formed the nefarious project of counter-plotting his associate, and betraying the trust which he had procured through the facility and precipitate confidence of the Queen. "[180]

The Duke of Queensbury immediately communicated the plot, disclosed by Lovat, to Queen Anne. In the main points the conduct of that able and influential Minister appears to have been tolerably free from blame during the inquiry into the Scottish plot which was afterwards instituted; but it is a proof of the horror and suspicion in which Lord Lovat was held, that the Duke of Queensbury's negotiations with so abandoned a tool for some time diminished the political sway which he had heretofore possessed in Scotland. [181]

Lord Lovat returned to Paris, where he had the effrontery to hand in a boasting memorial of his services, written with that particularity which gives an air of extreme accuracy to any statement. In this art he was generally accomplished, yet he seems on this occasion to have failed. For some time he flourished; alternately, one day at Versailles—one day at St. Germains; and, whilst an under-current of dislike and suspicion marked his course, all, apparently, went on successfully with this great dissembler. The Earl of Middleton, indeed, was undeceived.

"I doubt not, " he writes to the Marquis De Torcy, "you will be as much surprised at Lord Lovat's memorial as we have been; for although I never had a good opinion of him, yet, I did not believe him fool enough to accuse himself. He has not, in some places, been as careful as authors of romance to preserve probability. "

"If the King thinks proper to apprehend him, " concludes Lord Middleton, "it should be done without noise. His name should not be mentioned any more, and at the same time his papers should be seized. "[182] Such were the preparations for the secret incarceration which it was then the practice of the French Court to sanction.

Lord Lovat was not long in ignorance of the intrigues, as he calls them, which were carried on to blast his reputation at the Court of St. Germains. In other words, he perceived that the double game which he had been playing was discovered, and discovered in time to prevent any new or important trust being committed to his command. He fell ill, or perhaps feigned illness, probably in order to account for his absence from Court; and, although backed by the influence of the Earl of Melfort, brother of the Duke of Perth, and by the Marquis De Torcy, he found that he could never recover the confidence of the Queen Mother.

He took the usual plan adopted by servants who perceive that they are on the eve of being discarded—he announced his determination to retire. "My Lord, " he wrote to Lord Middleton, "I am daily informed, that the Queen has but a scurvy opinion of me, and that I did her Majesty bad rather than good service by my journey. My Lord, I find that my enemies have greater power with the Queen than I can have; and to please them, and ease her Majesty, I am resolved to meddle no more with any affairs till the King is of age."[183]

There seemed to have been little need of this voluntary surrender of his employments; for, after undergoing an examination, in writing from the Pope's Nuncio, and after several letters had passed between Lord Middleton and himself, the altercation was peremptorily closed by a *lettre de cachet,* and Lord Lovat was committed, according to some statements, to the Bastille, —as others relate, to the Castle of Angoulême. [184] Upon this occasion the hardihood of Lord Lovat's character, which shone out so conspicuously at his death, was thus exemplified.

"As they went along the Captain (by this name he was generally called among his friends) discoursed the officer with the same freedom as if he had been carrying him to some merry-meeting; and, on observing on his men's coats a badge all full of points, with this device—*monstrorum terror,* —'the terror of monsters, ' he said wittily, pointing to the men, 'Behold there the terror, and here the monster! ' meaning himself. 'And if either of the Kings had a hundred thousand of such, they would be fitter to fright their enemies than to hurt any one of them. ' He took occasion, also, to let his attendants know of what a great and noble family he was, and how much blood had been spent in the cause of the Monarchs by his ancestors. "[185]

According to Lord Lovat's manifesto, he was at dinner at Bourges, whither he had been sent on some pretext by the French Government, when "a grand fat prev't, accompanied by his lieutenant and twenty-four archers, stole into the drawing-room, and seized Lord Lovat as if he had been an assassin, demanding from him his sword in the King's name. The villain of a prev't, " adds his Lordship, "was so obliging as to attend Lord Lovat, with his archers, all the way to Angoulême. He had the luck to procure a cursed little chaise, where Lord Lovat was in a manner buried alive under the unwieldy bulk of this enormous porpoise. " This relation, so different from that given by Mr. Arbuthnot, weakens the veracity of both accounts, and leads one to infer that the long narrative by the reverend gentleman of Lord Lovat's adventures in the Bastille were written upon hearsay. [186]

In the Castle of Angoulême Lord Lovat continued for three years; at first, being treated with great severity: "thirty-five days in perfect darkness, where every moment he expected death, and prepared to meet it with becoming fortitude. He listened with eagerness and anxiety to every noise, and, when his door screached upon its hinges, he believed that it was the executioner come to put an end to his unfortunate days. "

In this predicament, finding that the last punishment was delayed, he "thought proper to address himself to a grim jailoress, who came every day to throw him something to eat, in the same silent and cautious manner in which you would feed a mad dog. "[187] By the "clink of a louis d'or, " the prisoner managed to subdue the fidelity of this fair jailoress; she supplied him with pens and paper, and he immediately began a correspondence with his absent friends at the French Court.

After a time, the severity of Lord Lovat's imprisonment was mitigated. The Castle of Angoulême was, in a manner, an open prison, having an extensive park within its walls, with walks open to the inhabitants; and here, through the influence of Monsieur De Torcy, Lord Lovat was permitted to take exercise. His insinuating manners won upon the inhabitants, and the prison of Angoulême became so agreeable to him, that he was often heard to say, that "if there was a beautiful and enchanting prison in the world, it was the Castle of Angoulême. "

Meantime, the scheme of invasion was by no means relinquished on the part of the Jacobites, although it had received a considerable check from the treachery of its agents.

It is stated by some historians that scarcely had Lord Lovat quitted England, than Sir John Maclean, his cousin-german, and Campbell, of Glendarnel, disclosed the plot to Lord Athole and Lord Tarbat. These noblemen instantly went to Queen Anne, and accused the Duke of Queensbury of high treason, in carrying on a villanous plot with the Court of St. Germains. Queensbury defended himself before the House of Lords, and the accusation, which rested chiefly on the assertions of Ferguson, the famous hatcher of plots, was declared false and scandalous, and Ferguson was committed to Newgate. The reluctance of the Duke of Queensbury to give up the correspondence, excited, however, suspicions of his integrity; which, as Harley, Lord Oxford, expressed it, could only be cleared up by Fraser, Lord Lovat; [188] but Lord Lovat was not then to be found.

In all this singular and complicated affair, it is impossible to help wondering at the folly and audacity which Lord Lovat had shown in returning to France, conscious of having placed himself at the mercy of ruthless politicians, and aware that in that country he could expect no redress nor protection from law. But the original crime for which he had been sent forth, an outlaw from his country, was the source of all his subsequent mistakes and misfortunes. France was open to him; Scotland was closed; and England was a scene of peril to one who trod on fragile ice, beneath which a deep gulf yawned.

Lord Lovat had been two years in prison before any of his former friends, for even he was not wholly devoid of partisans, interfered with success in his behalf; and it was the good, old-fashioned feeling of kindred that finally moved the Marquis De Frezelière, or Frezel, or Frezeau de la Frezelière, to interest himself in the fate of his despised, and perhaps forgotten, relative.

"The house of Frezelière, which ascends, " says Lord Lovat, "in an uninterrupted line, and without any unequal alliance, to the year 1030, with its sixty-four quarterings in its armorial bearings, and all noble, its titles of seven hundred years standing in the Abbey of N'tre Dame de Noyers in Touraine, and its many other circumstances of inherent dignity, " was, as we have seen, derived from the same blood with the family of Frezel, or Fraser. In former, and more prosperous days, a common and authentic Act of Recognition of this relationship had been drawn up at Paris by the Marquis and his many illustrious kinsmen, the three sons of the Marshal Luxembourg de Montmorenci; and executed, on the other hand, by Simon Fraser, Lord Lovat, and by his brother, and several of their nearest kin.

The Marquis De Frezelière appears to have been a fine specimen of that proud and valiant aristocracy, not even then wholly broken down in France by the effeminacy of the times. He was haughty and determined, "an eagle in the concerns of war, " and of a spirit not to be subdued. By his powerful intercession, checked only by the disgust which Mary of Modena felt towards Lovat, he procured from the King of France permission for his relative to repair to the waters of Bourbon for the restoration of his health. This order was signed by Louis the Fourteenth, and countersigned by the Marquis De Torcy, as "Colbert. " Four days afterwards, a second order was received by the authorities at Angoulême, by which his Majesty commanded that Lord Lovat, after the restoration of his health, should repair to his town of Saumur, until further orders. "At the same time, " says Lord Lovat, "he was permitted to take with him the Chevalier De Frezel, his brother. " These orders were dated August the second and August the fourteenth, 1707.

The brother, whom Lord Lovat always designates as the Chevalier de Fraser, had been placed with a Doctor of the Civil Law at Bourges, in order to learn French, and the profession of a civilian. He had been arrested at the same time with Lord Lovat; and was now, after a temporary separation, permitted to share the pleasures of a removal to Bourbon. According to Lord Lovat, a pension from the French Government was settled upon this young man as long as he resided in France; and Lord Lovat received also the ample income of four thousand francs, (one hundred and sixty-six pounds, thirteen shillings and fourpence,) from the same quarter: nor was it in the power of his enemies at St. Germains to induce Louis the Fourteenth to withdraw this allowance. [189]

The Marquis de Frezelière continued firm in his regard towards Lord Lovat. On his road to Saumur, Lord Lovat was received and entertained at the château of the Marquis with hospitality and kindness, and no opportunity was omitted by which the Marquis could testify the sincerity of his interest in the fate of his relative. Meantime daily reports were circulated that the projected insurrection, far from being abandoned, had been revived, and that the Chevalier was going to undertake the conduct of the invasion in person. But that young Prince was still inexorable to any petition in favour of Lovat, and was wisely resolved not to let him participate in the operations. "Were he not already in prison, " he is stated by Lovat himself to have said, "I would make it my first request to the King of France to throw him into one. " This fixed aversion was owing to the determined dislike of the Queen to abdicate, as it was her resolution, if there were no other person to be employed, never to make Lord Lovat an instrument of her affairs.

Lovat, therefore, now clearly perceived that, during the life of the Queen and of Lord Middleton, he must look for nothing favourable from the Court of St. Germains. That of Versailles, although, by his account, decidedly friendly to his release, refused to support those whom the Chevalier had renounced. He resolved, therefore, to make every exertion to return to his own country, and to place himself once more at the head of his clan, who, in spite of his crimes, in spite of his long absence and imprisonment, had still refused to acknowledge any other chief. The attempt was indeed desperate, but Lovat resolved to risk it, and to escape, at all events, from France.

To the vengeance of the Athole family, Lord Lovat always imputed much of the severity shown him by the Court at St. Germains: and it is probable that the representations of that powerful house may have contributed to the odium in which the character of Lord Lovat was universally held. His own deeds were, however, sufficient to ensure him universal hatred. The great source of surprise is, that this unscrupulous intriguer, this unprincipled member of society, seems, at times, during the course of his eventful life, to have met with friends, firm in their faith to him, and to have enjoyed, in that respect, the privilege of virtue.

The young heiress of Lovat, Amelia Fraser, was now married to Alexander Mackenzie, son of Lord Prestonhall; Mr. Mackenzie had adopted the title of Fraserdale; and a son had been born of this marriage, who had been named after his grandfather, Hugh. Fraserdale and his lady had taken possession both of the title and estates of Lord Lovat, during his absence; but, since the dignity and estates had always been enjoyed by an heir-male, from the origin of the house of Fraser, these claimants to the estate of the outlawed Lovat spread a report that the honours and lands had, in old times, belonged to the Bissets, whose daughter and only child had married a Fraser, from whom the estates had descended to the heir of that line. A suit was instituted against Lord Lovat and, on the ninth of March, 1703, Lord Prestonhall, the father of Fraserdale, himself adjudged the Lordship and Barony of Lovat to Amelia Fraser. An entail of the estates and honours upon the heirs of the marriage between Amelia Fraser and Mackenzie of Fraserdale, was then executed, and the former assumed the title of Lady Lovat, whilst her son was designated the Master of Lovat. [190]

Lord Prestonhall seems to have acted with the same unscrupulous spirit which characterizes most of the business transactions of those who intermeddled with the forfeited or disputed estates. It was his aim, as the Memorial for the Lovat case, subsequently tried, sets forth, to extirpate the clan of the Frasers, and to raise that of the Mackenzies upon its ruins. "Accordingly, " says Mr. Anderson, in his curious and elaborate account of the house of Fraser, "he framed a deed, with the sly contrivance of sinking the Frasers into the Mackenzies, by encouraging the former to change their names, and providing, as a condition of the estate, that should they return to, and reassume their ancient name of Fraser, they should forfeit their right. "[191]

The arms of Mackenzie, Macleod of Lewis, and Bisset, were to be quartered with those of Fraser, in this deed, which bore the signature of Robert Mackenzie, and was dated the twenty-third of February, 1706.

This decision, and the deed which followed it, appeared to complete the misfortunes of the disgraced and banished Lord Lovat. But, in fact, the act of injustice and rapacity, so repugnant to the spirit of the Highlanders, —this attempt to force upon the heirs of Fraser a foreign name, and thus to lower the dignity of the clan, was the most auspicious event that could happen to the wretched outlaw. What was his exact condition, or what were his circumstances, during the seven years of his imprisonment, three of which were passed under strict, though not harsh control, in the Castle of Angoulême, and four, apparently on his parole, in the Fortress of Saumur, it is not easy to describe. The cause of the obscurity of his fate at this time, is not that too little, but that too much, has been stated relative to his movements.

It is always an inconvenience when one cannot take a man's own story in evidence. According to Lord Lovat's own account, these weary years were spent in visits to different members of the nobility. The charming Countess de la Roche succeeded the Marquis de la Frezelière as his friend and patroness, after the death of the Marquis in 1711, an event which, according to Lord Lovat's statement, brought him nearly to the grave from grief. The Countess was a woman of a masculine understanding, and of admirable talents, bold, insinuating, and ambitious. Her education in the household of the great Condé, and her long attendance upon the Princess de Conti, the hero's daughter, had qualified her for those arduous and delicate intrigues, without which no woman of intellect at that period in France might think herself sufficiently distinguished.

The appointment of the Duke of Hamilton as ambassador at the Court of Louis, rendered such a friend as Madame de la Roche, who was also distantly related to him, very essential for the prosecution of Lord Lovat's present schemes, which were, to obtain his release, and to procure employment in any enterprise concerted by the Jacobites against England.

Fate, however, relieved Lord Lovat from one apprehension. The Duke of Hamilton was killed in a duel by Lord Mohun, in Hyde Park; and this fresh source of danger was thus annihilated. The kindness which the famous Colbert, Marquis de Torcy, had shown to Lord Lovat, and the promise which he had given to that nobleman, not to break his parole, and to return to England, seems to have been the only check to a long-cherished project on the part of Lord Lovat to escape to London, and to risk all that law might there inflict. It is uncertain in what manner, during the tedious interval between intrigues and intrigues, he solaced his leisure. It has been stated by one of his biographers that he actually joined a society of Jesuits, — by another, that he took priest's orders, and acted as parochial priest at St. Omers. Of course, in compiling a defence of his life, the wary man of the world omitted such particulars as would, at any rate, betray inconsistency, and beget suspicion. His object in becoming a Jesuit, is said to have been to hear confessions and to discover intrigues. With respect to the report of his having entered the order of Jesuits, it is justly alleged in answer, that no Jesuit is permitted to hear confessions until he has been fifteen years a member of the society, or, at least, in priest's orders. [192]

The rumour of his having become an ecclesiastic, in any way, no doubt originated in Lord Lovat's joke on a subsequent occasion, when "he declared that had he wished it, and had remained in priest's orders, which he did not deny having assumed for some purpose, he might have become Pope in time. "[193]

Whilst Lord Lovat, contrary to the advice of Madame la Roche, was deliberating whether he should not leave France, he was surprised, in the summer of 1714, by a visit from one of the principal gentlemen of his clan, Fraser of Castle Lader, son of Malcolm Fraser, of Culdelthel, a very considerable branch of the family of Lovat. This gentleman brought Lord Lovat a strong remonstrance from all his clan at his absence—an entreaty to him to return—a recommendation that he would join himself in an alliance with the Duke of Argyle, who was disposed to aid him; he added affectionate greetings from some of the principal gentry of his neighbourhood, and, among others, from John Forbes, of Culloden. This important ally was the father of the justly celebrated Duncan Forbes, afterwards Lord President. These messages decided Lord Lovat. After some indecision he left Saumur, and being allowed by his parole to travel to any place in France, he went on the twelfth of August, 1714, to Rouen, under pretence of paying a visit there. From Rouen he proceeded to Dieppe, but finding no vessel there, he travelled along the coast of Normandy, and from thence to

Boulogne. From that port he sailed in a small smack, in a rough sea, during the night, and landed at Dover, November the eleventh, 1714.

He met his kinsman, Alexander Fraser, on the quay at Dover, and with him proceeded to London. His former friend, the Duke of Argyle, was now dead; but alliances, as well as antipathies, are hereditary in Scotland, and John, Duke of Argyle, was well disposed to assist one whose family had been anciently connected with his own. Besides, the state of public affairs was now totally changed since Lord Lovat had left England, and it was incumbent upon the Government to avail themselves of any tool which they might require for certain ends and undertakings.

Queen Anne was now dead, —the last of the Stuart dynasty in this kingdom. Whatever were her failings and her weaknesses as a woman, she has left behind her the character of having loved her people; and she was endeared to them by her purely English birth, her homely virtue of economy, and her domestic unpretending qualities. Her reign had been one of mercy; no subject had suffered for treason during her rule: she had few relations with foreign powers; and when, in her opening speech to the Parliament, she expressed that her heart was "wholly English, " she spoke her real sentiments, and described, in that simple touch the true character of her mind.

She was succeeded by a German Prince, who immediately showered marks of his royal favour upon the Whigs; whilst the Tories, who formed so large a party in the kingdom, were alienated from the Government by the manifest aversion to them which George the First rather aimed to evince than laboured to conceal.

The Jacobites differed in some measure from the Tories, inasmuch as the latter were generally well affected to the accession of the Hanoverian family, until disgusted by the choice of the new administration. Dissensions quickly rose to their height; and when the Government was attacked in the House of Commons by Sir William Wyndham, the unusual sounds, "the Tower! the Tower! " were heard once more amid the inflamed assembly.

The spirit of disaffection quickly spread throughout England; the very life-guards were compelled by an angry populace, when celebrating the anniversary of the Restoration of the Stuarts, to join in the cry of "High Church and Ormond! " Lord Bolingbroke had withdrawn to France—treasonable papers were discovered and intercepted on their way from Jacobite emissaries to Dr. Swift, tumults were raised in the city of London and in Westminster, and were punished with a severity to which the metropolis had been unaccustomed since the reign of James the Second. All these manifestations had their origin in one common source, —the deeply concerted schemes which were now nearly brought into maturity at the Court of St. Germains.

The following extract of a letter dated from Luneville, and taken from the Macpherson Papers, shows what was meditated abroad; it is in Schrader's hand.

(Translation.)

"Luneville, June 5th, 1714.

"It is likely the Chevalier St. George is preparing for some great design, which is kept very private. It was believed he would drink the waters of Plombière for three weeks, as is customary, and that he would come afterwards to pass fifteen days at Luneville; but he changed his measures; he did not continue to drink the waters, which he drank only for ten days, and came back to Luneville on Saturday last. He sets out to-morrow very early for Bar. Lord Galmoy went before him, and set out this morning. Lord Talmo, who came lately from France, is with him, and some say that the Duke of Berwick is incognito in this neighbourhood.

"The Chevalier appears pensive, —that, indeed, is his ordinary humour. Mr. Floyd, who has been these five days at the Court of his Royal Highness, told a mistress he has there, that when he leaves her now, he will take his leave of her perhaps for the last time: —in short, it is certain that everything here seems sufficiently to announce preparations for a journey. It is said, likewise, in private, that the Chevalier has had letters that the Queen is very ill. I have done everything I could to discover something of his designs. I supped last night with several of his attendants, thinking to learn something; but they avoid to explain themselves. They only say that the Chevalier did not find himself the better for drinking the waters; that he would now go to repose himself for some time at Bar, until he goes, the beginning of next month, to the Prince De Vandemont's, at Commercie, where their Royal Highnesses will come likewise. They say they do not know yet if they will remain in this country or not; that they will follow the destiny of the Chevalier, and that it is not known yet what it shall be. "[194]

When Lord Lovat thus precipitately threw himself once more on the mercy of his country, he could not have been ignorant that the cabals which had long been carried on against the Hanoverian succession, were now shortly to break out in open rebellion; and it was, without doubt, in the hope of profiting in some measure during the confusion of the coming troubles, that he had hastened, at the risk of his life, to England.

He entrusted the secret of his arrival immediately to the Duke of Argyle, whom he met in London. That nobleman, one of the few disinterested men whose virtues might almost obtain the name of patriotism in those days, saw the danger which Lord Lovat would incur if he returned to Scotland. Sentence of death had been passed upon him; it might be acted upon by an adverse judge at any moment. He besought Lovat to remain in England until a remission of that sentence could be obtained; and for this purpose addresses to the Court for mercy were circulated for signature throughout the northern counties of Scotland. [195] To further the success of this scheme, Lord Lovat had recourse to his neighbour and early friend, John Forbes, laird of Culloden, whose after-services in the royal cause, and whose strict alliance of friendship with the Duke of Argyle, secured to him a considerable influence in that part of Scotland in which he resided.

"Much honoured and dear Sir, "—thus wrote Lord Lovat to the Laird, —"The real friendship that I know you have for my person and family makes me take the freedom to assure you of my kind service, and to entreat you to join with my other friends between Sky and Nesse, to sign the addresse which the Court requires, in order to give me my remission. Your cousin James, who has generously exposed himself to bring me out of chains, will inform you of all steps and circumstances of my affairs since he saw me. I wish, dear Sir, from my heart, you were here; I am confident you would speak to the Duke of Argyle and to the Earl of Isla, to let them know their own interest, and their reiterated promises to do for me. Perhaps they may have, sooner than they expect, a most serious occasion for my service. But it is needless to preach now that doctrine to them; they think themselves in ane infallible security; I wish they may not be mistaken. However, I think it's the interest of all who love this Government, betwixt Sky and Nesse, to see me at the head of my clan, ready to join them; so that I believe none of them will refuse to sign ane adresse to make me a Scotsman. I am perswaded, dear Sir, that you will be of good example to them on that head. But secrecy, above all, must be keept; without which all may go wrong. I hope you will be stirring for the Parliament, for I will not be reconciled to you if you let Prestonall outvote you. Brigadier Grant, to whom I am infinitely obliged, has written to Foyers to give you his vote, and he is ane ungrat villian if he refuses him. [If] I was at home, the little pitiful barons of the Aird durst not refuse you. But I am hopefull that the news of my going to Brittain will hinder Prestonall to go north; for I may come to meet him when he lest thinks of me. I am very impatient to see you, and to assure you most sincerely how much I am, with love and respect, Right Honourable, your most obedient and most humble servant,

"LOVAT. "

"The 24th of Nov. 1714. "

The nature of the address to which this letter refers was not only an appeal to the King in behalf of Lord Lovat, but also an engagement, on the part of his friends, to answer for the loyalty of Lord Lovat, in any sum required. It is remarkable that when James Fraser, the kinsman of Lovat, arrived in the county of Inverness, and declared the purpose of his journey, the lairds who were well-affected to the nobility, joined in giving their subscriptions; and the Earl of Sutherland, the Lord Strathallan, and the nobility of the counties of Ross and Sutherland, signed them also. The Duke of Montrose, however, boldly opposed them, and described Lord Lovat as a man unworthy of the King's confidence. [196]

A year, however, had elapsed, whilst Lovat was hanging about the Court, before the address was brought to London by Lord Isla, brother of the Duke of Argyle, and afterwards Archibald, Duke of Argyle. The address was presented on Sunday, the twenty-fourth of July, 1715. "The Earl of Orkney, " says Lord Lovat, "who was the lord in waiting, held out his hand to receive them from the King, according to custom. The King, however, drew them back, folded them up, and, as if he had been pre-advised of their contents, put them into his pocket. "[197] And with this sentence, denoting that the crisis of his affairs was at hand, end the memoirs which Lord Lovat either wrote or dictated to others, of the early portion of his life.

Meantime, the Earl of Stair, the English ambassador at Paris, had discovered the embryo scheme of invasion, and had communicated it to the British Court, although, unhappily for both parties, not in sufficient time to damp the hopes of the unfortunate Jacobites. On the sixth of September, 1715, the Earl of Mar set up his standard at Braemar. Consistent with the usual fatality attending every attempt of the Stuarts, this event was preceded only five days by the death of Louis the Fourteenth—the only real friend of the excluded family; but the Jacobites had now proceeded too far to recede. [198]

Lord Lovat resolved, however, to profit in the general disasters. His influence among his clansmen was obvious: whether for good or, in some instances, for evil, there is much to admire in the resolute adherence of those faithful mountaineers, who had resisted the assumption of a stranger, and invited back to their hills the long-absent and ruined chief, whom they regarded as their own.

Lord Lovat now found means to represent to the English Government, that if he could have a passport to go into the Highlands, he might be instrumental in quelling the rebellion. The Ministry, in their perplexities, availed themselves of his aid, and a pass was granted to him, under the name of Captain Brown.

He once more set out for his own country, and reached Edinburgh in safety, attended only by his kinsman, Major Fraser. From Edinburgh he resolved to proceed in a ship—when he could procure one, for the country was all in commotion. Meantime he took up his abode, still maintaining his disguise, in the Grass Market.

His real name was soon discovered, and information was given to the Lord Justice Clerk, who granted a warrant for his apprehension, as a person "outlawed and intercommuned; " and to prevent any difficulty in apprehending the prisoner, a party of the town guard was ordered to escort the peace officers to the lodgings of Lord Lovat.

The officer who had the command of the town guard happened, however, to be acquainted with Lovat, and he interposed his aid on this occasion. He listened to the account which Lovat gave of the business which had brought him to Edinburgh. The Provost was next gained over to the opinion, that it would be wrong to oppose any obstruction to one who had his Majesty's passport: he ordered Lord Lovat to be set at liberty; and in order to give some colour of justice to this act, he declared that the information must have been wrong, it being laid against Captain Fraser, —whereas, the person taken appeared to be Captain Brown.

Lovat was once more in safety: he changed his lodgings, however; and, as soon as possible, set sail for Inverness. Again danger, in another form, retarded his arrival among his clan. A storm arose, the ship was obliged to put into the nearest harbour, and Lord Lovat was driven into Fraserburgh, which happened to be within a few miles of the abode of his old enemy and rival Lord Saltoun.

Mr. Forbes, one of the Culloden family, was now fortunately for Lord Lovat, with him on his Majesty's service. After some consultation together, he and Lovat decided to make themselves known to Mr. Baillie, town-clerk of Fraserburgh: they did so, were kindly received, and provided with horses to convey them to Culloden House, the seat of the future Lord President of Scotland, Duncan Forbes. Here they arrived in November, after incurring great risks from the Jacobite troops, who were patroling in parties over the country. [199]

Culloden House, famed in history, was inhabited by a race whose views, conduct, and personal character present a singular contrast, with those of Lord Lovat, or with those of other adventurers in political life. The head of the family was, at the period of the first insurrection, John Forbes, a worthy representative of an honourable, consistent, and spirited family. The younger brother of John Forbes was the celebrated Duncan Forbes, a man whose toleration of Lord Lovat, not to say countenance of that compound of violence and duplicity, seems to be the only incomprehensible portion of his lofty and beautiful character.

"Duncan Forbes was born, " observes a modern writer, "of parents who transmitted their estate to his elder brother, and to all their children an hereditary aversion to the house of Stuart, which they appear to have resisted from the very commencement of the civil wars, and upon the true grounds on which that resistance ought to have been made. "[200] By a singular fortune the hereditary estates of Culloden and Ferintosh had been ravaged, the year after the Revolution, by the soldiers of Buchan and Cannon, on account of the Jacobite principles of the owners. A liberal compensation was made in the form of a perpetual grant of a liberty to distil into spirits the grain of the Barony of Ferintosh, —a name which has become almost as famous as that of Culloden. It was the subsequent fate of Culloden to witness on its Moors the total destruction of that cause which its owners had so long resisted and deprecated.

Duncan Forbes, who, during a course of many years, was bound by an inexplicable alliance with Lovat, was at this period about thirty years of age. He had already attained the highest reputation for eloquence, assiduity, and learning at the Scottish bar, and during his frequent opportunities for display before the House of Lords. But it was his personal character, during a period of vacillating principles, and almost of disturbed national reason, which obtained that singular and benignant influence over his fellow-countrymen for which the life of Duncan Forbes is far more remarkable, far more admirable, than for the exercise of his brilliant and varied talents. He had "raised himself, " observes the same discriminating commentator on his life and correspondence, "to the high station which he afterwards held by the unassisted excellence of a noble character, by the force of which he had previously won and adorned all the subordinate gradations of office. "[201] He adorned this unenvied and unsullied pinnacle of fame by virtues of which the record is ennobling to the mind. "He is, " observes another writer, "in every situation, so full of honour, of gentleness, of kindness, and intrepidity, that we doubt if there be any one public man in this part of the empire, or of the age that is gone, whose qualities ought to be so strongly recommended to the contemplation of all those who wish to serve their country. "

It was in such society as this that Lord Lovat, by a rare fortune, was brought, after his long and disgraceful exile. It was to such a home of virtue, of intelligence, of the purest and best affections, that he was introduced after a long course of contamination in the lowest scenes of French corruption, which had succeeded an equally demoralising initiation into the less graceful vices of the Court of George the First. The inestimable privilege came too late in one sense. Lord Lovat had gained nothing but wariness by the lapse of years; but the benefit to his worldly condition was considerable.

From this time until a few years before the insurrection of 1745, Lord Lovat may be regarded as a jealous partisan of the house of Hanover. No doubt, a general survey of the state of society in Scotland would, independent of his own personal views, have satisfied him that in such a course was the only chance of permanent safety. The wretchedness of the state of things at that period, can scarcely be adequately comprehended by those who live in times when liberty of opinion is universally an understood condition of civilized intercourse.

It is difficult for any person who lives now to carry himself back, by reading or conversation, into the prospects or feelings of the people of Scotland about a hundred years ago. The religious persecutions of the Stuarts had given a darker hue to the old austerity of their Calvinism. The expectation of change constantly held out by that family divided the nation into two parties, differing on a point which necessarily made each of them rebels in the eyes of the other; and thus the whole kingdom was racked by jealousies, heart-burnings, and suspicions. The removal, by the Union, of all the patronage and show of royalty, spread a gloom and discontent, not only over the lower, but over the higher ranks. The commencement of a strict system of general taxation was new, while the miserable poverty of the country rendered it unproductive and unpopular. The great families still lorded it over their dependants, and exercised legal jurisdiction within their own domains; by which the general police of the kingdom was crippled, and the grossest legal oppression practised. The remedy adopted for all these evils, which was to abate nothing and to enforce everything under the direction of English counsels or of English men, completed the national wretchedness, and infused its bitterest ingredient into the brim full cup.

The events of the year 1715 present but a feeble exemplification of the truth of this description compared with the annals of 1745, for the first Rebellion was, happily, soon closed.

Lord Lovat did not hesitate long on which side he should enlist himself; and the intelligence that his rival, Mackenzie of Fraserdale, had taken up arms in favour of the Chevalier, decided his course. [202] On the fifth of November he assembled all those of his clan who were still faithful to him, and who had been warned of his approach by his friends. He was received among them with exclamations of joy; and, hearing that a body of Mackintoshes, a Jacobite clan, were marching to reinforce Sir John Mackenzie, who commanded the castle at Inverness, he marched forward with his adherents to intercept them, and to prevent their joining what he then called "the rebel garrison. "

The citadel of Inverness, built in 1657 by Oliver Cromwell, and called Oliver's Fort, stood on the east bank of the river Ness, and was a regular pentagon, with bastions, ramparts, and a moat; the standard of the Protectorate, with the word "Emmanuel" inscribed upon it, had formerly been displayed upon its ramparts. It was calculated to hold two thousand men, and was washed on one side by the river. As a fortress it had many inconveniencies; approaches to it were easy, and the town afforded a quarter for an enemy's army. In 1662 it had been partly dismantled by Charles the Second, because it was the relic of usurpation, and constituted a check upon the adjacent Highlanders, who were then considered loyal. [203] It is said by one who saw it after the Restoration to have been a very superb work, and it was one of the regular places for the deposition of arms at the time of the Rebellion of 1715. Subsequently it was much augmented and enlarged, and bore, until its destruction after the battle of Culloden, the name of Fort George, an appellation now transferred to its modern successor on the promontory of Ardesseil.

It was against this important fortress that Lord Lovat now marched with as much zeal and intrepidity as if he had been fighting in the cause of that family for whom his ancestors had suffered. He proceeded straight to Inverness, and placing himself on the west side of the town despatched a party of troops to prevent any supply of arms or provisions from approaching the castle by the Firth. Forbes of Culloden lay to the east, and the Grants, to the number of eight hundred, to the south side of the town. Sir John Mackenzie finding himself thus invested on all sides, took advantage of a spring tide that came up to the town and made the river navigable, to escape with all his troops; and Lord Lovat immediately gained possession of the citadel. The fame of this inglorious triumph has, however, been divided between Lovat and Hugh Rose of Kilravock, [204] whose brother, in pursuing the Jacobite guard to the Tolbooth, was shot through the body. But whoever really deserved the laurel, Lord Lovat profited largely by his dishonest exertions in a cause which he began life by disliking, and ended by abjuring.

On the thirteenth of November Lord Lovat was joined by the Earl of Sutherland; and, leaving a garrison in Inverness, the two noblemen marched into the territory of the Earl of Seaforth, where they intimidated the natives into submission. Lord Lovat also despatched a friend to Perth, where the main portion of the Jacobite army lay, to claim the submission of his clansmen, who were led by his rival, Mackenzie of Fraserdale. They complied with his summons to the number of four hundred, and Lovat, after entering Murray and Strathspey, and exacting obedience to the King's troops in these districts, prepared to attack Lord Seaforth, who was threatening to invest Inverness. But Duncan Forbes, who was then serving with the army, restrained the ardour of his neighbour, and hostilities were terminated in the North without further bloodshed. [205]

Lord Lovat was quickly repaid for his exertions. From George the First he received three letters of thanks, and an invitation to go to Court; and in March, 1716, a remission of the sentence of death which had been passed upon him, received the royal signature. He was appointed governor of Inverness, with a free company of Highlanders. What, perhaps, still more gratified his natural thirst for vengeance was the fate of his rival, the husband of Amelia Lovat, Mackenzie of Fraserdale, who was attainted of high treason, and whose life-interest in the lands and barony of Lovat were forfeited and escheated to the Crown. To complete the good fortune of Lovat, the King was graciously pleased, in June, 1716, to make him a present of the forfeited lands; and Lovat immediately took possession of the estate, and entered his claim to the honours and dignities which were appended to the lands. [206] It was now that he added another motto to the arms of the Frasers, and struck out the quarterings of the Bisset family, which had been made a plea for his adversary. The ancient Frasers, or Frizells, had for their motto "*Je suis prest,* " to which this honour to their house now added the words, "*Sine sanguine victor,* " denoting that he had come peaceably to the estate. [207]

He was now the undisputed Lord Lovat; hitherto he had borne, generally, the convenient name of Captain Fraser, given to him in his military capacity; and it appears, in spite of all his boastings, that he had scarcely been called by any other title at the French Court than that of Fraser of Beaufort. He had now an admirable opportunity of obliterating the remembrance of his past life, and of conciliating good opinion by the consistency and regulation of his present conduct. Notwithstanding his crimes his clansmen turned towards him gladly; his neighbours were willing to assist him in the support of his honours, and he enjoyed what he had never before experienced, the confidence of his Sovereign.

Lord Lovat began his season of prosperity by litigations, which lasted between twelve and fourteen years. His first aim was to set aside the pretensions of Hugh Fraser, the son of Mackenzie of Fraserdale, who claimed the title of Lord Lovat after his father's death; and also, by virtue of settlements, asserted rights to the estate.

The contest was finally decided by the House of Lords in favour of Lord Lovat's enjoying the honours and lands during his life, the fee remaining with Fraserdale, who died in 1755.

Vexatious and expensive suits occupied the period between 1715 and 1732, when they were brought to a final conclusion.

Lovat now assumed a state corresponding to his station, and suitable to the turn of his mind for display. Not only the lands, heritages, tenements, annual rents, &c., of the unfortunate Mackenzie of Fraserdale were bestowed on him for his services in suppressing what in the deed of gift was termed "the late unnatural rebellion in the north of Scotland; " but also the "goods, jewels, gear, utensils and *domecills*, horses, sheep, cattle, corn, " and, in short, whatsoever had belonged to the Mackenzies, together with five hundred pounds of money, which had fallen into the King's hands. It was, indeed, some time before all this could be accomplished, as the correspondence between Lord Lovat and his friend Duncan Forbes sufficiently shows.

"Inverness, the 5th March, 1716.

"My Dearest General, [208]

"I send you the inclosed letter from the name of Macleod, which I hope you will make good use of; for it's most certain, I keep'd the M'Leods at home, which was considerable service done to the Government. The Earle went off from Cullodin to Cromarty last night; and tho' he got a kind letter from Marlbrugh, congratulating him on his glorious actions, yet he was obliged to own to General Wightman, that his Lordship would have got nothing done in the North without my dear General and me. I wish he may do us the same justice at Court: if not, I am sure, if I live, I will inform the King in person of all that passed here since the Rebellion. The Earle's creatures openly speak of the Duke of Argyle's being recalled. I could not bear it. You know my too great vivacity on that head. I was really sick with it, and could not sleep well since. I expect impatiently a letter from you to determinal my going to London, or my stay here, where I am very well with General Wightman, but always much mortified to see myself the servant of all, without a post or character. I go to-morrow to Castle Grant to take my leave of my dear Alister Dow. Your brother is to follow and to go with Alister to London this week. I find the Duke was gone before you could be at London. I hope, my dear General, you will take a start to London to serve his Grace, and do something for your poor old corporal; and, if you suffer Glengarry, Frazerdale, or the Chisholm, to be pardoned, I will never carry a musquet any more under your command, though I should be obliged to go to Affrick. However, you know how obedient I am to my General's orders. You forgot to give the order, signed by you and the other depicts, to meddle with Frazerdale's estate for the King's service. I intreat you send it me, for —— is afraid to meddle without authority. Adieu, mon aimable General; vous savez que je vous aime tendrement; et que je suis mille fois plus à vous qu'à moy-même pour la vie.

"LOVAT. "

In another letter, he observes—"The King has been pleased, this very day, to give me a gift of all Fraserdale's escheat. " Still, however, one thing was wanting; the rapacious Lovat had not obtained his former enemy's plate; General Wightman had taken possession of it as from the person with whom it was deposited; and he was celebrated for his unwillingness to part with what he had gained. At last, however, the greediness of Lovat was appeased if not satisfied by a present from General Cadogan of the plate which he had taken, belonging to Fraserdale; and by a compromise with General Wightman, Lovat paying the General one-half of the value of the plate which was worth only one hundred and fifty pounds. Thus were the remains of the unhappy Jacobites parcelled out among these military plunderers.

During this year, the avocations of Lord Lovat's turbulent leisure were pleasingly varied by the cares of a love suit. The young lady who was persuaded to link her fate to his, was Margaret, the fourth daughter of Ludovick Grant, of Grant; she is said to have been young and beautiful. But several obstacles retarded for awhile her union with Lord Lovat. In the first place, he was not wholly unmarried to the Dowager of Lovat, who was still alive. The family of Athole had, it is true, annulled that marriage, yet there were still legal doubts and difficulties in the way of a fresh bond. Lord Lovat was now, however, according to his own report to his "dearest General" at Culloden, in high favour with King George and the Prince of Wales; and to them he broached the subject of his marriage.

"I had a private audience of King George this day; and I can tell you, dear General, that no man ever spoke freer language to his Majesty or to the Prince than I did. " "They still behave to me like kind brothers; and I spoke to them both of my marriage, they approve of it mightily, and my Lord Islay brother of the Duke [of Argyle], is to make the proposition to the King; and, so that I believe it will do, with that agreement that my two great friends wish and desire it. "[209]

He could, however, do nothing except in a sinister manner; nor was there ever one motive which sprang from a right source. Again he thus addresses Duncan Forbes: —

"I spoke to the Duke and my Lord Islay about my marriage, and told them that one of my greatest motifs to that design, was to secure them the joint interest of the North. " This must have been a pleasing consideration for the young lady, but that which follows is scarcely less promising and agreeable.

"They [the Duke and Lord Islay] are both to speak of it to the King; but Islay desired me to write to you, to know if there would be any fear of a poursuit of adherence from that other person [the Dowager Lady Lovat], which is a chimirical business, and tender fear for me in my dear Islay. But when I told him that the lady denyed, before the Justice Court, that I had anything to do with her, and that the pretended marriage is declared nul (which Islay says should be done by the Commissarys only), yet, when I told him that the witnesses were all dead who were at the pretended marriage, he was satisfyed that they could make nothing of it, though they would endeavour it."[210]

This letter, which shows in too clear colours how unscrupulous even men of reputed honour, such as Lord Islay, were on some points in those days, seems to have removed all obstacles; and, during the following year (1717), Lord Lovat was united to Margaret Grant. Her father was the head of a numerous and powerful clan, and this marriage tended greatly to increase the influence of Lord Lovat among the Highlanders. Two children, a son and a daughter, were the result of this union. Prosperity once more shone upon the chieftain of the Frasers; and he now restored to his home, Castle Downie, all the baronial state which must so well have accorded with that ancient structure. The famous Sergeant Macleod, in his Memoirs, gives a graphic account of his reception at Castle Downie by Lord Lovat, where the old soldier repaired to seek a commission in the celebrated Highland company, afterwards called the Highland Watch. [211]

"At three o'clock, " says the biographer of Macleod, [212] "on a summer's morning, he set out on foot from Edinburgh; and about the same hour, on the second day thereafter, he stood on the green of Castle Downie, Lord Lovat's residence, about five or six miles beyond Inverness; having performed in forty-eight hours a journey of a hundred miles and upwards, and the greater part of it through a mountainous country. His sustenance on this march was bread and cheese, with an onion, all which he carried in his pocket, and a dram of whiskey at each of the three great stages on the road, —and at Falkland, the half-way house between Edinburgh, by the way of Kinghorn and Perth. He never went to bed during the whole of this journey; though he slept once or twice for an hour or two together, in the open air, on the road side.

"By the time he arrived at Lord Lovat's park the sun had risen upwards of an hour, and shone pleasantly, according to the remark of our hero, well pleased to find himself in this spot, on the walls of Castle Downie, and those of the ancient abbey of Beaulieu in the near neighbourhood. Between the hours of five and six Lord Lovat appeared walking about in his hall, in a morning dress, and at the same time a servant flung open the great folding doors, and all the outer doors and windows of the house. It is about this time that many of the great families of the present day go to bed.

"As Macleod walked up and down on the lawn before the house, he was soon observed by Lord Lovat who immediately went out, and, bowing to the Sergeant with great courtesy, invited him to come in. Lovat was a fine-looking tall man, and had something very insinuating in his manners and address. He lived in the fullness of hospitality, being more solicitous, according to the genius of the feudal times, to retain and multiply adherents than to accumulate wealth by the improvement of his estate. As scarcely any fortune, and certainly not *his* fortune, was adequate to the extent of his views, he was obliged to regulate his unbounded hospitality by rules of prudent economy. As his spacious hall was crowded by kindred visitors, neighbours, vassals, and tenants of all ranks, the table, that extended from one end of it nearly to the other, was covered at different places with different kinds of meat and drink—though of each kind there was always great abundance. At the head of the table the lords and lairds pledged his Lordship in claret, and sometimes champagne; the tacksmen, or demiwassals, drank port or whiskey-punch; tenants, or common husbandmen, refreshed themselves with strong beer; and below the utmost extent of the table, at the door, and sometimes without the door of the hall, you might see a multitude of Frasers, without shoes or bonnets, regaling themselves with bread and onions, with a little cheese, perhaps, and small beer. Yet amidst the whole of the aristocratic inequality, Lord Lovat had the address to keep all his guests in perfectly good humour. 'Cousin, ' he would say to such and such a tacksman or demiwassal, 'I told my pantry lads to hand you some claret, but they tell me you like port or punch best. ' In like manner to the beer drinkers he would say, 'Gentlemen, there is what you please at your service; but I send you ale because I understand you like ale. ' Everybody was thus well pleased; and none were so ill bred as to gainsay what had been reported to his Lordship.

"This introduction was followed by still further condescension on the part of Lord Lovat. He looked at the veteran who had served in Lord Orkney's regiment, under Marlborough, at Ramilies and Malplaquet, with approbation.

"'I know, ' said his Lordship, 'without your telling me, that you have come to enlist in the Highland Watch; for a thousand men like you I would give an estate. ' Donald Macleod then, at Lovat's request, related his history and pedigree, —that subject which most delights the heart of a Highlander. Lord Lovat clasped him in his arms, and kissed him, and then led him into an adjoining bedchamber, where Lady Lovat then lay, to whom he introduced the Sergeant. Lady Lovat raised herself in her bed, called for a bottle of brandy, and drank prosperity to Lord Lovat, to the Highland Watch, and to Donald Macleod. 'It is superfluous to say, ' adds the Sergeant, 'that in this toast the lady was pledged by the gentlemen. '"

In contradiction to this attractive account of Lord Lovat's splendour and hospitality we must quote a very different description, given by the astronomer Ferguson. Lord Lovat's abode, according to his account, boasted, indeed, a numerous feudal retinue within its walls, but presented little or no comfort. It was a rude tower with only four apartments in it, and none of these spacious. Lord Lovat's own room served at once as his place for constant residence, his room for receiving company, and his bedchamber. Lady Lovat's bedchamber was allotted to her for all these purposes also. The domestics and a herd of retainers were lodged in the four lower rooms of the tower, a quantity of straw constituting their bed-furniture. Sometimes above four hundred persons were thus huddled together here; the power which their savage and ungrateful chieftain exercised over them was despotic; and Ferguson himself had occasionally the pleasurable sight of some half dozen of them hung up by the heels for hours, on a few trees near the house. [213]

The pretended loyalty of the chief to the exiled family constituted a strong bond of union between Lovat and his followers; and having them once under his command, "that indefinable magic by which he all his life swayed those who neither loved nor esteemed him, " to borrow Mrs. Grant's expression, caused them afterwards to follow his desperate fortunes. "He resembled, in this respect, " says the same admirable writer, "David when in the cave of Adullam, for every one that was discontented, and every one that was in debt, literally resorted to him. " Lovat, once settled in the abode of his ancestors, did all that he could do to efface the memory of the past, and to redeem the good opinion of his neighbours. One thing he alone left undone, —he did not amend his life. Crafty, vindictive, gross, tyrannical, few men ever continued long such a career with impunity.

He was long distrusted by the good of both parties; by the one he was regarded as a spy of Government, by the other as one whose Jacobite loyalty was only a pretext to win the affections of the honest and simple Highlanders. Yet, at last, he succeeded in obtaining influence, partly by his real talents, partly by his artifices and knowledge of character. "When one considers, " observes Mrs. Grant, "that his appearance was disgusting and repulsive, his manners, except when he had some deep part to play, grossly familiar, and meanly cajoling, and that he was not only stained with crimes, but well known to possess no one amiable quality but fortitude, which he certainly displayed in the last extremity, his influence over others is to be regarded as inexplicable. " Although the most valuable possessions of his family were on the Aird, the chief centre of his popularity was in Stratheric, a wild hilly district between Inverness and Fort Augustus. There he was beloved by the common people, who looked upon him as a patriot, and there he made it his chief study to secure their affections, often going unlooked for to spend the day and night with his tenants there, and banishing reserve, he indulged in a peculiar strain of jocularity perfectly suited to his audience. His conversation, composed of ludicrous fancies and blandishments, was often intermingled with sound practical advice and displays of good sense. The following curious account of his table deportment, and ordinary mode of living, is from the pen of Mrs. Grant of Laggan, who was well acquainted with those who had personally known Lord Lovat.

"If he met a boy on the road, he was sure to ask whom he belonged to, and tell him of his consequence and felicity in belonging to the memorable clan of Fraser, and if he said his name was Simon to give him half-a-crown, at that time no small gift in Stratheric; but the old women, of all others, were those he was at most pains to win, even in the lowest ranks. He never was unprovided with snuff and flattery, both which he dealt liberally among them, listened patiently to their old stories, and told them others of the King of France, and King James, by which they were quite captivated, and concluded by entreating that they impress their children with attachment and duty to their chief, and they would not fail to come to his funeral and assist in the coranach *keir*. At Castle Downie he always kept an open table to which all comers were welcome, for of all his visitors he contrived to make some use; —from the nobleman and general by whose interest he could provide for some of his followers, and by that means strengthen his interest with the rest, to the idle hanger-on whose excursions might procure the fish and game which he was barely suffered to eat a part of at his patron's table. Never was there a mixture of society so miscellaneous as was there assembled. From an affectation of loyalty to his new masters Lovat paid a great court to the military stationed in the North; such of the nobility in that quarter as were not in the sunshine, received his advances as from a man who enjoyed court favour, and he failed not to bend to his own purposes every new connection he formed. In the mean time the greatest profusion appeared at table while the meanest parsimony reigned through the household. The servants who attended had little if any wages; their reward was to be recommended to better service afterwards; and meantime they had no other food allowed to them but what they carried off on the plates: the consequence was, that you durst not quit your knife and fork for a moment, your plate was snatched while you looked another way; if you were not very diligent, you might fare as ill amidst abundance as the Governor of Barataria. A surly guest once cut the fingers of one of these harpies when snatching his favourite morsel away untasted. I have heard a military gentleman who occasionally dined at Castle Downie describe those extraordinary repasts. There was a very long table loaded with a great variety of dishes, some of the most luxurious, others of the plainest—nay, coarsest kind: these were very oddly arranged; at the head were all the dainties of the season, well dressed and neatly sent in; about the middle appeared good substantial dishes, roasted mutton, plain pudding and such like. At the bottom coarse pieces of beef, sheeps' heads, haggiss, and other national but inelegant dishes, were served in a slovenly manner in great pewter platters; at the head of the table were placed guests of distinction, to whom alone the dainties were offered; the middle was occupied by gentlemen of his own tribe, who well knew their allotment, and were satisfied with the share assigned to them. At the foot of the table sat hungry retainers, the younger sons of younger brothers, who had at some remote period branched out from the family; for which reason he always addressed them by the title of 'cousin. ' This, and a place, however low, at his table, so flattered these hopeless hangers-on, that they were as ready to do Lovat's bidding "in the earth or in the air" as the spirits are to obey the command of Prospero. "

"The contents of his sideboard were as oddly assorted as those of his table, and served the same purpose. He began, —'My lord, here is excellent venison, here turbot, &c. : call for any wine you please; there is excellent claret and champagne on the sideboard. Pray, now, Dunballock or Killbockie, help yourselves to what is before you; there are port and lisbon, strong ale and porter, excellent in their kind; ' then calling to the other end of the table, —'Pray, dear cousin, help yourself and my other cousins to that fine beef and cabbage; there is whiskey-punch and excellent table-beer. ' His conversation, like his table, was varied to suit the character of every guest. The retainers soon retired, and Lovat (on whom drink made no impression) found means to unlock every other mind, and keep his own designs impenetrably secret; while the ludicrous and careless air of his discourse helped to put people off their guard; and searchless cunning and boundless ambition were hid under the mask of careless hilarity. "

But darker deeds even than these diversified the pursuits of a man who had quitted the prisons of Angoulême and of Saumur only to wreak, upon his own faithful and trusting clansmen, or his neighbours, as well as his foes, the vindictive cruelty of a nature utterly depraved, not softened even by kindness, still less chastened by a long series of misfortunes.

Lovat's re-establishment at the head of his clan seems to have intoxicated him, and the display of his power to have risen into a ruling passion. Above all, he boasted of it to Duncan Forbes, whose endurance of this wretched ally's correspondence lasted until the pretended friendship was succeeded by avowed treachery to the Government to which he had professed such gratitude, and to the King and Prince whom he was wont to call "the bravest fellows in the world. "[214]

In accordance with this spirit of self-glorification was Lovat's erection of two monuments, —filial piety dictating the inscription on one of them, that dedicated to his father, and his own audacious vanity assisting in the composition of the tribute to his own virtues.

It was his Lordship's favourite boast that at his birth a number of swords which hung up in the hall of his paternal home leaped themselves out of their scabbards, denoting that he was to be a mighty man of arms. The presage was not fulfilled, but Lord Lovat's ingenuity suggested the following means of imposing upon the credulity of his simple clansmen, by the composition of an epitaph which he erected in the old church of Kirkhill, a few miles from Castle Downie.

TO THE MEMORY OF

THOMAS LORD FRASER, OF LOVAT,

Who chose rather to undergo the greatest hardships of fortune than to part with the ancient honours of his house, and bore these hardships with undaunted fortitude of mind.

This monument was erected by

SIMON LORD FRASER OF LOVAT, HIS SON.

Who, likewise, having undergone many and great vicissitudes of good and bad fortune, through the malice of his enemies, he, in the end, at the head of his clan, forced his way to his paternal inheritance with his sword in his hand, and relieved his kindred and followers from oppression and slavery; and both at home and in foreign countries, by his eminent actions in the war and the state, he has acquired great honours and reputation.

Hic tegit ossa lapis Simonis fortis in armis,
Restituit pressum nam genus ille suum:

Hoc marmor posuit cari genitoris honori,
In genus afflictum par erat ejus amor.

Sir Robert Munro, who was killed at the battle of Falkirk, being on a visit to Lord Lovat, went with his host to see this monument. "Simon, " said the brave and free-spoken Scotsman, "how the devil came you to put up such boasting romantic stuff? " "The monument and inscription, " replied Lovat, "are chiefly for the Frasers, who must believe whatever I require, their chief, of them, and then posterity will think it as true as the Gospel. " Yet he did not scruple, when it suited his purpose, to designate his clansmen, the lairds around him, as "the little pitiful barons of the Aird; "—this was, however, when writing to his friends of opposite politics to the Frasers, generally to Duncan Forbes.

The devotion of his unfortunate adherents can hardly be conceived in the present day. In the early part of his career, before his rapacity, his licentiousness, and falsehood were fully known, one may imagine a fearless and ardent young leader, of known bravery, engaging the passions even of the most wary among his followers in his personal quarrels: but it is wonderful how, when the character of the man stood revealed before them, any could be found to lend their aid to deeds which had not the colour of justice, nor even the pretence of a generous ardour, to recommend them to the brave. But Lovat was not the only melancholy instance in which that extraordinary feature in the Highland character, loyalty to a chieftain, was employed in aiding the darkest treachery, and in deeds of violence and cruelty.

For many years, Lovat revelled in the indulgence of the fiercest passions; but he paid in time the usual penalty of guilt. His name came to be a bye-word. Every act of violence, done in the darkness of night, —the oppressions of the helpless, the corruption of the innocent, —every plot which was based upon the lowest principles, were attributed to him. His vengeance was such, that while the public knew the hand that dealt out destruction, they dared not to name the man. The hated word was whispered by the hearth; it was muttered with curses in the hovel; but the voice which breathed it was hushed when the band of numerous retainers, swift to execute the will of the feudal tyrant, was remembered. His power, thus tremblingly acknowledged, was fearful; his wrath, never was appeased except by the ruin of those who had offended him. With all this, the manners of Lord Lovat were courteous, and, for the times, polished; whilst beneath that superficial varnish lay the coarsest thoughts, the most degrading tastes. His address must have been consummate; and to that charm of manner may be ascribed the wonderful ascendancy which he acquired even over the respectable part of the community.

Something of his ready humour was displayed soon after Lord Lovat's restoration to his title, in his rencontre with his early friend, Lord Mungo Murray, in the streets of Edinburgh. Lord Mungo had sworn to avenge the wrongs and insults inflicted by Lord Lovat on himself and Lord Saltoun, whenever he had an opportunity. Seeing Lord Lovat approaching, he drew his sword and made towards him as fast as he could. Lord Lovat, being near-sighted, did not perceive him, but was apprised of his danger by a friend who was walking with him; upon which his Lordship also drew, and prepared for his defence. Lord Mungo, seeing this, thought proper to decline the engagement, and wheeled round in order to retire. The people crowded about the parties, and somewhat impeded Lord Mungo's retreat; upon which Lord Lovat called out to the people, "Pray, gentlemen, make room for Lord Mungo Murray, " Lord Mungo slank away, and the affair ended without bloodshed.

An affair with the profligate Duke of Wharton, was very near ending more fatally. Lord Lovat, during the year 1724, happening to be in London, mingled there in the fashionable society for which his long residence in France had, in some measure, qualified him. In the course of his different amusements, he encountered one evening, at the Haymarket, the beautiful Doña Eleanora Sperria, a Spanish lady who had visited England under the character of the Ambassador's niece. His attentions to this lady, and his admiration of her attractions, were observed by the jealous eye of the Duke of Wharton, who immediately sent him a challenge. Lord Lovat accepted it, replying, that "none of the family of Lovat were ever cowards, " and appointing to meet the Duke with sword and pistol. The encounter took place in Hyde-park. They first fired at each other, and then had recourse to the usual weapon, the sword. Lovat was unlucky enough to fall over the stump of a tree, and was disarmed by Wharton, who gave him his life, and what was in those days perhaps even still more generous, never boasted of the affair until some years afterwards.

Lovat lived, however, chiefly in Scotland. Four children were born to writhe under his sway; the eldest, Simon, the Master of Lovat, gentle, sincere, of promising abilities, and upright in conduct, suffered early and late from the jealousy of his father, who could not comprehend his mild virtues. This unfortunate young man was treated with the utmost harshness by Lord Lovat, who kept him in slavish subjection to his own imperious will, and treated him as if he had been the offspring of some low-born dependant, instead of his heir. Still, those who were well-wishers to the Lovat family, built their hopes upon the virtues of the young Master of Lovat, and they were not deceived. Although forced by his father to quit the University of St. Andrews, where he was studying in 1745, and to enter into the Rebellion, he retrieved that early act by a subsequent respectability of life, and by long and faithful services.

But there was another victim still more to be pitied, and over whose destiny the vices of Lord Lovat exercised a still more fatal sway than on those of his son. The story of Primrose Campbell is, perhaps, the saddest among this catalogue of crimes and calamities.

She was the daughter of John Campbell, of Mamore, and the sister of John Duke of Argyle, the friend and patron of Duncan Forbes; and she had been, by Lovat's introduction, for some time a companion of his first wife. [215] Lord Lovat, about the year 1732, became a widower. He then cast his eyes upon the ill-fated Miss Campbell, and sought her in marriage. The match was of great importance to him, on account of the family connection; and Lord Lovat had reason to believe, that whatever the young lady might think of it, her friends were not opposed to the union. She was staying with her sister, Lady Roseberry, when Lovat proffered his odious addresses. She to whom they were addressed, knew him well: for she entertained the utmost abhorrence of her suitor, and repeatedly rejected his proposals. At last, he gained her consent to the union which he sought, by the following stratagem. Miss Campbell, while residing still with her sister in the country, received a letter, written apparently by her mother, and, beseeching her immediate attendance at a particular house in Edinburgh, in which she lay at the point of death. The young lady instantly set out, and reached the appointed place: here, instead of beholding her mother, she was received by the hated and dreaded Lovat. [216] She was constrained to listen to his proffers of marriage; but she still firmly refused her assent. Upon this, Lord Lovat told the unhappy creature that the house to which she had been brought was one in which no respectable woman ought ever to enter; —and he threatened to blast her character upon her continued refusal to become his wife.

Distracted, intimidated by a confinement of several days, the young lady finally consented. She was married to the tyrant, who conveyed her to one of his castles in the North, probably to Downie, the scene of his previous crimes. Here she was secluded in a lonely tower, and treated with the utmost barbarity, probably because she could neither conceal nor conquer her disgust to the husband of her forced acceptance. Yet outward appearances were preserved: a lady, the intimate friend of her youth, was advised to visit, as if by accident, the unhappy Lady Lovat, in order to ascertain the truth of the reports which prevailed of Lord Lovat's cruelty. The visitor was received by Lovat with extravagant expressions of welcome, and many assurances of the pleasure which it would afford Lady Lovat to see her. His Lordship then retired, and hastening to his wife, who was secluded without even tolerable clothes, and almost in a state of starvation, placed a costly dress before her, and desired her to attire herself, and to appear before her friend. His commands were obeyed; he watched his prisoner and her visitor so closely, that no information could be conveyed of the unhappiness of the one, or of the intentions of the other. [217] This outrageous treatment, which Lord Lovat is reported, also, to have exercised over his first wife, went on for some time. Lady Lovat was daily locked up in a room by herself, a scanty supply of food being sent her, which she was obliged to devour in silence. The monotony of her hapless solitude was only broken by rare visits from his Lordship. Under these circumstances, she bore a son, who was named Archibald Campbell Fraser, and who eventually succeeded to the title. In after years, when he frowned at any contradiction that she gave him, Lady Lovat used to exclaim, "Oh, boy! Dinna look that gate—ye look so like your father. " These words spoke volumes.

The character of the lady whose best years were thus blighted by cruelty, and who was condemned through a long life to bear the name of her infamous husband, was one peculiarly Scotch. Homely in her habits, and possessing little refinement of manner, she had the kindest heart, the most generous and self-denying nature that ever gladdened a house, or bore up a woman's weakness under oppression. The eldest son of Lord Lovat, Simon, was a sickly child. His father, who was very anxious to have him to his house, placed him under Lady Lovat's charge; and, whenever he went to the Highlands, left her with this pleasing intimation, "that if he found either of the boys dead on his return, he would shoot her through the head. " Partly through fear, and partly from the goodness and rectitude of her mind, Lady Lovat devoted her attentions so entirely to the care of the delicate and motherless boy, that she saved his life, and won his filial reverence and affection by her attention. He loved her as a real parent. The skill in nursing and in the practical part of medicine thus acquired, was never lost; and Lady Lovat was noted ever after, among those who knew her, as the "old lady of the faculty. "

Family archives, it is said, reveal a tissue of almost unprecedented acts of cruelty towards this excellent lady. They were borne with the same spirit that in all her life guided her conduct, —a strict dependance upon Providence. She regarded her calamities as trials, or tests, sent from Heaven, and received them with meek submission. In after years, during the peaceful decline of her honoured life, when a house near her residence in Blackfriars Wynd, Edinburgh, took fire, she sat calmly knitting a stocking, and watching, occasionally, the progress of the flames. The magistrates and ministers came, in vain, to entreat her to leave her house in a sedan; she refused, saying, that if her hour was come, it was in vain for her to think of eluding her fate: if it were not come, she was safe where she was. At length she permitted the people around her to fling wet blankets over the house, by which it was protected from the sparks.

She seems, however, to have made considerable exertions to rid herself from an unholy bond with her husband. Like many other Scottish ladies of quality, in those days, her education had been limited; and it was not until late in life that she acquired the art of writing, which she then learned by herself without a master. She never attained the more difficult process of spelling accurately.

She now, however, contrived to make herself understood by her friends in this her dire distress: and to acquaint them with her situation and injuries, by rolling a letter up in a clue of yarn, and dropping it out of her window to a confidential person below. Her family then interfered, and the wretched lady was released, by a legal separation, from her miseries. She retired to the house of her sister, and eventually to Edinburgh. When, in after times, her grand nephews and nieces crowded around her, she would talk to them of these days of sorrow. "Listen, bairns, " she was known to observe, "the events of my life would make a good novel; but they have been of sae strange a nature, that I'm sure naebody wad believe them. "[218]

But domestic tyranny was a sphere of far too limited a scope for Lord Lovat: his main object was to make himself absolute over that territory of which he was the feudal chieftain; to bear down everything before him, either by the arts of cunning, or through intimidation. Some instances, singular, as giving some insight into the state of society in the Highlands at that period, have been recorded. [219] Very few years after the restitution of his family honours had elapsed, before he happened to have some misunderstanding with one of the Dowager Lady Lovat's agents, a Mr. Robertson, whom her Ladyship had appointed as receiver of her rents. One night, during the year 1719, a number of persons, armed and disguised, were seen in the dead of night, very busy among Mr. Robertson's barns and outhouses. That night, the whole of his stacks of corn and hay were set on fire and entirely consumed. Lord Lovat was suspected of being the instigator of this destruction; yet such was the dread of his power, that Mr. Robertson chose rather to submit to the loss in silence than to prosecute, or even to name, the destroyer.

A worse outrage was perpetrated against Fraser of Phopachy, a gentleman of learning and character, and one who had befriended Lord Lovat in all his troubles, and had refused to join with Fraserdale in the Rebellion of 1715. Mr. Fraser had the charge of Lord Lovat's domestic affairs, more especially of his law contests, both in Edinburgh and in London. When accounts were balanced between Lord Lovat and Mr. Fraser, it was found that a considerable sum was due to the latter. Among his other peculiarities Lord Lovat had a great objection to pay his debts. As usual, he insulted Fraser, and even threatened him with a suit. Mr. Fraser, knowing well the man with whom he had to deal, submitted the affair to arbitration. A Mr. Cuthbert of Castlehill was chosen on the part of his Lordship; the result was, a decision that a very considerable sum was due to Fraser. Lord Lovat was violently enraged at this, and declared that Castlehill had broken his trust. Not many days afterwards, Castlehill Park, near Inverness, was invaded by a party of Highlanders, armed and disguised; the fences and enclosures were broken down, and a hundred of his best milch-cows killed. Again the finger of public opinion pointed at Lovat, but pointed in silence, as the author of this wicked attack. None dared to name him; all dreaded a summary vengeance: his crimes were detailed with a shudder of horror and disgust; their author was not mentioned.

Lord Lovat, moreover, instantly commenced a law-suit against Fraser, in order to set aside the arbitration. This process, which lasted during the lifetime of the victim, was scarcely begun when one night Fraser's seat at Phopachy, which, unhappily, was near the den of horrors, Castle Downie, was beset by Highlanders, armed and disguised, who broke into the house and inquired for Mr. Fraser. He was, luckily, abroad. The daughters of the unfortunate gentleman were, however, in the house; they were bound to the bed-posts and gagged; and, doubtless, the whole premises would have been pillaged or destroyed, had not a female servant snatched a dirk from the hands of one of the ruffians; and although wounded, defended herself, while by her shrieks she roused the servants and neighbours. The villains fled, all save two, who were taken, and who, after a desperate resistance, were carried off to the gaol at Inverness; they were afterwards tried, and capitally convicted of housebreaking, or *hamesaken,* as it is called in Scotland, and eventually hung. It appeared, from the confession of one of these men to a clergyman at Inverness, that the same head which planned the destruction of Mr. Robertson's stacks had contrived this outrage, and had even determined on the murder of his former friend, Mr. Fraser. But the hour was now at hand in which retribution for these crimes was to be signally visited upon this disgrace to his species. [220]

One more sufferer under his vile designs must be recorded, the unhappy Lady Grange. In that story which has been related of her fate, and which might, indeed, furnish a theme for romance, she is said to have ever alluded to Lord Lovat as the remorseless contriver of that scheme which doomed her to sufferings far worse than death, and to years of imbecility and wanderings. [221] The subtlety of Lord Lovat equalled his fierceness; it is not often that such qualities are combined in such fearful perfection. He could stoop to the smallest attentions to gain an influence or promote an alliance: a tradition is even believed of his going to the dancing-school with two young ladies, and buying them *sweeties,* in order to conciliate the favour of their father, Lord Alva.

His habitual cunning and management were manifested in his discipline of his clan. It was his chief aim to impress upon the minds of his vassals that his authority among them was absolute, and that no power on earth could absolve them from it; that they had no right to inquire into the merits or justifiableness of the action they were ordered to engage in; his will ought to be their law, his resentment a sufficient reason for taking his part in a quarrel, whether it were right or wrong.

One can hardly conceive that it could be requisite for the Frasers to give any fresh proof of their obedience and fealty; yet it seems to have required a continual effort on the part of Lord Lovat to establish his authority and to keep up his dignity among the Frasers. The reason assigned for this is, that though they were his vassals, tenants, and dependants, yet they must be brought to acknowledge his sovereignty; otherwise, when on some emergency he might require their assistance, they might assume their natural right of independence, and refuse to rise. It was Lord Lovat's policy, therefore, to discourage all disposition in his clansmen to enter trade or to go to sea and seek their fortunes abroad, lest they should both shake off their dependence on him, and also, by emigrating, diminish the broad and pompous retinue with which he chose to appear on all occasions. It was therefore his endeavour to check industry, to oppose improvement, to preach up the heroism of his ancestors, who never stooped to the meannesses of commerce, but made themselves famous by martial deeds. "Never, " thus argued the chieftain, "had those brave men enervated their bodies and debased their minds by labours fit only for beasts or stupid drudges. Should not the generous blood which flowed in their veins still animate the brave Frasers to deeds of heroism? "[222]

Notwithstanding all these exalted sentiments, the chief, who was set upon this pinnacle of power, hesitated not to retain a hired assassin for the purpose of executing any of his dark projects. Donald Gramoach, a notorious robber, was long in the employ of Lovat, who lavished large sums upon him. At length, in the year 1742, this man was apprehended, lodged in Dingwall Gaol; and being convicted of robbery, was sentenced to be hanged. Lord Lovat immediately despatched a body of his Highlanders to rescue the prisoner; but the magistrates were aware of his intentions; the prison was doubly guarded, and the culprit met with his due punishment.

Lord Lovat had long thrown off the mask of courtesy, and had laid aside the arts of fawning to which he had had recourse before his claims to the honours and estates had been fully acknowledged. His tenants now felt the iron rule of a merciless and necessitous master; for Lord Lovat's expenditure far exceeded his means and revenue. He raised his rents, and many of the farmers were forced to quit their farms; but his *vassals by tenure* were even more ruinously oppressed by suits of law, compelling them to make out their titles to their estates; if they failed in so doing, he insisted on forfeiture or escheate; and, in some instances, these suits were so expensive that it was almost wiser to relinquish an estate, than to be plundered in long and anxious processes.

At last, to prevent their utter ruin, the gentlemen who held lands under Lord Lovat determined upon resistance; after twenty-seven years of bondage they resolved to free themselves. They met together, and unanimously resolved to unite their arms, and to deliver themselves by their swords; to this extremity were reduced these brave and devoted adherents, who had blindly rushed into every crime and every danger at the command of their ungrateful chieftain. Their resolution alarmed the tyrant; he ordered the suits against his vassals to be stopped, and excused, as well as he could, and with his usual odious courtesy, the severities into which he had been led. He was playing a desperate game; and the adherence of these unhappy dependants was soon to be put to the test.

His oppression of his stewards and agents was consistent with the rest of his conduct. They could rarely induce him to settle his accounts; and if they ventured to ask for sums due to them, he threatened them with actions at law. He was all powerful, and they were forced to submit. His inferior servants were treated even still more oppressively. If they wished to leave his Lordship's service, or asked for their wages, he alleged some crime against them, which he always found sufficient witnesses to prove. They were then sent off to the cave of Beauly, a dismal retreat, about a mile from his castle, where they were confined until they were reduced to submission. That such enormities should have been tolerated in a land of liberty, seems almost incredible; but the slavery of the clans, the poverty and ignorance of the people, the vast power and influence of the chief, account, in some measure, for this degrading bondage on the one hand, this absolute monarchy on the other. [223]

This long-endured course of tyranny had not tended to humble the heart of him who indulged in such an immoderate exercise of power. The ambition of Lord Lovat, always of a low and personal nature, increased with years. He watched the state of public affairs, and built upon their threatening character a scheme by which he might, as he afterwards said, "be in a condition of humbling his neighbours. "

His allegiance was henceforth given to the Jacobites, and his fidelity, if such a word could ever be used as applied to him, seems actually to have lasted two years, —that is from 1717 to 1719, when a Spanish invasion was undertaken in favour of the Pretender. To that Lord Lovat promised to lend his aid, and wrote to Lord Seaforth, promising to join him. But the invasion was then defeated, and Lovat continued to enjoy royal favour at home. On this occasion the letter which Lord Lovat had written to Lord Seaforth, was shown to Chisholm of Knoebsford before it was delivered, and an affidavit of its contents was sent up to Court. Upon Lord Lovat becoming acquainted with this, he immediately got himself introduced at Court, possibly with a view to deceiving the public mind. Lady Seaforth having asked some favour from him, he refused to grant it, unless she would return that letter, which had been addressed to her son. With his usual cunning he had omitted to sign the letter, which he thought could not therefore be fixed upon him. Upon receiving it back, Lovat showed it to a friend, who remarked that there was enough in it to condemn thirty lords. He immediately threw it into the fire.

During many years of iniquity, Lord Lovat had preserved, to all appearance, the good will of Duncan Forbes. That great lawyer had been Lovat's legal advocate during the long and expensive suits for the establishment of his claims, and had generously refused all fees or remuneration for his exertions. The letters addressed by Lovat to him breathe the utmost regard, and speak an intimacy which, as Sir Walter Scott observes, "is less wonderful when we consider that Duncan Forbes could endure the society of the infamous Charteris. "[224] Lovat's expressions of regard were frequently written in French. "Mon aimable General: " he writes to Mr. John Forbes, also, the President's elder brother. —"My dear Culloden. " "Your affectionate friend, and most obedient and most humble servant. "

To the President, whom he always addressed with some allusion to his brief military service, —"My dear General. " "Your own Lovat. " In 1716 such professions as these are made to Mr. John Forbes.

"My dearest Provost (we must give you your title, since it is to last but short), my dear General's letter and yours are terrible; but I was long ere now prepared for all that could happen to me on your illustrious brother's account: I'll stand by him to the last; and if I fall, as I do not doubt but I will, I'll receive the blow without regret. But all I can tell you is this, that we are very like to see a troublesome world, and my Generall and you will be yet useful; and I am ready to be with you to the last drop, for I am yours eternally, Lovat. " His frequent style to the President was thus, —"The most faithfull and affectionat of your slaves. " It is indeed evident, in almost every letter, what real obligations Lovat received from both Culloden and his brother; and how strenuously they supported his claim against Fraserdale. [225]

At the hospitable house of Culloden he was a frequent guest, —"a house, or castle, " says the author of "Letters from the North, " written previous to the year 1730, "belonging to a gentleman whose hospitality knows no bounds. It is the custom of that house, at the first visit or introduction, to take up war freedom, by cracking his nut, as he terms it; that is, a cocoa-shell, which holds a pint, filled with champagne, or such other sort of wine as you shall chuse. You may guess, by the introduction, of the contents of the volume. Few go away sober at any time; and for the greatest part of his guests, in the conclusion, they cannot go at all. "

"This he partly brings about artfully, by proposing, after the public healths (which always imply bumpers), such private ones as he knows will pique the interest or inclination of each particular person of the company, whose turn it is to take the lead, to begin it in a brimmer; and he himself being always cheerful, and sometimes saying good things, his guests soon lose their guard, and then—I need say no more. "[226]

In this hospitable house, a strange contrast to the penuriousness and despotic management of Castle Downie, Lord Lovat was on the most intimate footing. His professions of friendship to the laird were unceasing. "I dare freely say, " he observes in one of his characteristic letters, "that there is not a Forbes alive wishes your personal health and prosperity more than I do, affectionate and sincerely; and I should be a very ungrateful man if it was otherways, for no man gave me more proofs of love and friendship at home and abroad than John Forbes of Colodin did.

"As to carrying your lime to Lovat, I shall do more in it than if it was for my own use. I shall give the most pressing orders to my officers to send in my tenants' horses; and to show them the zeal and desire that I have to serve you, I shall send my own labouring horses to carry it, with as much pleasure as if it was to build a house in Castle Downie. "

Even his wife and his "bearns" are "Colodin's faithful slaves—" "I'll never see a laird of Culodin I love so much, " he declares in another letter; —in which, also, he reminds Mr. Forbes of a promise that he "will do him the honour, since he cannot himself at this time be present, to hold up his forthcoming child to receive the holy water of baptisme, and make it a better Christian than the father. I expect this mark of friendship from my dear John Forbes of Culodin. "[227]

Yet all these professions were wholly forgotten, when Lord Lovat, being fairly established in his honours, no longer deemed the friendship of the Forbes family necessary to him. An occasion then occurred, in which Mr. Forbes's "grateful slave" showed the caprice inherent in his nature. Forbes of Culloden had long been the representative of Inverness, chiefly through the interest of Lord Lovat; but when Sir William Grant came forward to oppose the return of Forbes, to the dismay of that gentleman, Lord Lovat turned round, and, upon the plea of consanguinity, used his interest in favour of the new candidate. The disappointment resulting from this defeat is said to have preyed upon the spirits of the worthy Laird of Culloden, and to have caused his death. [228]

The decline of this alliance between the Forbes family and Lord Lovat, was the prelude to greater changes.

In order to repress the local disturbances in the Highlands, Government had adopted a remedy, well termed by Sir Walter Scott, "of a doubtful and dangerous character. " This was the raising of a number of independent companies among the Highlanders, to be commanded by chieftains, and officered by their sons, by tackmen, or by *Dnihne* vassals. At the period when those great military roads were formed in the Highlands between the year 1715 and 1745, these companies were better calculated, it was supposed, to maintain the repose of a country with which they were well acquainted, than regular troops. But the experiment did not succeed. The Highland companies, known by the famous name of the Black Watch, traversed the country, it is true, night and day, and tracked its inmost recesses; they knew the most dangerous characters; they were supposed to suppress all internal disorders. But they were Highlanders. Whilst they looked leniently upon robberies and outrages to which they had been familiarized from their youth, they revived in their countrymen the military spirit which the late Act for disarming the clans had subdued. Upon their removal from the Highlands, and their exportation to Flanders, the mischief became apparent; and no regular force being sent to the Highlands in their stead, those chieftains who were favourable to the exiled family, found it easy to turn the restless temper and martial habits of their clansmen to their own purposes.

Lord Lovat was one of those who thus acted. The Ministry, irritated by his patronage of Sir William Grant's interests, in preference to those of Forbes, at the election for Inverness, suddenly deprived him of his pension in 1739, and also of the command of the free company of Highlanders. This was a rash proceeding, and contrary to the advice of President Forbes. Lord Lovat, who had caused his clansmen to enter his regiment by rotation, and had thus, without suspicion, been training his clan to the use of arms, soon showed how dangerous a weapon had been placed in his hand, and at how critical a period he had been incensed to turn it against Government.

He had long been suspected. Even in 1737, information had been given of his buying up muskets, broadswords, and targets, in numbers. When challenged to defend himself from the imputation of Jacobitism by a friend, he insisted upon the services he had done in 1715 as a reason why he should for ever be free from the imputation of disloyalty; and he continued to play the same subtle part, and to pretend indifference to all fresh enterprises, to his friends at Culloden, as that which he had always affected.

"Everybody expects we shall have a war very soon, " he writes to his friend John Forbes in 1729—"which I am not fond of; for being now growne old, I desire and wish to live in peace with all mankind, except some damned Presbyterian ministers who dayly plague me. "[229] Yet, even then he was engaged in a plot to restore the Stuarts. In 1736, when he was Sheriff for the county, he received the celebrated Roy Stuart, who was imprisoned at Inverness for high treason, when he broke out of gaol, and kept him six weeks in his house; sending by him an assurance to the Pretender of his fidelity, and at the same time desiring Roy Stuart to procure him a commission as lieutenant-general, and a patent of dukedom.

This was the secret spring of his whole proceeding. It is degrading to the rest of the Jacobites, to give this double traitor an epithet ever applied to honourable, and fervent, and disinterested men. The sole business of Lovat was personal aggrandizement; revenge was his amusement.

Henderson, in his "History of the Rebellion, " attributes to Lord Lovat the entire suggestion of the invasion of 1745. It is true that the Chevalier refused to accede to the proposal made by Roy Stuart of an invasion in 1735, not considering, as he said, that the "time for his deliverance was as yet come. " But, after consulting the Pope, it was agreed that the present time might be well employed in "whetting the minds of the Highlanders, and in sowing in them the seeds of loyalty that so frequently appeared. " In consequence of this, Lord Lovat's request was granted; a letter was written to him from the Court, then at Albano, giving him full power to act in the name of James, and the title of Duke of Fraser and Lieutenant-General of the Highlands was conferred upon the man who seems to have had the art of infatuating all with whom he dealt. [230]

Lord Lovat immediately changed the whole style of his deportment. He quitted the comparative retirement of Castle Downie; went to Edinburgh, where he set up a chariot, and lived there in a sumptuous manner, though with little of those ceremonials which we generally associate with rank and opulence. He now sought and obtained a very general acquaintance. Few men had more to tell; and he could converse about his former hardships, relate the account of his introduction to Louis the Fourteenth, and to the gracious Maintenon. He returned to Castle Downie. That seat, conducted hitherto on the most penurious scale, suddenly became the scene of a plenteous hospitality; and its lord, once churlish and severe, became liberal and free. He entertained the clans after their hearts' desire, and he kept a purse of sixpences for the poor. As his castle was almost in the middle of the Highlands, it was much frequented; and the crafty Lovat now adapted his conversation to his own secret ends. He expatiated to the Highlanders, always greedy of fame, and vain beyond all parallel of their country, upon the victories of Montrose on the fields of Killicrankie and Cromdale.

"Such a sword and target, " he would say to a listener, "your honest grandfather wore that day, and with it he forced his way through a hundred men. Well did I know him; he was my great friend, and an honest man. Few are like him now-a-days; —you resemble him pretty much. "

Then he began to interpret prophecies and dreams, and to relate to his superstitious listeners the dreams their fathers had before the battle, in which they fought. He would trace genealogies as far back as the clansmen pleased, and show their connection with their chieftains. They were all his "cousins and friends; " for he knew every person that had lived in the country for years.

Then he spoke of the superiority of the broad-sword and target over the gun and the bayonet; he sneered at the weakness of an army, after so many years of peace, commanded by boys; he boasted of the valour of the Scots in Sweden and France; he even unriddled the prophecies of Bede and of Merlin. By these methods he prepared the minds of those over whom he ruled for the Rebellion; but in the event, as it has been truly said, "the thread of his policy was spun so fine that at last it failed in the maker's hand. "[231]

The shrewdness of Lovat's judgment might indeed be called in question, when he decided to risk the undisturbed possession of his Highland property for a dukedom and prospect. But there were many persons of rank and influence who believed, with Prince Charles Edward, that "the Hanoverian yoke was severely felt in England, and that now was the time to shake it off. " "The intruders of the family of Hanover, " observes a strenuous Jacobite, [232] "conscious of the lameness of their title and the precariousness of their tenure, seem to have had nothing in view but increasing their power, and gratifying their insatiable avarice: by the former, they proposed to get above the caprice of the people; and by the latter, they made sure of something, happen what would. " "Abundance of the Tories, " he further remarks, "had still a warm side for the family of Stuart; and as for the old stanch Whigs, their attachment and aversion to families had no other spring but their love of liberty, which they saw expiring with the family of Hanover: they had still this, and but this chance to recover it. In fine, there was little opposition to be dreaded from any quarter but from the army, — gentlemen of that profession being accustomed to follow their leaders, and obey orders without asking any questions. But there were malcontents among them, too; such as were men of property, whose estates exceeded the value of their commissions, did by no means approve of the present measures. "[233]

Upon the whole the conjuncture seemed favourable, and Lord Lovat, whose political views were very limited, was the first to sign the association despatched in 1736, according to some accounts, by others in 1740, and signed and sealed by many persons of note in Scotland, inviting the Chevalier to come over to that country. His belief was, that France had at all times the power to bring in James

Stuart if she had the will; that, indeed, was the general expectation of the Jacobites.

"Most of the powers in Europe, " writes Mr. Maxwell, "were engaged, either as principals or auxiliaries, in a war about the succession to the Austrian dominions. France and England were hitherto only auxiliaries, but so deeply concerned, and so sanguine, that it was visible they would soon come to an open rupture with one another; and Spain had been at war with England some years, nor was there the least prospect of an accommodation. From those circumstances it seemed highly probable that France and Spain would concur in forwarding the Prince's views. "

Influenced by these considerations, Lovat now became chiefly involved in all the schemes of the Chevalier. In 1743, when the invasion was actually resolved upon, Lovat was fixed upon as a person of importance to conduct the insurrection in the Highlands. Nor did the failure of that project deter him from continued exertions. During the two succeeding years, and until after the battle of Preston Pans, he acted with such caution and dissimulation, that, had his party lost, he might still have made terms, as he thought, with the Hanoverians.

In the beginning of the year 1745, Prince Charles despatched several commissions to be distributed among his friends in Scotland, with certain letters delivered by Sir Hector Maclean, begging his friends in the Highlands to be in readiness to receive him, and desiring, "if possible, that all the castles and fortresses in Scotland might be taken before his arrival. "[234] On the twenty-fifth of July, [235] the gallant Charles Edward landed in a remote corner of the Western Highlands, with only seven adherents. Lord Lovat was informed of this event, but he continued to play the deep game which his perfidious mind suggested on all occasions. He sent one of his principal agents into Lochaber to receive the young Prince's commands, as Regent of the three kingdoms, and to express his joy at his arrival. He sent also secretly for his son, who was then a student at the University of St. Andrews, and compelled him to leave his pursuits there, appointing him colonel of his clan. Arms, money, and provisions were collected; and the fiery cross was circulated throughout the country.

Such proceedings could not be concealed, and the Lord Advocate, Craigie, wrote to Lord Lovat from Edinburgh, in the month of

August, calling upon him to prove his allegiance, referring to Lovat's son as well able to assist him, and asking his counsels on the state of the Highlands. The epistle alluded to a long cessation of any friendly correspondence between the Lord Advocate and Lord Lovat.

It was answered by assurances of loyalty. "I am as ready this day (as far as I am able) to serve the King and Government as I was in the year 1715, &c. But my clan and I have been so neglected these many years past, that I have not twelve stand of arms in my country, though I thank God I could bring twelve hundred good men to the field for the King's service if I had arms and other accoutrements for them. " He then entreats a supply of arms, names a thousand stand to be sent to Inverness, and promises to engage himself in the King's service. He continues, —"Therefore, my good Lord, I earnestly entreat that as you wish that I would do good service to the Government on this critical occasion, you may order immediately a thousand stand of arms to be delivered to me and my clan at Inverness, and then your Lordship shall see that I will exert myself for the King's service; and if we do not get these arms immediately, we will certainly be undone; for these madmen that are in arms with the pretended Prince of Wales, threaten every day to burn and destroy my country if we do not rise in arms and join them; so that my people cry hourly that they have no arms to defend themselves, nor no protection or support from the Government. So I earnestly entreat your Lordship may consider seriously on this, for it will be an essential and singular loss to the Government if my clan and kindred be destroyed, who possess the centre of the Highlands of Scotland, and the countries most proper, by their situation, to serve the King and Government. "

"As to my son, my Lord, that you are so good as to mention, he is very young, and just done with his colleges at St. Andrews, under the care of a relation of yours, Mr. Thomas Craigie, professor of Hebrew, who I truly think one of the prettiest, most complete gentlemen that I ever conversed with in any country: and I think I never saw a youth that pleased him more than my eldest son; he says he is a very good scholar, and has the best genius for learning of any he has seen, and it is by Mr. Thomas Craigie's positive advice, which he will tell you when you see him, that I send my son immediately to Utrecht to complete his education. But I have many a one of my family more fitted to command than he is at his tender age; and I do assure your Lordship that they will behave well if they are supported as they ought from the Government. "

This artful letter, wherein he talks of sending his son to Utrecht, when he was, at that time, by threats and persuasion driving him into the field of civil war, is finished thus: —

"I hear that mad and unaccountable gentleman" (thus he designates the Prince) "has set up a standard at a place called Glenfinnin—Monday last. This place is the inlet from Moydart to Lochaber; and I hear of none that joined him as yet, except the Camerons and Macdonells. "

But this masterpiece of art could not deceive the honest yet discerning mind of him to whom it was addressed.

Since the death of Mr. Forbes, the President had resided frequently at Culloden, now his own property; his observing eye was turned upon the proceedings of his neighbour at Castle Downie, but still appearances were maintained between him and Lovat. "This day, " writes the President to a friend, "the Lord Lovat came to dine with me. He said he had heard with uneasiness the reports that were scattered abroad; but that he looked on the attempt as very desperate; that though he thought himself but indifferently used lately, in taking his company from him, yet his wishes still being, as well as his interest, led him to support the present Royal Family; that he had lain absolutely still and quiet, lest his stirring in any sort might have been misrepresented or misconstrued; and he said his business with me was, to be advised what was to be done on this occasion. I approved greatly of his disposition, and advised him, until the scene should open a little, to lay himself out to gain the most certain intelligence he could come at, which the situation of his clan will enable him to execute, and to prevent his kinsmen from being seduced by their mad neighbours, which he readily promised to do. "

Consistent with these professions were the letters of Lovat to the President.

"I have but melancholy news to tell you, my dear Lord, of my own country; for I have a strong report that mad Foyers is either gone, or preparing to go, to the West; and I have the same report of poor Kilbockie; but I don't believe it. However, if I be able to ride in my chariot the length of Inverness, I am resolved to go to Stratherrick next week, and endeavour to keep my people in order. I forgot to tell you that the man yesterday assured me that they were resolved to burn and destroy all the countries where the men would not join them, with fire and sword, which truly frights me much, and has made me think of the best expedient I could imagine to preserve my people.

"As I know that the Laird of Lochiel has always a very affectionate friendship for me, as his relation, and a man that did him singular services, and as he is perfectly well acquainted with Gortuleg, I endeavoured all I could to persuade Tom to go there, and that he should endeavour in my name to persuade Lochiel to protect my country; in which I think I could succeed; but I cannot persuade Gortuleg to go; he is so nice with his points of honour that he thinks his going would bring upon him the character of a spy, and that he swears he would not have for the creation. I used all the arguments that I was capable of, and told him plainly that it was the greatest service he could do to me and to my country, as I knew he could bring me a full account of their situation, and that is the only effectual means that I can think of to keep the Stratherrick men and the rest of my people at home. He told me at last he would take some days to consider of it until he comes out of Stratherrick; but I am afraid that will be too late. I own I was not well pleased with him, and we parted in a cooler manner than we used to do. "[236]

In all his letters he characterizes Charles Edward, to whom he had just pledged his allegiance, as the "pretended Prince. " His affectation of zeal in the cause of Government, his pretence of an earnest endeavour to arrest the career of the very persons whom he was exciting to action, his exertions with my "cousin Gortuleg, " and his delight to find that "honest Kilbockie, " whom he had been vilifying, had not stirred, and would do nothing without his consent, might be amusing if they were not traits of such wanton irreclaimable falsehood in an aged man, soon to be called to an account, before a heavenly tribunal, for a long career of crime and injury to his neighbours.

If any further instance of his duplicity can be read with patience, the following letter to Lochiel, who, according to Lovat, had a very affectionate friendship for him, affords a curious specimen of cunning. [237]

"1745.

"Dear Lochiel,

"I fear you have been over rash in going ere affairs were ripe. You are in a dangerous state. The Elector's General, Cope, is in your rear, hanging at your tail with three thousand men, such as have not been seen here since Dundee's affair, and we have no force to meet him. If the Macphersons will take the field I would bring out my lads to help the work; and 'twixt the two we might cause Cope to keep his Christmas here; but only Cluny is earnest in the cause, and my Lord Advocate plays at cat and mouse with me; but times may change, I may bring him to Saint Johnstone's tippet. Meantime look to yourselves, for ye may expect many a sour face and sharp weapons in the South. I'll aid when I can, but my prayers are all I can give at present. My service to the Prince, but I wish he had not come here so empty-handed. Siller would go far in the Highlands. I send this by Evan Fraser, whom I have charged to give it to yourself; for were Duncan to find it, it would be my head to an onion. Farewell!

"Your faithful friend, "LOVAT. "

"For the Laird of Lochiel. "Yese. "

But perhaps the most odious feature in this part of Lovat's career was his treachery to Duncan Forbes, whose exertions had placed his unworthy client in possession of his property, and whose early ties of neighbourhood ought, at any rate, to have secured him from danger. A party of the Stratherric Frasers, kinsmen and clansmen of Lovat's, attacked Culloden House, as there was every reason to believe with the full concurrence of Lovat. Forbes, who was perfectly aware of the source whence the assault proceeded, appeared to treat it lightly, talked of it as an "idle attempt, " never hinting that he guessed Lovat's participation in the affair, and only lamenting that the ruffians had "robbed the gardener and the poor weaver, who was a common benefit to the country. " Lovat, as it has been sagaciously remarked, the guilty man, took it up much more knowingly.

This tissue of artifice was carried on for some weeks; first by a vehement desire to have arms sent in order to repel the rebels, then by hints that the inclinations of his people, and the extensive popularity of the cause began to make it doubtful whether he could control their rash ardour. "Your Lordship may remember, " he wrote to Forbes, "that I had a vast deal of trouble to prevent my men rising at the beginning of this affair; but now the contagion is so general, by the late success of the Highlanders, that they laugh at any man that would dissuade them from going; so that I really know not how to behave. I really wish I had been in any part of Britain these twelve months past, both for my health and other considerations. "[238] The feebleness of his health was a point on which, for some reasons or other, he continually insisted. It is not often that one can hear an aged man complain, without responding by pity and sympathy.

"I'm exceeding glad to know that your Lordship is in great health and spirits: I am so unlucky that my condition is the reverse; for I have neither health nor spirits. I have entirely lost the use of my limbs, for I can neither walk nor mount a horseback without the help of three or four men, which makes my life both uneasy and melancholy. But I submit to the will of God. " This account, indeed, rather confirms a tradition that Lord Lovat, after the separation from his wife, sank into a state of despondency, and lay two years in bed previous to the Rebellion of 1745. When the news of the Prince's landing was brought to him, he cried out, "Lassie, bring me my brogues. —I'll rise too. "[239]

At length, this wary traitor took a decisive step. His dilatoriness had made many of the Pretender's friends uneasy, and showed too plainly that he had been playing a double game. He was urged by some emissaries of Charles Edward "to throw off the mask, " upon which he pulled off his hat and exclaimed "there it is! " He then, in the midst of his assembled vassals, drank "confusion to the white horse, and all the generation of them. "[240] He declared that he would "cut off" in a moment any of his tenants who refused to join the cause, and expressed his conviction that as sure as the sun shined his "master would prevail. "

This was in the latter part of the summer: on the twenty-first of September the battle of Preston Pans raised the hopes of the Jacobites to the highest pitch, and Alexander Macleod was sent to the Highland chieftains to stimulate their loyalty and to secure their rising. Upon his visiting Castle Downie he found Lovat greatly elated by the recent victory, which he declared was not to be paralleled. He now began to assemble his men, and to prepare in earnest for that part which he had long intended to adopt; "but, " observes Sir Walter Scott, "with that machiavelism inherent in his nature, he resolved that his own personal interest in the insurrection should be as little evident as possible, and determined that his son, whose safety he was bound, by the laws of God and man, to prefer to his own, should be his stalking-horse, and in case of need his scape-goat. "[241]

Lord President Forbes, who had been addressing himself to the Highland chieftains, exhorting the well-affected to bestir themselves, and entreating those who were devoted to the Pretender not to involve themselves and their families in ruin, expostulated by letter with Lord Lovat upon the course which his son was now openly pursuing, pointing out how greatly it would reflect upon the father, whose co-operation or countenance he supposed to be impossible. The letters written on this subject by Forbes are admirable, and show a deep interest not only in the security of his country, but also in the fate of the young man, who afterwards redeemed his involuntary errors by a career of the highest respectability.

"You have now so far pulled off the mask, " writes the President, "that we can see the mark you aimed at. " "You sent away your son, and the best part of your clan, " he adds, after a remonstrance full of good sense and candour, "to join the Pretender, with as little concern as if no danger had attended such a step. And I am sorry to tell you, my Lord, that I could sooner undertake to plead the cause of any one of those unhappy gentlemen who are actually in arms against his Majesty; and I could say more in defence of their conduct, than I could in defence of your Lordship's. "[242]

Can any instance of moral degradation be adduced more complete than this? The implication of a son by a father, who had used his absolute authority to drive his son into an active part in the affairs of the day?

"I received the honour of your Lordship's letter, " writes Lovat, in reply, "late last night, of yesterday's date; and I own that I never received any one like it since I was born; and I give your Lordship the thousand thanks for the kind freedom you use with me in it; for I see by it that for my misfortune of having ane obstinate stubborn son, and ane ungrateful kindred, my family must go to destruction, and I must lose my life in my old age. Such usage looks rather like a Turkish or Persian government than like a British. Am I, my Lord, the first father that had ane undutiful and unnatural son? or am I the first man that has made a good estate, and saw it destroyed in his own time? but I never heard till now, that the foolishness of a son, would take away the liberty and life of a father, that lived peaceably, that was ane honest man, and well inclined to the rest of mankind. But I find the longer a man lives, the more wonders, and extraordinary things he sees.

"Now, my Lord, as to the civil war that occasions my misfortune; and in which, almost the whole kingdom is involved on one side or other. I humbly think that men should be moderate on both sides, since it is morally impossible to know the event. For thousands, nay, ten thousands on both sides are positive that their own party will carry; and suppose that this Highland army should be utterly defeat, and that the Government should carry all in triumph, no man can think that any king upon the throne would destroy so many ancient families that are engaged in it. "

Upon the news of the Pretender's troops marching to England, the Frasers, headed by the Master of Lovat, formed a sort of blockade round Fort Augustus; upon which the Earl of Loudon, with a large body of the well-affected clans, marched, in a very severe frost during the month of December, to the relief of Fort Augustus. His route lay through Stratherric, Lord Lovat's estate, on the south side of Loch Ness. Fort Augustus surrendered without opposition; and the next visit which Lord Loudon paid was to Castle Downie, where he prevailed on Lord Lovat to go with him to Inverness, and to remain there under Loudon's eye, until his clan should have been compelled to bring in their arms. Lord Lovat was now very submissive; he promised that this should be done in three days, and highly condemned the conduct of his son. But he still delayed to surrender the arms; and, at last, found means, in spite of his lameness which he was always lamenting, to get out of the house where he was lodged by a back passage, and to make his escape to the Isle of Muily, in Glenstrathfarrer. Here he occupied himself in exciting all the clans, especially his own Frasers, to join in the insurrection. A scheme having been submitted to the Duke of Cumberland, for the prevention of all future disturbances by transporting all those who had been found in arms to America, Lord Lovat had this document translated into Gaelic, and circulated in the Highlands, in order to exasperate the natives against the Duke, and to show that that General intended to extirpate them root and branch. Unhappily, the event did not serve to dispel those suspicions. This manifesto, as it was called, was read publicly in the churches every Sunday.

The march of the rebels to Inverness drove Lord Loudon to retire into Sutherland early in 1746, and President Forbes had accompanied him in his retreat. It was, therefore, again practicable for Lord Lovat to return to his own territory; and we find him, before the battle of Culloden, alternately at Castle Downie, or among some of his adherents, chiefly at the House of Fraser of Gortuleg, from which the following letter which exemplifies much of the character of Lovat, appears to have been written.

"March 20, 1746.

"My dearest Child,

"Gortulegg came home last night, with Inocralachy's brother; and the two Sandy Fairfield's son, and mine: and I am glad to know, that you are in perfect health, which you may be sure I wish the continuance of. I am sure for all Sandy's reluctance to come to this country, he will be better pleased with it than any where else; for he has his commerade, Gortuleg's son, to travell up and down with him; I shall not desire him to stay ane hour in the house but when he pleases.

"My cousin, Mr. William Fraser, tells me that the Prince sent notice to Sir Alexander Bennerman, by Sir John M'Donell, that he would go some of these days, and view my country of the Aird, and fish salmon upon my river of Beauly, I do not much covet that great honour at this time as my house is quite out of order, and that I am not at home myself nor you: however, if the Prince takes the fancy to go, you must offer to go along with him, and offer him a glass of wine and any cold meat you can get there. I shall send Sanday Doan over immediately, if you think that the Prince is to go: so I have ordered the glyd post to be here precisely this night.

"Mr. William Fraser says, that Sir Alexander Bennerman will not give his answer to Sir John M'Donell, till he return about the Prince's going to Beaufort; and that cannot be before Saturday morning. So I beg, my dearest child, you may consider seriously of this, not to let us be affronted; for after Sir Alexander and other gentlemen were entertained at your house, if the Prince should go and meet with no reception, it will be ane affront, and a stain upon you and me while we breathe. So, my dearest child, don't neglect this; for it is truely of greater consequence to our honour than you can imagine, tho' in itself it's but a maggot: but, I fancy, since Cumberland is comeing so near, that these fancy's will be out of head. However, I beg you may not neglect to acquaint me (if it was by ane express) when you are rightly informed that the Prince is going. I have been extreamly bad these four days past with a fever and a cough; but I thank God I am better since yesterday affernoon. I shall be glad to see you here, if you think it proper for as short or as long a time as you please. All in this family offer you their compliments: and I ever am, more than I can express, my dearest child, your most affected and dutiful father,

"— —."

"P. S.—The Prince's reason for going to my house is, to see a salmon kill'd with the rod, which he never saw before; and if he proposes that fancy, he must not be disappointed.

"I long to hear from you by the glyd post some time this night. I beg, my dear child, you may send me any news you have from the east, and from the north, and from the south. "[243]

It was not until after the battle of Culloden that Charles Edward and Lord Lovat first met. In that engagement, Lovat's infirmities, as well as his precautions, had prevented his taking an active part; but his son, the Master of Lovat, whose energy in the cause which he had unwillingly espoused, met the praise of Prince Charles, led his clan up to the encounter, and was one of the few who effected a junction with the Prince on the morning of the battle. Fresh auxiliaries from the clan Fraser were hastening in at the very moment of that ill-judged action; and they behaved with their accustomed bravery, and were permitted to march off unattacked, with their pipes playing, and their colours flying. The great body of the clan Fraser were led by Charles Fraser, junior, of Inverlaltochy, as Lieutenant-Colonel in the absence of the Master of Lovat, who was coming up with three hundred men, but met the Highlanders flying. The brave Inverlaltochy was killed; and the fugitives were sorely harassed by Kingston's light horse.

The battle of Culloden occurring shortly afterwards, decided the question of Lord Lovat's political bias. Very different accounts have been transmitted of the feelings and conduct of Prince Charles after the fury of the contest had been decided. By some it has been stated, that he lost on that sad occasion those claims to a character for valour which even his enemies had not hitherto refused him;

but Mr. Maxwell has justified the unfortunate and inexperienced young man.
"The Prince, " he says, "seeing his army entirely routed, and all his endeavours to rally the men fruitless, was at last prevailed upon to retire. Most of his horse assembled around his person to secure his retreat, which was made without any danger, for the enemy advanced very leisurely over the ground. They were too happy to have got so cheap a victory over a Prince and an enemy that they had so much reason to dread. They made no attack where there was any body of the Prince's men together, but contented themselves with sabering such unfortunate people as fell in his way single and disarmed. "[244]

"If he did less at Culloden than was expected from him, " adds this partial, but honest follower, "'twas only because he had formerly done more than could be expected. " He justly blames the Prince's having come over without any officer of experience to guide him. "He was too young himself, and had too little experience to perform all the functions of a general; and though there are examples of princes that seem to have been born generals, they had the advice and assistance of old experienced officers, men that understood, in detail, all that belongs to any army. "[245]

Lord Elcho, in his manuscript, thus accounts for the censures which were cast upon the Prince by those who shared his misfortunes.

"What displeased the people of fashion (consequence) was, that he did not seem to have the least sense of what they had done for him; but, after all, would afterwards say they had done nothing but their duty, as his father's subjects were bound to do.

"And there were people about him that took advantage to represent the Scotch to him as a mutinous people, and that it was not so much for him they were fighting as for themselves; and repeated to him all their bad behaviour to Charles the First and Charles the Second, and put it to him in the worst light, that at the battle of Culloden he thought that all the Scots in general were a parcel of traitors. And he would have continued in the same mind had he got out of the country immediately; but the care they took of his person when he was hiding made him change his mind, and affix treason only to particulars. "[246]

After the battle was decided, and the plain of Culloden abandoned to the fury of an enemy more merciless and insatiable than any who ever before or after answered to an English name, the Prince retired across a moor in the direction of Fort Augustus, and, according to Maxwell, slept that night at the house of Fraser of Gortuleg; and there for the first time saw Lord Lovat. But this interview is declared by Arbuthnot, who appears to have gathered his facts chiefly from local information, in the Castle of Downie; and the testimony of Sir Walter Scott confirms the assertion. "A lady, " writes Sir Walter, "who, then a girl, was residing in Lord Lovat's family, described to us the unexpected appearance of Prince Charles and his flying attendants at Castle Downie. The wild and desolate vale on which she was gazing with indolent composure, was at once so suddenly filled with horsemen riding furiously towards the Castle, that, impressed with the idea that they were fairies, who, according to men, are visible only from one twinkle of the eyelid to another, she strove to refrain from the vibration which she believed would occasion the strange and magnificent apparition to become invisible. To Lord Lovat it brought a certainty more dreadful than the presence of fairies or even demons. The tower on which he had depended had fallen to crush him, and he only met the Chevalier to exchange mutual condolences. "[247]

The Prince, it is affirmed, rushed into the chamber where Lovat, supported by men, for he could not stand without assistance, awaited his approach. The unhappy fugitive broke into lamentations. "My Lord, " he exclaimed, "we are undone; my army is routed: what will become of poor Scotland? " Unable to utter any more, he sank fainting on a bed near him. Lord Lovat immediately summoned assistance, and by proper remedies the Prince was restored to a consciousness of his misfortunes, and to the recollection that Castle Downie, a spot upon which the vengeance of the Government was sure to fall, could be no safe abiding place for him or for his followers. [248]

Such was the commencement of those wanderings, to the interest and romance of which no fiction can add. After this conference was ended, Prince Charles went to Invergarie; Lord Lovat prepared for flight.

His first place of retreat was to a mountain, whence he could behold the field of battle; he collected his officers and men around him, and they gazed with mournful interest upon the plain of Culloden. Heaps of wounded men were lying in their blood; others were still pursued by the soldiers of an army whose orders were, from their royal General, *to give no quarter*; fire and sword were everywhere; vengeance and fury raged on the moor watered by the river Nairn. Here, too, the unhappy Frasers and their chief might view Culloden House, a large fabric of stone, graced with a noble avenue of great length leading to the house, and surrounded by a park covered with heather. Here Charles Edward had slept the night before the battle. The remembrance of many social hours, of the hospitality of that old hall, might recur at this moment to the mind of Lovat. But whatever might be his reflections, his fortitude remained unbroken. He turned to the sorrowful clan around them, and addressed them. He recurred to his former predictions: "I have foretold, " he said, still attempting to keep up his old influence over the minds of his clans, "that our enemies would destroy us with the fire and sword; they have begun with me, nor will they cease until they have ravaged all the country. " He still, however, exhorted his captains to keep together their men, and to maintain a mountain war, so that at least they might obtain better terms of peace. Having thus counselled them, he was carried upon the shoulders of his followers to the still farther mountains, from one of which he is said, by a singular stroke of retributive justice, to have beheld Castle Downie, the scene of his crime, to maintain the splendour of which he had sacrificed every principle, and compassed every crime, burned by the infuriated enemy. Nine hundred men, under Brigadier Mordaunt, were detached for this purpose.

In one of the Highland fastnesses Lovat remained some time; but the blood-thirsty Cumberland was eager in pursuit. Parties of soldiers were sent out in search of Lovat, and he soon found that it was no longer safe to remain in the vicinity of Beaufort. He fled, in the first instance, to Cawdor Castle. In this famous structure, with its iron-grated doors, its ancient tapestry hanging over secret passages and obscure approaches, he took refuge. In one of its towers, in a small low chamber beneath the roof, the wretched old man concealed himself for some months. When he was at last obliged to quit it, he descended by means of a rope from his chamber.

He had still lost neither resolution nor energy. On the fourth of May, fifteen of the Jacobite chieftains, Lord Lovat among the number, met in the Island of Mortlaig, to concert measures for raising a body of men to resist the victorious troops. On this occasion Lord Lovat declared that they need not be uneasy, since he had no doubt but that they should be able to collect eight or ten thousand men to fight the Elector of Hanover's troops. Cameron of Lochiel, Murray of Broughton, and several other leaders of distinction were present; Lord Lovat was attended by many of his own clan, who were armed with dirks, swords, and pistols, and marked by wearing sprays of yew in their bonnets. But the conference broke up without any important result. The leaders embraced each other, drank to Prince Charles's health, and separated. On this occasion Lord Lovat headed that party among the Jacobites who still looked for aid from France, and abjured the notion of surrendering to the conqueror. [249] Still hunted, to use his own expression, "like a fox, " through the main land, Lovat now got off in a boat to the Island of Morar, where he thought himself secure from his enemies; but it was decreed that his iniquitous life should not close in peaceful obscurity. It was not long before he heard that a party of the King's troops had arrived in pursuit of him, and a detachment of the garrison of Fort William, on board the Terror and Furnace sloops, was also despatched, to make descents on different parts of the island. Lovat retreated into the woods; Captain Mellon, who commanded the detachment searched every town, village, and house; but not finding the fugitive, he resolved to traverse the woods, planting parties at the openings to intercept an escape. In the course of his researches he passed a very old tree, which, from some slits in its trunk, he and his men perceived to be hollow. One of the soldiers, peeping into the aperture, thought he saw a man's leg; upon which he summoned his captain, who, on investigating farther, found on one side a large opening, in which stood a pair of legs, the rest of the figure being hidden within the hollow of the tree. This was, however, quickly discovered to be Lord Lovat, for whom this party had then been three days in search. He was wrapped in blankets, to protect his aged limbs from the cold.

Thus discovered, Lovat was forced to surrender, but his spirit rose with the occasion: he told Captain Mellon that "he had best take care of him; for if he did not, he should make him answer for his conduct before a set of gentlemen the very sight of whom would make him tremble. " He was taken, in the first instance, to Fort William, where he was treated with humanity, in obedience to the express orders of the Duke of Cumberland. From this prison Lovat wrote a letter to the Duke, reminding his Royal Highness of the services which he had performed in 1715, and of the favour shown him by George the First. "I often carried your Royal Highness, " pursues the unhappy old man, "in my arms, in the palaces of Kensington and of Hampton Court, to hold you up to your royal grandfather, that he might embrace you, for he was very fond of you and the young princesses. " He then represented to the Duke that if mercy were shown him, and he "might have the honour to kiss the Duke's hand, he might do more service to the King and Government than destroying a hundred such old and very infirm men like me, (past seventy, without the least use of my hands, legs, or knees,) can be of advantage in any shape to the Government. "

He was conveyed soon after this letter, which is dated June the twenty-second, 1746, to Fort Augustus. He had requested that a litter might be prepared for him, for he was not able either to stand, walk, or ride. On the fifteenth of July he was removed, under a strong guard, to Stirling, where a party of Lord Mark Ker's dragoons received him. After a few days rest he passed through Edinburgh for the last time; thence to Berwick, and on the twenty-fifth he began his last journey under the escort of sixty dragoons commanded by Major Gardner. His journey to London was divided into twenty stages, and he was to travel one stage a day. It was, indeed, of importance to the Government that he should reach London alive, since many disclosures were expected from Lovat. On reaching Newcastle three days afterwards he appeared to be in a very feeble state, and walked from his coach to his lodgings supported by two of the dragoons. As he travelled along in a sort of cage, or horse-litter, the acclamations and hisses of the populace everywhere assailed him; but his spirits were unbroken, and he talked confidently of his return.

But as he drew near London this security diminished. He happened to reach London a few days before the unhappy Jacobite noblemen were beheaded on Tower Hill. On his way to the Tower he passed the scaffold which was erected for their execution. "Ah! " he exclaimed, "I suppose it will not be long before I shall make my exit there. "

He was received in the Tower by the Lieutenant-Governor, who conducted him to the apartment prepared for his reception. Here, reclining in an elbow chair, he is said to have broken out into reflections upon his eventful and singular career. He uttered many moral sentiments, and expressed himself, as many other men have done on similar occasions, perfectly satisfied with his own intentions. Such was the self-deception of this extraordinary man. [250]

In this prison Lovat remained during five months without being brought to trial. But the delay was of infinite importance; it prepared him to quit, with what may be almost termed heroism, a life which he had employed in iniquity. Without remembering this interval, during which ample time for preparation had been afforded, the hardihood which could sport with the most solemn of all subjects, would shock rather than astonish. In consideration of the conduct of many of our state prisoners on the scaffold, we must recollect how familiarized they had previously become with death, in those gloomy chambers whence they could see many a fellow sufferer issue, to shed his blood on the same scaffold which would soon be re-erected for themselves.

During his imprisonment, Lovat had the affliction of hearing that his estates, after being plundered of everything and destroyed by fire, were given by the Duke of Cumberland to James Fraser of Cullen Castle. [251] He was therefore left without a shilling of revenue during his confinement, and was thus treated as a convicted prisoner. In this situation he was reduced to the utmost distress, and indebted solely to the bounty of a kinsman, administered through Governor Williamson, for subsistence. At length, early in the year 1747, upon preferring a petition to the House of Lords, these grievances were in a great measure redressed. Yet the unhappy prisoner had sustained many hardships. Among others the legal plunder of his strong box, containing the sum of seven hundred pounds, and of many valuables. [252]

After much deliberation on the part of the Crown lawyers, Lord Lovat was impeached of high treason. "We learn, " says Mr. Anderson, "from Lord Mansfield's speech in the Sutherland cause, that much deliberation was necessary. It was foreseen that his Lordship would have recourse to art. If he was tried as a commoner he might claim to be a peer; if tried as a peer he might claim to be a commoner. Everything was fully considered; the true solid ground upon which he was tried as a peer, was the presumption in favour of the heirs male. "[253]

On Monday, the ninth of March, the proceedings were commenced against Lord Lovat; and a renewal took place of that scene which Horace Walpole declared to be "most solemn and fine; —a coronation is a puppet-show, and all the splendour of it idle; but this sight at once feasted the eyes, and engaged all one's passions. "

Lord Lovat was now dragged forth to play the last scene of his eventful life. His size had by this time become enormous, so that when he had first entered the Tower it was jestingly said that the doors must be enlarged to receive him. He could neither walk nor ride, as he was almost helpless; he was deaf, purblind, eighty years of age, ignorant of English law, and it was therefore not a matter of surprise that the high-born tribes, who thronged to his trial, were disappointed in the brilliancy of his parts, and in the readiness of his wit. "I see little of parts in him, " observes Walpole, "nor attribute much to that cunning for which he is so famous; it might catch wild Highlanders. " Singular, indeed, must have been the contrast between Lord Lovat and the polished assembly around him: the Lord High Steward, Hardwicke, comely, and endowed with a fine voice, but "curiously searching for occasions to bow to the Minister, Henry Pelham, " and asking at all hands what he was to do. The rude Highland clansmen, vassals of Lord Lovat's, but witnesses against him; above all, the blot and scourge of the Jacobite cause, Murray of Broughton, who was the chief witness against the prisoner, must have formed an assembly of differing characters not often to be seen, and never to be forgotten.

The trial lasted five days; it affords, as has been well remarked, a history of the whole of the Rebellion of 1745. Robert Chevis of Muirtown, a near neighbour of Lovat's, but, as the counsel for the Crown observed, a man of very different principles, gave testimony against the prisoner. At the end of the third day, Lord Lovat, pleading that he had been up at four o'clock in the morning, "to attend their Lordships, " and declaring that he would rather "die on the road than not pay them that respect, " prayed a respite of a day, which was granted. It appeared, indeed, doubtful in what form death would seize him first, and whether disease and age might not cheat the scaffold of its victim.

Lord Lovat spoke long in his defence, but without producing any revulsion in his favour. Throughout the whole of the proceedings he appears not to have dreaded the rigour of the law; when the defence was closed, and the Lord High Steward was about to put the question, guilty or not guilty, to the House, the Lieutenant of the Tower was ordered by the Lord Steward to take the prisoner from the bar, but not back to the Tower.

"If your Lordships, " said Lovat, "would send me to the Highlands, I would not go to the Tower any more. " He was pronounced guilty by the unanimous votes of one hundred and seventeen Lords present. He was then informed of his sentence, and remanded to his prison. On the following day, March the nineteenth, he was brought up to receive sentence. On that occasion, in reply to the question "why judgment of death should not be passed upon him, " he made a long and, considering his fatigues and infirmities, an extraordinary speech, giving the Lords "millions of thanks for being so good in their patience and attendance, " and drawing a parallel between the two different men of the name of Murray, who had figured in the trial. The one was Murray of Broughton; the other, Murray afterwards Lord Mansfield. He then went into the history of his life; or, at least, into such passages of it as were proper for the public ear. He was interrupted by the Lord High Steward, whose conduct to the unhappy State prisoner is said to have been peevish and overbearing.

Judgment of death was then pronounced upon him, and the barbarous sentence which had been passed upon the Earl of Wintoun was pronounced; "to be hanged by the neck, but not till you are dead, " &c. The prisoner then spoke again; hoping by this reiterated reference to his services, to obtain a mitigation of the sentence; but he spoke to those who heard, without compassion, the petitions for mercy which fell from an aged, tottering, and miserable old man. Well has it been said, "Whatever his character or his crimes might be, the humanity of the British Government incurred a deep reproach, from the execution of an old man on the very verge of the grave. "[254]

At last, the Lord High Steward put the final question; "Would you offer anything further? "

"Nothing, " was the reply, "but to thank your Lordships for your goodness to me. God bless you all; I bid you an everlasting farewell. We shall not meet all again in the same place, —I am sure of that. "

Lord Lovat was reconducted to the Tower—that prison on entering which he had boasted, that if he were not old and infirm they would have found it difficult to have kept him there. The people told him they had kept those who were much younger. "Yes, " he answered, "but they had not broken so many gaols as I have. "

He now met his approaching fate with a composure that it is difficult not to admire, even in Lovat. And yet reflection may perhaps suggest that the insensibility to the fear of death—an emotion incident to conscientious minds—bespeaks, in one whose responsibilities had been so grossly abused, an insensibility springing from utter depravity. Let us, however, give to the wretched man every possible allowance. He wrote, in terms of affection, a letter full of religious sentiments to his son, after his own condemnation. When the warrant came down for his execution, he exclaimed, "God's will be done! " With the courtesy that had charmed and had betrayed others all his life, he took the gentleman who brought the warrant by the hand, thanked him, drank his health, and assured him that he would not then change places with any prince in Christendom. He appears, indeed, to have had no misgivings, or he affected to have none, as to his eternal prospects. When the Lieutenant of the fortress in the Tower asked him how he did? "Do? " was his reply; "why I am about doing very well, for I am going to a place where hardly any majors, and very few lieutenant-generals go. "

Some friends still remained warmly attached to this singular man. Mr. William Fraser, his cousin, advanced a large sum of money to General Williamson, to provide for his wants; and, after acting as his solicitor, attended him to the last. But Lord Lovat felt deeply the circumstance of his having been convicted by his own servants: "It is shocking, " he observed, "to human nature. I believe that they will carry about with them a sting that will accompany them to their grave; yet I wish them no evil. "

He prayed daily, and fervently; and expressed unbounded confidence in the Divine mercy. "So, my dear child, " he thus wrote to his son, "do not be in the least concerned for me; for I bless God I have strong reasons to hope that when it is God's will to call me out of this world, it will be by his mercy, and the suffering of my Saviour, Jesus Christ, to enjoy everlasting happiness in the other world. I wish this may be yours. " After he had penned this remarkable letter, he asked a gentleman who was in his room how he liked the letter? The reply was, "I like it very well; it is a very good letter. " "I think, " answered Lord Lovat, "it is a Christian letter. "[255]

In this last extremity of his singular fortunes, the wife, whom he had so cruelly treated, forgetful of every thing but her Christian duty, wrote to him, and offered to repair immediately to London, and to go to him in the Tower, if he desired it. But Lord Lovat returned an answer, in which, for the first time, he adopted the language of conjugal kindness to Lady Lovat, and refused the generous proposal, worthy of the disinterestedness of woman's nature. He declared that he could not take advantage of it, after all that had occurred. [256]

Meantime, an application was made in favour of Lovat by a Mr. Painter, of St. John's College, Oxford, in the form of three letters, one of which was addressed to the King, another to Lord Chesterfield, a third to Henry Pelham. The courage of the intercession can scarcely be appreciated in the present day; in that melancholy period, the slightest word uttered in behalf of the Insurgents, brought on the interceder the imputation of secret Jacobitism, a suspicion which even President Forbes incurred. The petitions for mercy were worded fearlessly; "In a word, " thus concludes that which was addressed to the King, "bid Lovat live; punish the vile traytor with life; but let me die; let me bow down my head to the block, and receive without fear the friendly blow, which, I verily believe, will only separate the soul from its body and miseries together. "[257] In his letter to Lord Chesterfield the Oxonian repeats his offer of undergoing the punishment instead of the decrepid old man: "This I will be bold to say, " he adds: "I will not disgrace your patronage by want of intrepidity in the hour of death, and that all the devils in Milton, with all the ghastly ghosts of Scotsmen that fell at Culloden, if they could be conjured there, should never move me to say, coming upon the scaffold, 'Sir, this is terrible. '"[258] To Mr. Pelham he declared, that "the post that he wanted was not of the same nature with other Court preferments, for which there is generally a great number of competitors, but may be enjoyed without a rival. "

The observations which Lord Lovat made upon this well-meant but absurd proposal, show his natural shrewdness, or his disbelief in all that is good and generous. "This, " he exclaimed, on being told of these remarkable letters, "is an extraordinary man indeed. I should like to know what countryman he is, and whether the thing is fact. Perhaps it may be only some *finesse* in politics, to cast an odium on some particular person. In short, Sir, I'm afraid the poor gentleman is weary of living in this wicked world; in that case, the obligation is altered, because a part of the benefit is intended for himself. "

In his last days, Lovat avowed himself a Roman Catholic; but his known duplicity caused even this profession of faith to be distrusted. It is probable that like many men who have seen much of the world, and have mingled with those of different persuasions, Lord Lovat attached but little importance to different modes of faith. He was as unscrupulous in his religious professions as in all other respects. Early in his career, he thought it expedient to obtain the favour of the Pope's nuncio at Paris by conforming to the Romish faith. He declared to the Duke of Argyle and to Lord Leven that he could not get the Court of St. Germains to listen to his projects until he had declared himself a papist. One can scarcely term this venal conversion[259] an adoption of the principles of any church. The outward symbols of his pretended persuasion had, however, become dear to him, from habit: he carried about his person a silver crucifix, which he often kissed. "Observe, " he said, "this crucifix! Did you ever see a better? How strongly the passions are marked, how fine the expression is! We keep pictures of our best friends, of our parents, and others, but why should we not keep a picture of Him who has done more than all the world for us? " When asked, "Of what particular sort of Catholic are you? A Jesuit? " He answered to the nobleman who inquired, (and whose name was not known,) "No, no, my Lord, I am a Jansenist; " he then avowed his intimacy with that body of men, and assured the nobleman, that in *his* sense of being a Roman Catholic, he "was as far from being one as his Lordship, or as any other nobleman in the House. "

"This is my faith, " he observed on another occasion, after affirming that he had studied controversy for three years, and then turned Roman Catholic; "but I have charity for all mankind, and I believe every honest man bids fair for Heaven, let his persuasion be what it may; for the mercies of the Almighty are great, and his ways past finding out. "

The allusion to his funeral had something touching, coming from the old Highland chieftain. Almost the solitary good trait in Lovat's character was the fondness for his Highland home—a pride in his clan—a yearning to the last for the mountains, the straths, the burns, now ravaged by the despoiler, and red with the blood of the Frasers. "Bury me, " he said, "in my own tomb in the church of Kirk Hill; in former days, I had made a codicil to my will, that all the pipers from

John O'Groat's house to Edinburgh should be invited to play at my funeral: that may not be now—but still I am sure there will be some good old Highland women to sing a coronach at my funeral; and there will be a crying and clapping of hands—for I am one of the greatest of the Highland chieftains. " The circumstance which gave him the most uneasiness was the bill then depending for destroying the ancient privileges and jurisdiction of the Highland chiefs. "For my part, " he exclaimed, when referring to the measure, "I die a martyr to my country. "

He became much attached to one of his warders, and the usual influence which he seems to have possessed over every being with whom he came into collision, attracted the regards of this man to him. "Go with me to the scaffold, " said Lovat—"and leave me not till you see this head cut off the body. Tell my son, the Master of Lovat, with what tenderness I have parted from you. " "Do you think, " he exclaimed, on the man's expressing some sympathy with his approaching fate, "I am afraid of an axe? 'Tis a debt we all owe, and what we must all pay; and do you not think it better to go off so, than to linger with a fever, gout, or consumption? Though my constitution is so good, I might have lived twenty years longer had I not been brought hither. "

During the week which elapsed between the warrant for his being brought down to the Tower, and his death, although, says a gentleman who attended him to the scaffold, "he had a great share of memory and understanding, and an awful idea of religion and a future state, I never could observe, in his gesture or speech, the least symptom of fear, or indeed any symptoms of uneasiness. "[260] "I die, " was his own expression, "as a Christian, and a Highland chieftain should do, —that is, not in my bed. " Throughout the whole of that solemn interval, the certainty of his fate never dulled the remarkable vivacity of his conversation, nor the gay courtesy of his manners. No man ever died less consistently with his life. "It is impossible, "—such is the admission of a writer who detests his crimes, —"not to admire the fearlessness even of this monster in his last moments. But, in another view, it is somewhat difficult to resist a laugh of scorn at his impudent project of atoning for all the vices of a long and odious career, by going off with a fine sentiment on his lips. "[261]

On Thursday, the ninth of April, and the day appointed for his death, Lord Lovat awoke about three in the morning, and then called for a glass of wine and water, as was his custom. He took the greatest pains that every outward arrangement should bear the marks of composure and decency, —a care which may certainly incline one to fancy, that the heroism of his last moments may have had effect, in part, for its aim, and that, as Talleyrand said of Mirabeau, "he dramatized his death. " But, it must be remembered, that in those days, it was the custom and the aim of the state prisoners to go to the scaffold gallantly; and thus virtuous men and true penitents walked to their doom attired with the precision of coxcombs. Lord Lovat, who had smoked his pipe merrily during his imprisonment with those about him, and had heard the last apprisal of his fate without emotion, was angry, when within a few hours of death and judgment, that his wig was not so much powdered as usual. "If he had had a suit of velvet embroidered, he would wear it, " he said, "on that occasion. " He then conversed with his barber, whose father was a Muggletonian, about the nature of the soul, adding with a smile, "I hope to be in Heaven at one o'clock, or I should not be so merry now. " But, with all this loquacity, and display of what was, perhaps, in part, the insensibility of extreme age, the "behaviour that was said to have had neither dignity nor gravity"[262] in it at the trial, had lost the buffoonish character which characterized it in the House of Lords.

At ten o'clock, a scaffold which had been erected near the block fell down, and several persons were killed, and many injured; but the proceedings of the day went on. No reprieve, no thoughts of mercy ever came to shake the fortitude of the old man. At eleven, the Sheriffs of London sent to demand the prisoner's body: Lord Lovat retired for a few moments to pray; then, saying, "I am ready, " he left his chamber, and descended the stairs, complaining as he went, "that they were very troublesome to him. "

He was carried to the outer gate in the Governor's coach, and then delivered to the Sheriffs, and was by them conveyed to a house, lined with black, near to the scaffold. He was promised that his head should not be exposed on the four corners of the scaffold, that practice, in similar cases, having been abandoned: and that his clothes might be delivered with his corpse to his friends, as a compensation for which, to the executioner, he presented ten guineas contained in a purse of rich texture. He then thanked the Sheriff, and saluted his friends, saying, "My blood, I hope, will be the last shed upon this occasion. "

He then walked towards the scaffold. It was a memorable and a mournful sight to behold the aged prisoner ascending those steps, supported by others, thus to close a life which must, at any rate, soon have been extinguished in a natural decay. As he looked round and saw the multitudes assembled to witness this disgraceful execution, "God save us! " he exclaimed; "why should there be such a bustle about taking off an old grey head, that cannot get up three steps without two men to support it? " Seeing one of his friends deeply dejected, "Cheer up, " he said, clapping him on the shoulder; "I am not afraid, why should you be? "

He then gave the executioner his last gift, begging him not to hack and cut about his shoulders, under pain of his rising to reproach him. He felt the edge of the axe, and said "he believed it would do; " then his eyes rested for some moments on the inscription on his coffin. "Simon Dominus Fraser de Lovat, decollat. April 9, 1747. Ætat 80. " He repeated the line from Horace: —

"Dulce et decorum est pro patriâ mori. "

Then quoted Ovid: —"Nam genus et proavos, et quæ non fecimus ipsi, vix ea nostra voco. "

He took leave of his solicitor, Mr. William Fraser, and presented him with his gold cane, as a mark of his confidence and token of remembrance. Then he embraced another relative, Mr. James Fraser. "James, " said the old chieftain, "I am going to Heaven, but you must continue to crawl a little longer in this evil world. " He made no address to the assembled crowds, but left a paper, which he delivered to the Sheriffs, containing his last protestations. After his sentence, Lovat had accustomed his crippled limbs to kneel, that he might be able to assume that posture at the block. He now kneeled down, and after a short prayer gave the preconcerted signal that he was ready; this was the throwing of a handkerchief upon the floor. The executioner severed his head from his body at one blow. A piece of scarlet cloth received his head, which was placed in the coffin with his body and conveyed to the Tower, where it remained until four o'clock. It was then given to an undertaker.

In the paper delivered to the Sheriff there were these words, which would have partly been deemed excellent had they proceeded from any other man: —"As it may reasonably be expected of me that I should say something of myself in this place, I declare I die a true but unworthy member of the Holy, Catholic, Apostolic Church. As to my death, I cannot look upon it but as glorious. I sincerely pardon all my enemies, persecutors, and slanderers, from the highest to the lowest, whom God forgive as I heartily do. I die in perfect charity with all mankind. I sincerely repent of all my sins, and firmly hope to obtain pardon and forgiveness for them through the merits and passion of my blessed Lord and Redeemer, Jesus Christ, into whose hands I recommend my soul. Amen.

LOVAT. "

"In the Tower, April 9, 1747. "

The public might well contrast the relentless hand of justice, in this instance, with the mercy of Queen Anne. She, like her brother the Chevalier, averse from shedding blood, had spared the life of an old man, who had been condemned in her reign for treason. Many other precedents of a similar kind have been adduced. [263] But this act of inhumanity was only part of a system of what was called justice; but which was the justice of the heathen, and not of the Christian.

If the character of Lord Lovat cannot be deduced from his actions, it must be impossible to understand the motives of man from any course of life; for never was a career more strongly marked by the manifestation of the passions, than that of this unworthy descendant of a great line. His selfishness was unbounded, his rapacity insatiable; his brutality seems incredible. In the foregoing narrative, the mildest view has been adopted of his remorseless cruelty: of his gross and revolting indulgences, of his daily demeanour, which is said to have outraged everything that is seemly, everything that is holy, in private life, little has been written. Much that was alleged to Lovat, in this particular, has been contradicted: much may be ascribed to the universal hatred of his name, which tinted, perhaps too highly, his vices, in his own day. Something may be ascribed to party prejudice, which gladly seized upon every occasion of reproach to an adversary. Yet still, there is too much that is probable, too much that is too true, to permit a hope that the private and moral character of Lord Lovat can be vindicated from the deepest stains.

By his public life, he has left an indelible stain upon the honour of the Highland character, upon his party, upon his country. Of principle he had none: —for prudence, he substituted a low description of time-serving: he never would have promoted the interests of the Hanoverians in the reign of George the First, if the

Court of St. Germains had tolerated his alliance: he never would have sided with Charles Edward, if the Court of St. James's had not withdrawn its confidence. His pride and his revengeful spirit went hand in hand together. The former quality had nothing in it of that lofty character which raises it almost to a virtue, in the stern Scottish character: it was the narrow-minded love of power which is generated in a narrow sphere.

In the different relations of his guilty life, only one redeeming feature is apparent, —the reverence which Lord Lovat bore to his father. With that parent, seems to have been buried every gentle affection: he regarded his wives as slaves; he looked upon his sons with no other regard and solicitude, than as being heirs of his estates. As a chief and a master, his conduct has been variously represented; the prevailing belief is, that it was marked by oppression, violence, and treachery: yet, as no man in existence ever was so abandoned as not to have his advocates, even the truth of this popular belief has been questioned, on the ground that the influence which he exercised over them, in being able to urge them to engage in whatsoever side he pleased, argues some qualities which must have engaged their affections. [264]

He who pleads thus, must, however, have forgotten the hereditary sway of a Highland chieftain, existing in unbroken force in those days: he must have forgotten the sentiment which was inculcated from the cradle, the loyalty of clanship, —a sentiment which led on the brave hearts in which it was cherished to far more remarkable exertions and proofs of fidelity than even the history of the Frasers can supply.

But the deepest dye of guilt appears in Lord Lovat's conduct as a father. It was not only that he was, in the infancy and boyhood of his eldest born, harsh and imperious: such was the custom of the period. It was not only that he impelled the young man into a course which his own reason disapproved, and which he undertook with reluctance and disgust throwing, on one occasion, his white cockade into the fire, and only complying with his father's orders upon force. This was unjustifiable compulsion in any father, but it might be excused on the plea of zeal for the cause. But it appeared on the trial that the putting forward the Master of Lovat was a mere feint to save himself at the expense of his son, if affairs went wrong. In Lord Lovat's letters to President Forbes the poor young man was made to bear the brunt of the whole blame;

although Lord Lovat had frequently complained of his son's backwardness to certain members of his clan. On the trial it appeared that the whole aim of Lord Lovat was, as Sir John Strange expressed it, "an endeavour to avoid being fixed himself and to throw it all upon his son, —that son whom he had, in a manner, forced into the Rebellion. "

Rare, indeed, is such a case; —with that, let these few remarks on the character of Lord Lovat, conclude. Human nature can sink to no lower depth of degradation.

Lord Lovat left, by his first wife, three children: —Simon, Master of Lovat; Janet, who was married to Ewan Macpherson of Cluny, —a match which Lord Lovat projected in order to increase his influence, and to strengthen his Highland connections. This daughter was grandmother to the present chief, and died in 1765. He had also another daughter, Sybilla.

This daughter was one of those rare beings whose elevated minds seem to expand in despite of every evil influence around them. Her mother died in giving her birth; and Lord Lovat, perhaps from remorse for the uncomplaining and ill-used wife, evinced much concern at the death of his first lady, and showed a degree of consideration for his daughters which could hardly have been expected from one so steeped in vice. Although his private life at Castle Downie, after the death of their mother was disgusting in detail, and therefore, better consigned to oblivion, the gentle presence of his two daughters restrained the coarse witticisms of their father, and he seemed to regard them both with affection and respect, and to be proud of the decorum of their conduct and manners. Disgusted with the profligacy which, as they grew up, they could not but observe at Castle Downie, the young ladies generally chose to reside at Leatwell, with Lady Mackenzie, their only aunt; and Lord Lovat did not resent their leaving him, but rather applauded a delicacy of feeling which cast so deep a reproach upon him. He was to them a kind indulgent father. When Janet, Lady Clunie, was confined of her first child, he brought her to Castle Downie that she might have the attendance of physicians more easily than in the remote country where the Macphersons lived. He always expressed regret that her mother had not been sufficiently attended to when her last child was born.

The fate of Sybilla Fraser presents her as another victim to the hardness and impiety of Lovat. "She possessed, " says Mrs. Grant, "a high degree of sensibility, which when strongly excited by the misfortunes of her family, exalted her habitual piety into all the fervour of enthusiasm. " When Lovat passed through Badenoch, after his apprehension, Sybilla, who was there with Lady Clunie, followed him to Dalwhinney, and there, in an agony of mind which may be readily conceived, entreated her aged father to reconcile himself to his Maker, and to withdraw his thoughts from the world. She was answered by taunts at her "womanish weakness, " as Lovat called it, and by coarse ridicule of his enemies, with a levity of mind shocking under such circumstances. The sequel cannot be better told than in these few simple words: "Sybilla departed almost in despair; prayed night and day, not for his life, but for his soul; and when she heard soon after, that 'he had died and made no sign, ' grief in a short time put an end to her life."[265]

The Master of Lovat was implicated, as we have shown, in the troubles of 1745. Early in that year, he had the misery of discovering the treachery of his father, by accidentally finding the rough draught of a letter which Lord Lovat had written to the President, in order to excuse himself at the expense of his son. "Good God! " exclaimed the young man, "how can he use me so? I will go at once to the President, and put the saddle on the right horse. " In spite of this provocation, he did not, however, reveal his father's treachery; whilst Lord Lovat was balancing between hopes and fears, and irresolute which side to choose, the Master at last entreated, with tears in his eyes, that "he might no longer be made a tool of—but might have such orders as his father might stand by."

Having received these orders, and engaged in the insurrection, the Master of Lovat was zealous in discharging the duties in which he had thus unwillingly engaged. His clan were among the few who came up at Culloden in time to effect a junction with Prince Charles. In 1746 an Act of Attainder was passed against him; he surrendered himself to Government, and was confined nine months in Edinburgh Castle. In 1750 a full and free pardon passed the seals for him. He afterwards became an advocate, but eventually returned to a military life, and was permitted to enter the English army. In 1757 he raised a regiment of one thousand eight hundred men, of which he was constituted colonel, at the head of which he distinguished himself at Louisbourg and Quebec. He was afterwards appointed colonel of the 71st foot, and performed eminent services in the American war.

The title of his father had been forfeited, and his lands attainted. But in 1774 the lands and estates were restored upon certain conditions, in consideration of Colonel Fraser's eminent services, and in consideration of his having been involved in "the late unnatural Rebellion" at a tender age. Colonel Fraser rose to the rank of lieutenant-general, and died in 1782 without issue; he was generally respected and compassionated. He was succeeded in the estates by his half-brother, Archibald Campbell Fraser, the only child whom Lord Lovat had by his second wife. This young man had mingled, when a boy, from childish curiosity among the Jacobite troops at the battle of Culloden, and had narrowly escaped from the dragoons.

He afterwards entered into the Portuguese service, where he remained some years; but, being greatly attached to his own country, he returned. He could not, however, conscientiously take the oaths to Government, and therefore never had any other military employment. "With much truth, honour, and humanity, " relates Mrs. Grant, "he inherited his father's wit and self-possession, with a vein of keen satire which he indulged in bitter expressions against the enemies of his family. Some of these I have seen, and heard many songs of his composing, which showed no contemptible power of poetic genius, although rude and careless of polish. " He sank into habits of dissipation and over-conviviality, which impaired a reputation otherwise high in his neighbourhood, and became careless and hopeless of himself. What little he had to bequeath was left to a lady of his own name to whom he was attached, and who remained unmarried long after his death.

It is rather remarkable that Archibald Campbell Fraser, generally, from his command of the Invernessshire militia, called Colonel Fraser, should survive his five sons, and that the estates which Lord Lovat had sacrificed so much to secure to his own line should revert to another family of the clan Fraser, —the Frasers of Stricken, the present proprietors of Lovat and Stricken, being in Aberdeenshire the twenty-second in succession from Simon Fraser of Invernessshire. [266]

FOOTNOTES:

[118] Anderson's Historical Account of the Family of Frisel or Fraser, p. 5.

[119] One of Lord Lovat's family—it is not easy to ascertain which—emigrated after the Rebellion of 1745 into Ireland, and settled in that country, where he possessed considerable landed property, which is still enjoyed by one of his descendants. There is an epitaph on the family vault of this branch of the Frizells or Frazers, in the churchyard of Old Ross, in the County of Wexford, bearing this inscription: —"The burial place of Charles Frizell, son of Charles Fraser Frizell of Ross, and formerly of Beaufort, North Britain. " For this information I am indebted to the Rev. John Frizell, of Great Normanton, Derbyshire, and one of this Irish branch of the family, of which his brother is the lineal representative.

[120] Anderson's Historical Account of the Family of Fraser.

[121] Memoirs of the Life of Lord Lovat, written by himself in the French Language, p. 7.

[122] Memoirs of the Life of Lord Lovat, p. 7.

[123] In speaking of the other members of the family, Mr. Anderson remarks: —"The parish registers of Kiltarlity, Kirkill, and Kilmorack, were at the same time examined with the view of tracing the other children of Thomas of Beaufort, but the communications of the various clergymen led to the knowledge that no memorials of them exist. The remote branches called to the succession in General Fraser's entail proves, to a certainty, that these children died unmarried. "—*Anderson's Historical Account of the Family of Fraser.* It appears, however, from a previous note, that a branch of the family still exists in Ireland.

[124] See State Trials. Lovat.

[125] Letter from Fort Augustus in Gentleman's Magazine for 1746.

[126] Introduction to Culloden Papers, p. 36. Gentleman's Magazine, vol. xvi. p. 339.

[127] See Lord Lovat's Memoirs, p. 7. Also Anderson and Woods.

[128] Lord Lovat's Memoirs, p. 18.

[129] Lord Lovat's Memoirs, p. 27.

[130] Chambers's Biography.

[131] Anderson, p. 120.

[132] Lord Lovat's Memoirs, p. 75.

[133] Lord Lovat's Memoirs, p. 75.

[134] Arnot on the State Trials, p. 84.

[135] Memoirs.

[136] Stewart's Sketches, p. 21.

[137] Brown's Highlands, vol. i. p. 120.

[138] Memoirs, p. 51.

[139] Id. p. 53

[140] Memoirs, p. 53.

[141] Arnot, p. 84.

[142] Arnot, p. 84. Anderson, p. 121.

[143] Arnot, p. 89.

[144] Anderson, p. 124.

[145] Lord Lovat's Manifesto, p. 72.

[146] Ibid.

[147] Anderson, p. 124.

[148] Life and Adventures of Lord Lovat, by the Rev. Archibald Arbuthnot, one of the Society for propagating Christian Knowledge, and Minister of Killarlaty, Presbytery of Inverness. London, 1748.

[149] Life and Adventures, p. 42.

[150] Manifesto.

[151] Arnot, p. 79.

[152] Chambers's Dictionary.

[153] Manifesto, p. 71.

[154] Arnot, p. 79.

[155] Arnot, p. 90.

[156] Life of Lord Lovat, p. 47.

[157] Anderson, p. 123.

[158] Manifesto, p. 99.

[159] Arbuthnot, p. 53.

[160] Macpherson. Stuart Papers, vol. i. p. 665.

[161] Manifesto.

[162] Arbuthnot, p. 55.

[163] Arbuthnot, p. 52.

[164] Anderson, p. 130.

[165] Macpherson Papers.

[166] See Smollet, vol. ix. pp. 245 and 255.

[167] Lockhart Memoirs, vol. i. p. 75.

[168] Macpherson. Stuart Papers, vol. i. p. 629.

[169] Manifesto, p. 116.

[170] Two thousand five hundred pounds.

[171] Manifesto, p. 152.

[172] See Murray Papers. Advocate's Library in Edinburgh.

[173] Lockhart Memoirs, vol. i. p. 80.

[174] Stuart Papers. Macpherson, vol. i. p. 641.

[175] Stuart Papers. Macpherson, vol. i. p. 646.

[176] Stuart Papers. Macpherson, vol. i. p. 678.

[177] Ibid. p. 682.

[178] Letter from James Earl of Perth, Chancellor of Scotland, &c. — Edited by William Jerdan, Esq., and printed for the Camden Society, p. 50.

[179] Arbuthnot, p, 63.

[180] Somerville, p. 177.

[181] Somerville, p. 182. Also, Lockhart's Memoirs, p. 180; Macpherson, vol. i. p. 640.

[182] Stuart Papers, p. 652.

[183] Id. p. 655.

[184] Anderson. Chambers.

[185] Arbuthnot, p. 89.

[186] Of the two accounts of Lord Lovat's imprisonment, namely, Mr. Arbuthnot's and Lord Lovat's, the latter bears, strange to say, the greatest air of truth. Mr. Arbuthnot's, independent of his erring in the place of imprisonment, appears to me a pure romance.

[187] Manifesto, p. 301.

[188] Carstares. State Papers, p. 718.

[189] Manifesto, p. 328.

[190] Anderson, p. 137.

[191] Id. p. 138.

[192] Free Examination of the Memoir of Lord Lovat, quoted in Arbuthnot, p. 201.

[193] Anderson, p. 136.

[194] From the Macpherson Papers, vol. ii. p. 622.

[195] Culloden Papers, p. 32.

[196] Manifesto, p. 466.

[197] Ibid. p. 468.

[198] Smollet, p. xi. Patten's History of the Rebellion, p. 2.

[199] Arbuthnot, p. 210.

[200] Edinburgh Review, No. li. art. *Culloden Papers,* 1826. This article is attributed to the Honourable Lord Cockburn.

[201] See Introduction to the Culloden Papers.

[202] Arbuthnot, p. 211.

[203] Shaw's Hist. of Moray, p. 252.

[204] Ibid.

[205] Anderson, p. 141.

[206] Arbuthnot, p. 218.

[207] Shaw, p. 186.

[208] Such was the style in which Lovat, to be complimentary, usually addressed Duncan Forbes, on account of the military capacity in which the future Lord President had acted during the Rebellion.

[209] Culloden Papers, p. 55.

[210] Culloden Papers, p. 56.

[211] Sergeant Macleod served in 1703, when only thirteen years of age, in the Scots Royals, afterwards under Marlborough, then at the battle of Sherriff Muir in 1715. After a variety of campaigns he was wounded in the battle of Quebec, in 1759, and came home in the same ship that brought General Wolf's body to England. Macleod died in Chelsea Hospital at the age of one hundred and three. His Memoirs are interesting.

[212] Memoirs of the Life of Sergeant Donald Macleod, p. 45. London, 1791.

[213] Anderson. From King's Monumenta Antiqua.

[214] Culloden Papers.

[215] Mrs. Grant's MS.

[216] Anderson, p. 159. From family archives.

[217] Chambers's Traditions of Edinburgh.

[218] Chambers's Traditions of Edinburgh, p. 21.

[219] Culloden Papers, "Quarterly Review, " vol. xiv. This article is written by Sir Walter Scott, and the anecdote is given on his personal knowledge.

[220] Arbuthnot, p. 249.

[221] Lady Grange's Memoirs.

[222] Arbuthnot, p. 241.

[223] Arbuthnot.

[224] Quarterly Review, vol. xiv. Culloden Papers.

[225] Culloden Papers, p. 72.

[226] Burt's Letters from the North, vol. xxi.

[227] Culloden Papers, p. 106.

[228] Arbuthnot, p. 250.

[229] Culloden Papers, p. 106.

[230] Henderson's History of the Rebellion, p. 8.

[231] Henderson, p. 10.

[232] James Maxwell, of Kirkconnell; his narrative, of which I have a copy, has been printed for the Maitland Club, in Edinburgh; it is remarkably clear, and ably and dispassionately written, and was composed immediately after the events of the year 1745, of which Mr. Maxwell was an eye-witness.

[233] Maxwell of Kirkconnell's Narrative of the Prince's Expedition, p. 10.

[234] See Lord Elcho's Narrative. MS.

[235] Some say the fifteenth. See Henderson.

[236] Culloden Papers, pp. 211, 372.

[237] Anderson, p. 150.

[238] Culloden Papers, p. 230.

[239] Chambers's Traditions of Edinburgh, p. 9.

[240] Explained in the trial, by Chevis, one of the witnesses, to be in allusion to the royal arms.

[241] Quarterly Review, vol. xiv. p. 327.

[242] Edinburgh Review, 1816, vol. xxvi. p. 131.

[243] State Trials, vol. xviii.

[244] Maxwell of Kirkconnel, p. 167.

[245] Id.

[246] Lord Elcho's MSS.

[247] Quarterly Review, vol. xiv. p. 328.

[248] Arbuthnot, p. 270.

[249] State Trials, vol. xviii. p. 734.

[250] Arbuthnot, p. 279.

[251] Chambers's Biography. Art. *Fraser*.

[252] State Trials.

[253] Anderson, p. 153.

[254] Laing's History of Scotland, p. 299.

[255] State Trials, vol. xviii. p. 846.

[256] Chambers's Traditions of Edinburgh, p. 12.

[257] Gentleman's Magazine, vol. xvii. p. 184. These letters were afterwards collected and sold for a guinea.

[258] In allusion to the expression of agony and dismay used some time before by Lord Kilmarnock.

[259] Somerville's Reign of Queen Anne, p. 175, 4to edition; from Lockhart and Macpherson.

[260] State Trials.

[261] Edinburgh Review, vol. xxvi. p 132.

[262] Horace Walpole.

[263] State Trials, vol. xviii. p. 326.

[264] Free Examination of the Life of Lord Lovat; London 1746.

[265] Mrs. Grant's MS.

[266] Anderson, p. 187.

END OF THE SECOND VOLUME.

Printed in the United Kingdom
by Lightning Source UK Ltd.
134525UK00003B/88/P

9 781409 906599